Making t

Also by John A. Fortunato

Sports Sponsorship: Principles and Practices
(McFarland, 2013)

Making the Cut

Life Inside the PGA Tour System

JOHN A. FORTUNATO

McFarland & Company, Inc., Publishers

Jefferson, North Carolina

This book has not been prepared, endorsed
or sponsored by the PGA TOUR.

LIBRARY OF CONGRESS CATALOGUING-IN-PUBLICATION DATA

Names: Fortunato, John A., author.
Title: Making the cut : life inside the PGA tour system / John A. Fortunato.
Description: Jefferson, North Carolina : McFarland & Company, Inc.,
    Publishers, 2019]| Includes bibliographical references and index.
Identifiers: LCCN 2018054290 | ISBN 9781476676197 (softcover : acid free
    paper) ∞
Subjects: LCSH: PGA Tour (Association) | Golf—United States. | Golf—
    Tournaments—United States. | Golfers—United States. | Professional
    Golfers' Association of America.
Classification: LCC GV969.P75 F67 2019 | DDC 796.352/640973—dc23
LC record available at https://lccn.loc.gov/2018054290

BRITISH LIBRARY CATALOGUING DATA ARE AVAILABLE

ISBN (print) 978-1-4766-7619-7
ISBN (ebook) 978-1-4766-3517-0

Front cover photograph by Jacob Lund (iStock)

Printed in the United States of America

*McFarland & Company, Inc., Publishers
    Box 611, Jefferson, North Carolina 28640
    www.mcfarlandpub.com*

In loving memory
of Maria L. Fortunato,
January 28, 1939–May 2, 2017

Table of Contents

Table of Contents

Preface

The ramifications of every tournament outcome on the PGA Tour* are far-reaching, beyond what the casual golf fan may be aware of. While it is the professional golfers who provide the moments of exhilaration, the drama of the PGA Tour is in part created by a system that offers a series of dividing lines, with a golfer's positioning in relation to these dividing lines determining his career opportunities. The dividing lines on the PGA Tour are all based on performance. First, a golfer needs to make it onto the PGA Tour by graduating from the Web.com Tour. Each golfer on the PGA Tour is placed in a ranking group for the season, referred to as his exempt status, that provides his position in the priority selection process that is used for determining entrance into a regular season PGA tournament. A golfer tries to qualify to play in the major championships, the World Golf Championships tournaments, or invitational tournaments. In every tournament exist two of the most commonly recognized dividing lines on the PGA Tour: making the cut and winning. Finally, every season a golfer aims to be in the top 125 in the FedEx Cup points standings to qualify for the end-of-season FedEx Cup Playoffs. He then attempts to be high enough in the FedEx Cup points standings to advance to the next tournament that comprises the FedEx Cup Playoffs.

Success in crossing the threshold to the positive side of any of these dividing lines equates to significant opportunities for a professional golfer: the opportunity to play, the opportunity to earn. The golfers on the unfortunate side of any of the PGA Tour's dividing lines seek their opportunity to improve their situation and cross a critical dividing line.

This book explains the complex qualification system of the PGA Tour

*Although the organization refers to itself and to its top tour in all-caps (PGA TOUR), the publisher has followed the mixed-case style adopted by much of the media (PGA Tour), which preserves all-caps treatment only for the acronym PGA.

and depicts a series of compelling, life-changing stories that exist on both sides of the Tour's many dividing lines. The PGA Tour system thrives because it creates such engaging storylines that lie within a golfer's quest for achievement. This book is a collection of recent career storylines of some professional golfers' tournament outcomes, the confluence of events that created the outcome, and the opportunities for the golfers that result from that outcome.

The stories of *Making the Cut* that document the competitive nature of the PGA Tour and the stories of achievement, with golfers ending up on the positive side of one of golf's many dividing lines, are inevitably about pointing out some of the missed opportunities and the consequences for the golfers who find themselves on the negative side of a dividing line. Every season, there is going to be someone on the wrong side of the dividing line to graduate from the Web.com Tour onto the PGA Tour, who just misses qualifying for the FedEx Cup Playoffs, just misses qualifying to play in a major tournament, or just misses being placed into a higher priority ranking group for the following season. The system ensures it. The system demands it.

Life on the PGA Tour is about navigating this system of dividing lines. The PGA Tour had a grueling schedule of 43 regular season tournaments played over 39 weeks in the 2016–2017 season, followed by four FedEx Cup Playoff tournaments. The opportunities can be limited in that only a certain number of golfers are able to play in each tournament, and only a certain number of golfers make the cut in each tournament. The PGA Tour does have unique schedule opportunities with tournaments which highly-ranked golfers tend not to play. These tournaments occur in the autumn portion of the regular season schedule, are held the week before or after a major, or are held simultaneously with more elite tournaments that attract the high-profile golfers on the Tour. Finally, when one season concludes, the next regular season quickly begins.

A golfer must be poised to take advantage of the opportunities. The PGA Tour is the ultimate meritocracy. Only when a golfer performs well is the opportunity to play in more tournaments granted, especially the opportunity to play in the more elite and more lucrative tournaments, such as the majors, World Golf Championships, The Players Championship, and the FedEx Cup Playoffs. On the PGA Tour there are no multi-year, guaranteed contracts like the players in Major League Baseball or the National Basketball Association have, and no extravagant signing bonuses like the players get in the National Football League.

The dividing lines of the PGA Tour are profoundly stark in the opportunities provided or not provided for a golfer, and the outcomes can be determined by the slightest margin. Often, it is only one made or missed shot, or some good fortune or misfortune, that provides the difference in tournament outcomes. Every week there is someone who comes up just one stroke short of the cut line, or it is one stroke that determines higher or lower prize money or FedEx Cup points accumulated for that tournament. To illustrate, in the 2015–2016 PGA season, there were 44 stroke-play tournaments (the Greenbrier Classic was canceled due to heavy rain and flooding). In these tournaments, 13 were decided in a playoff, and in 16 other tournaments the margin of victory was one stroke. In the 2016–2017 season, there were 45 stroke-play tournaments. Ten were decided in a playoff, and in 15 other tournaments the margin of victory was one stroke.

Tournament outcomes are decided by a perfectly read and struck putt, a ball rolling to the ideal yardage for a golfer's particular club selection, a slightly missed approach shot after the ball had a bad lie because it happened to roll into a divot, a slightly awkward stance when striking the ball, a ball landing up against the lip of a sand trap, playing a round in severe wind while other golfers playing at a different time of day did not have to confront the more difficult weather conditions, or playing when the course is firm rather than during softer conditions.

Moreover, for a golfer on the PGA Tour, every time he swings a club there are direct financial consequences. A golfer can always recover from a bad shot with a spectacular shot, but that errant shot remains part of his tally (in football, an incomplete pass on first down only means that it is second and ten). Furthermore, while a golfer is playing against the course, his position on the leaderboard is changed not only by his own great or poor play, but the great or poor play of other golfers. It is a system where the game is never over. There is no "garbage time."

Being successful in this "every shot counts" world of the PGA Tour requires a combination of immense talent, intense love of competition, and a capacity to maintain focus. For a professional golfer, there is a need to persevere, maintain composure, demonstrate resolve, have a short memory, and focus on "this shot" throughout the entirety of a tournament. It takes more than a mechanically sound golf swing to survive and thrive in this type of competitive environment.

A golfer also has to be better than the incredibly talented competition for that tournament. While there are certainly degrees of talent, the fact that all of the golfers on the PGA Tour have incredible ability is a given. Many golfers are capable of winning a tournament. For the 2014–2015, 2015–2016, and 2016–2017 seasons, including the Zurich Classic of New Orleans, which became a two-player team event in the 2016–2017 season, there have been 83 different winners in the 140 tournaments played on the PGA Tour.

Success on the PGA Tour requires proper decision-making regarding course management. Golfers decide which club to play, how hard to swing, whether to play a fade or a draw, whether to lay-up or go for the green, where to land the ball on the green knowing how its contours will help roll the ball toward the hole, and the speed and line of a putt. Then, of course, they must have the skill to execute these strategic decisions.

Golfers have to retain the knowledge of the many courses where the PGA tournaments are played. In their course management, golfers seek to acquire every piece of information that they can. Golfers play some courses so often that they are familiar with how they need to approach each hole. They know where they need to hit the ball on a specific hole and how the greens normally play. Other golf courses are less familiar. Certainly, this is the case with the major tournaments, as aside from the Masters the location for these events shifts every year. Even if the major is played at a golf course that is used for a regular season PGA Tour event, the conditions of the course are made considerably more difficult for the major championship tournament.

Golfers will spend hours on the practice green and the chipping area to gauge the speed of the greens in the days prior to the tournament. Their caddies will walk the course to help develop a strategy. Sometimes, even the television broadcast can provide a useful piece of information. Justin Thomas, FedEx Cup Champion in 2016–2017, was waiting to play a round at the U.S. Open in 2017 and picked up a tip for how to approach a hole while watching the broadcast. He explained at his press conference at the Quicken Loans National tournament that during the U.S. Open, "I watched a bunch of coverage just because you're learning stuff about the course. I did the same thing on Saturday. I remember I birdied eight because of watching the coverage in the morning. I saw someone hit one up the slope and it came down. I'm in the fairway. I'm like all I have to do is hit it on that slope and I've got a kick-in [short putt]."

The dividing lines of the PGA Tour, and the opportunities on each side of those lines, are such that every golfer has his own unique storyline. While golfers dream of putting on the Green Jacket for winning the Masters or hoisting the Claret Jug at St. Andrews or one of the historic golf courses of Great Britain for winning The Open Championship, for some there is the mere practicality of earning a living and being able to compete on the PGA Tour. For all of the different golfer storylines that will be identified in this book, there are certainly countless others worthy of profile. This book represents only some of the stories of the golfers on the PGA Tour.

I approached the researching and writing of this book from the perspective of a fan. I enjoyed watching golf tournaments, witnessing the competition and the great play, but at times I was not aware of all of the consequences of what I was seeing. I wanted to learn more about the system of the PGA Tour. I was interested in a deeper understanding of what these tournament outcomes mean in terms of a golfer's season and career. What I found was a complex system that continuously produces compelling stories along this series of dividing lines. It is these stories of how the golfers navigate this system and the opportunities that come with their personal success that became the core of this book. I share these stories and my new understanding and appreciation of the PGA Tour with other fans to make them more knowledgeable and in many ways enhance their enjoyment of professional golf.

The first person who provided the needed assistance on this project was James Cramer, former PGA Tour Vice President of Communications (he is now the Vice President of Communications for the World Golf Foundation). James replied to my three-paragraph email, and we had a conversation about my idea of explaining the PGA Tour system and the types of stories that I wanted to include. He opened many doors and facilitated my visits to tournaments. I am extremely grateful for his faith in me and this project. Also, at the PGA Tour, Tracey Veal responded to every email and answered every question (any inaccuracy that you may find in the following pages is an error on my part, not the PGA Tour).

I gathered information from interviews with golfers, watching golf broadcasts, using the PGA Tour web site that contains an incredible amount of information about the golfers and tournament outcomes, and reading books and articles about the Tour. I want to acknowledge the excellent reporting that is done about the PGA Tour. I hope all of those writers who informed and inspired me find that this book is a complement to their work.

I am very appreciative of all of the golfers who spoke to me. They all provided considerable insight about navigating the PGA Tour system as well as the details about their own careers. The golfers I interviewed over the phone are Greg Chalmers, Joel Dahmen (I also spoke with Joel at the Web.com Tour Championship), Martin Flores, Cody Gribble, Jim Herman, Kevin Kisner, Ben Kohles, D. A. Points, and Brian Stuard. At the Quicken Loans National Tournament, I interviewed Morgan Hoffmann, Mackenzie Hughes, Rod Pampling, Xander Schauffele, Brendan Steele, and Robert Streb. Finally, at the Web.com Tour Championship, I spoke with Roberto Diaz, Ken Duke, Chesson Hadley, Troy Merritt, Keith Mitchell, and Rob Oppenheim.

I could write about how every interview that I conducted provided me with a valuable piece of information about the Tour and led me to another idea to go research, in addition to the golfer's own personal story. I do want to highlight some of these interviews. For the golfers I spoke with early in the process, I thank them for their patience in explaining some of the basic information about the system of the PGA Tour and the Web.com Tour. Cody Gribble was the first golfer that I interviewed. He told me about some of the close calls that he had in reaching the PGA Tour and then about his win at the Sanderson Farms Championship. After speaking with him, I felt more confident that these golfers' stories are worth telling. I cannot thank him enough for his contributions to this book.

Greg Chalmers is a true testament to the perseverance of a professional golfer. It was incredible hearing about his first tournament victory in his 386th career start. D. A. Points provided me great insight and a veteran's perspective of having won a tournament, having some seasons where he was not as successful, and then returning to being a tournament champion. His story demonstrates how quickly things can change for a professional golfer. Hearing how Jim Herman made it to the PGA Tour and the story of his first tournament win at the Shell Houston Open in 2016 added to this book. The conversations with Chalmers, Points, and Herman ended with me thinking that they are so deserving of being called a tournament champion. Speaking to Martin Flores about how tense the final tournament of the regular season is for the golfers who are on the borderline between keeping their PGA Tour card and qualifying for the FedEx Cup playoffs, as opposed to having to go play in the Web.com Tour Finals, was an important story to include.

Having overcome cancer to reach the PGA Tour, Joel Dahmen is simply an inspiration. Speaking with Joel and later meeting him at the Web.com Tour Championship was a gratifying experience for me. Joel, along with Keith Mitchell and Rob Oppenheim, provided dramatic stories of the precarious dividing line between the Web.com Tour and graduating onto the PGA Tour. Having Keith Mitchell go through the details of a difficult outcome in the final regular season tournament of the Web.com Tour season in which he did not earn his PGA Tour card, to his performance only a few weeks later that did get him to the Tour, demonstrated his resolve and some of the needed characteristics of a professional golfer. Rob Oppenheim, having teetered on the Web.com Tour/PGA Tour dividing line for many seasons, provided me the practical reality of the life of a professional golfer.

There are several of the golfers' agents who helped facilitate interviews. I thank them for responding to my requests and coordinating these interviews. They are: Brad Buffoni, Wasserman Media Group–Wisconsin (D. A. Points); Tony Bouffler, AJB Sports Management (Greg Chalmers); Allen Hobbs, Players Group, Inc. (Ben Kohles); Butler Melnyk, Wasserman Media Group–Virginia (Kevin Kisner); Jordan Millice, Sterling Sports Management (Joel Dahmen); Blake Smith, Hambric Sports Management (Martin Flores, Cody Gribble); John Wilner, IMG (Brian Stuard); and Michael Wolff, 228 LLC (Jim Herman). My conversation with Chris Kosiba, Meister Sports Management, was insightful.

When you attend a PGA Tour event in person and have the opportunity to watch the professional golfers practice on the driving range, chipping area, and putting greens, it is extremely evident that their talent is beyond extraordinary. While television broadcasts capture these tournaments beautifully with their enhanced technological techniques and announcer analysis, seeing these golfers in person provides an even greater appreciation of their skill. The other aspect you witness is the great amount of time and attention to detail that is put into their craft. The golfers are diligent in working on their swing mechanics, using an assortment of drills and apparatus to perfect their swings. It is also common to see a golfer in the practice area after completing a five-hour round. I do hope that my admiration for their skill and their dedication to their sport comes through in this book.

The staff that helped me during my visit to the Quicken Loans National tournament was sensational. Greg Ball was instrumental in making this visit possible. He also put me in touch with Peter Ripa, the tournament director of the Farmers Insurance Open. Learning about that perspective and the role of each individual event staff in putting on a PGA tournament was interesting and necessary for me to learn.

The media relations staff of the PGA Tour on-site at the tournaments is simply outstanding. At the Quicken Loans, I had the pleasure of meeting John Bush, Amanda Herrington, and Mark Williams. I cannot thank them enough for their patience, generosity, and professionalism. They provided me with information, answered questions, and facilitated interview requests. It was an above-and-beyond level of hospitality provided to me as a college professor (and not a regular golf reporter). I am extremely appreciative.

From the web site to the tournament notes that the PGA Tour media staff develops, the level of information that I had access to made this book possible and illuminated what I felt the reader needed to know about the Tour and the golfers. The dedication of the PGA media staff to the Tour and the golfers is commendable.

I also got to visit the Web.com Tour Championship. Royce Thompson was the lead media representative at that event, and I simply would not have obtained the amount of information that I did nor had access to the golfers I wanted to interview without his help. What I consider important parts of this book can be directly attributed to his time and effort. Also at the Web.com Tour Championship, my conversation with Kathy Mobley about how tournament fields are formed was insightful. I am also thankful to Nick Parker of the media staff, whom I got to meet during my week in Florida.

This is my second book with McFarland & Company Publishers. Gary Mitchem and his staff continue to support my ideas and make my research and writing better. I am appreciative of all of their efforts. The Fordham University research office provided support that allowed me to travel to PGA tournaments, as did the Center for Communication in the Area of Communication and Media Management of the Fordham University Gabelli School of Business. Three of my former students assisted in some of the fact-checking for this project: Michael Boss, Sean Johnson, and Thomas Strazzeri (again, any error in this book is my responsibility). Finally, there are many family members and friends who heard me talk about this book as it was being researched. I thank them for their interest and the motivation to keep me pursuing this project. For those family and friends whom I often play golf with, please note that working on this book has not improved my golf swing—you are still going to have to give me a few strokes.

In addition to any readers, I have the opportunity to communicate what I learned in researching this book about the inner workings of a major professional sport and its athletes with my students. This book was in part inspired by students in class asking me questions about the PGA Tour and my not being completely certain of the answers. I hope I now have some of those answers.

This book was also inspired by a golf tournament in 2013. For myself, awareness and interest in professional golf's dividing lines were heightened when on Sunday, June 23, 2013, I came upon the broadcast of the final round of the Travelers Championship from TPC River Highlands in Cromwell, Connecticut. One of the golfers in contention for the tournament championship was 44-year-old Ken Duke. Duke, who first played in a PGA Tour event in 1996, was making his 187th start on the Tour, but was still seeking his first tournament championship. Duke had some very successful seasons on the PGA Tour, earning almost $2 million in 2007 and more than $2 million in 2008. Duke had one second-place finish in 2007, two second-place finishes in 2008, and, overall, five top ten tournament finishes in each of those seasons. In 2012, Duke earned more than $1.5 million with six top ten tournament finishes. The CBS broadcasters highlighted Duke's storyline and some of the opportunities that would come with his first tournament victory on that Sunday of the 2013 Travelers Championship. As a fan of the sport, I simply wanted to see this compelling storyline unfold.

Duke arrived at the tenth hole in the final round with a score of nine under par. His approach shot to the green from 138 yards hooked badly left, but the ball ricocheted off of a tree and dropped onto the green, rolling inside six feet of the hole. Duke dropped his birdie putt. Duke says of his shot at the tenth hole, "that's just golf. There are plenty of shots where you get a bad break." Duke also points out that the key is to keep your composure and to stay focused in that the good fortune he experienced on the tenth hole was only meaningful because he made the putt.

Another birdie on the 11th hole put Duke into a tie for the lead. After a par on 12, a 45-foot birdie putt on 13 gave Duke the tournament lead at 12 under par. Duke responded to a bogey on 14 with a birdie on the 15th hole to once again tie for the lead.

Bubba Watson also birdied 15, giving him a one-stroke lead. Watson won four PGA tournaments at that point in his career, including the 2012 Masters and the 2010 Travelers Championship. On the 178-yard, par-3 16th hole, Watson hit his nine iron tee-shot into the water. His next shot from the drop zone went past the green, and Watson scored an uncharacteristic triple-bogey on the hole. Watson finished the tournament in fourth place at ten under par. He won $292,800 and accumulated 135 FedEx Cup points.

At the 18th hole, Ken Duke's putt from just off the green easily allowed him to make par. On the strength of a three under par 65 in the third round and a four under par 66 in the final round, Duke took his 12 under par score to the clubhouse with the tournament lead.

Chris Stroud emerged as the final challenger to Duke. At the time, Stroud was 31 years old and playing in his seventh full season on the PGA Tour. Stroud never won a PGA tournament at that time in his career. Stroud showed some consistency on the Tour, earning more than $900,000 with at least six top 25 finishes in each of the 2010, 2011, and 2012 seasons. Stroud came to the 18th hole one stroke behind Duke. After his approach shot left him off the green, a Duke victory appeared at hand. However, Stroud would improbably sink the 50-foot chip to tie for the lead and force a playoff.

On the first playoff hole, both players scored a par, with Stroud completing an up-and-down from the green-side bunker. Duke hit the defining shot of his career on the second playoff hole. His approach shot closely cleared a bunker and rolled less than three feet from the hole. Duke says of his shot in the playoff, "that is why you practice. You spend hours on the range so that you have a makeable putt." After Stroud's birdie attempt drifted slightly right, Duke made his birdie putt to earn the victory. He became the oldest first-time PGA tournament winner since 1995. The win at the TPC River Highlands golf course had special meaning for Duke as his teacher and mentor, Bob Toski, won his first PGA tournament on that same course in 1953.

For Duke, his victory earned him more than $1 million, the highest tournament earning for his career. In finally crossing the significant dividing line to tournament champion, Duke obtained the opportunities that come with a PGA Tour victory. Duke played in The Open Championship in 2013, and the Masters and U.S. Open in 2014, all tournaments that he had not played since 2009. He also became part of the tournament winners priority ranking group for the remainder of the current season and the following two seasons that ensured his entrance into all regular season tournaments on the PGA Tour.

Duke has not won another PGA Tour event, with his best finish being a tie for third in The Players Championship in 2016. Chris Stroud earned more than $650,000 at the 2013 Travelers Championship, at the time the highest tournament earning for his career. Stroud entered the 2016–2017 season having not yet won a PGA Tour event, and his performance at the 2013 Travelers remained his only second-place finish. Bubba Watson continued to have a stellar career. He claimed his second Masters Championship in 2014, and he returned to TPC River Highlands in 2015 to once again win the Travelers Championship. Watson had nine PGA tournament wins at the conclusion of the 2016–2017 season.

Sports are defined by moments. Professional athletes strive for their moment—the moment that changes the trajectory of their career and possibly even defines their career. For Ken Duke in 2013 in Connecticut, he had a career-changing, career-defining moment. All of the golfers whose moments of achievement are profiled in this book could just as easily point to the moments on the PGA Tour when they were on the losing end—when the putt did not roll in, or the tee-shot just drifted slightly into the difficult rough. The PGA Tour has these dramatic moments of triumph and misfortune every week.

The thrill of being a sports fan is witnessing these moments and being aware of their significance. It is about competition and rooting for the storylines that are occurring. Watching Ken Duke at the Travelers Championship began to raise my interest in seeking a better understanding of the PGA Tour system. I came to have a new appreciation for watching golf by seeing that tournament and knowing the opportunities that come from winning even one tournament championship, or making the tournament cut, and what they mean to a golfer's career. I hope this book does the same for the reader.

Introduction

The Pebble Beach Golf Links in California is one of the most historic locations in professional golf. It hosted the PGA Championship in 1977 and five U.S. Open Championship tournaments. Pebble Beach is hosting a sixth U.S. Open in 2019 to celebrate the 100-year anniversary of the golf course opening, and a seventh U.S. Open in 2027. Pebble Beach was host to the U.S. Open in 1982, when Tom Watson narrowly defeated Jack Nicklaus after he chipped in from the rough on the par-3 17th hole in the final round. This gave Watson his only U.S. Open victory among his eight major tournament championships. Pebble Beach witnessed two historic events while hosting the U.S. Open in 2000: Tiger Woods' first U.S. Open Championship, a 15-stroke win that remains the largest margin of victory in a major, and Jack Nicklaus playing in his final U.S. Open Championship. Nicklaus won the U.S. Open four times, including the 1972 tournament at Pebble Beach. In 2000, Nicklaus joined the traditional championship pairing for the first two rounds of the tournament after Payne Stewart, the 1999 U.S. Open champion, tragically passed away in a plane crash eight months earlier. At age 60, Nicklaus did not make the cut in the 2000 U.S. Open.

Pebble Beach also features one of the most popular annual stops on the PGA Tour, the AT&T Pebble Beach Pro-Am, originally known as the Bing Crosby Pro-Am. On Saturday, February 11, 2017, in the third round, Jordan Spieth was separating himself from the field at that year's tournament. Spieth shot a third-round, seven under par 65 that featured 13 one-putts. He needed 23 putts for the entire third round, and his back nine score of 31 required only ten strokes with his putter. Spieth finished the third round with a six-stroke lead. The closest any player would get in Sunday's final round was three strokes as Spieth achieved his first tournament championship at Pebble Beach. Spieth earned just under $1.3 million and accumulated 500 FedEx Cup points for the victory.

On that same Saturday at the Pebble Beach Golf Links course, playing the picturesque par-5, 543-yard 18th hole that bends left along the Pacific Ocean, D. A. Points teed off not chasing history, nor was he in contention for the tournament championship. Points was just trying to make the tournament cut, one of the fundamental weekly accomplishments for a professional golfer. By making the cut, a golfer simply gets to continue competing in the tournament, leading to his earning prize money and accumulating FedEx Cup points for that week. At the AT&T Pebble Beach Pro-Am, golfers play the Pebble Beach Golf Links, the Spyglass Hill Golf Course, and the Monterey Peninsula Country Club's Shore Course one round each before the tournament cut is administered. The third-round, 54-hole cut is different from the customary second-round, 36-hole cut. A golfer must be in the top 70, plus ties, to make the cut.

Points, champion of the 2011 AT&T Pebble Beach Pro-Am, was playing with his customary partner for the tournament, comedian and actor Bill Murray. Points had an up-and-down performance of six bogeys and five birdies to finish one over par in round one at the Monterey Peninsula course. He had another one over par score in round two at Spyglass Hill to put him at two over par for the tournament.

In round three on Saturday at the Pebble Beach Golf Links course, Points birdied the 2nd, 4th, and 6th holes and had no bogeys on his scorecard with one hole left to play. At 18, Points stood over his third shot, 112 yards from the green. He hit safely onto the green. Although Points left his birdie putt just short, he tapped in for his 12th consecutive par. His three under par round on Saturday put his tournament total score at one under par and placed him in a tie along with 13 other golfers for 53rd. Points' performance in the third round allowed him to make the tournament cut.

All golfers play the Pebble Beach Golf Links course in the final round on Sunday. Points shot a three under par 69 for the second consecutive round. He ended the tournament at four under par, in a tie for 39th. Points earned $26,640 and 13 FedEx Cup points at the 2017 AT&T Pebble Beach Pro-Am.

On the PGA Tour, for every golfer who makes the cut and continues to play, another golfer is coming up short and missing the cut. Jim Furyk found himself at even par at the 2017 AT&T Pebble Beach Pro-Am heading into his third round on Saturday at the Monterey Peninsula golf course. Entering the 2016–2017 season, Furyk won 17 PGA tournaments, made the cut in 465 tournaments, and ranked fourth on the Tour's career money list. Furyk earned more than $67 million in tournament prize money. Furyk moved to one under par in the third round when he scored a birdie on the 10th hole. He would take that score to the 17th hole. A bogey on the par-4, 430-yard 17th pushed him back to even par for the tournament. Furyk ended up one of 12 players tied for 66th at even par after the third round.

While the cut line is the top 70 golfers plus ties after 36 holes, if that total exceeds 78 golfers, another cut is administered after 54 holes. This 54-hole cut line is the closest to the top 70 golfers on the leaderboard. The golfers outside of that cut line number after the third round do not advance to the fourth round of that tournament. These golfers have to settle for a tournament result of MDF: made the cut, did not finish. The golfers who finish a tournament with the MDF designation are awarded prize money and FedEx Cup points. At the 2017 AT&T Pebble Beach Pro-Am, having only one cut after the third round, with 13 golfers tied at one under par for 53rd place, the position of D. A. Points, and 12 golfers tied at even par for 66th place, the position of Jim Furyk, meant that Furyk's tournament would end with an MDF result. For his play at the 2017 AT&T Pebble Beach Pro-Am, Furyk earned $14,184 and accumulated three FedEx Cup points.

Furyk could point to the third-round bogey on 17 as the reason for his not making the cut and being denied competing in Sunday's fourth round. Or, perhaps, it was the 13th hole in round two at Pebble Beach. With it raining, Furyk hit his tee-shot at the par-4 into the sand trap on the left side of the fairway, which happens to have a wooden walkway going through it. With his ball just short of the wooden walkway and his stance having him on an angle back toward the fairway, Furyk would have to stand on the slippery wooden surface for his second shot. Furyk decided to remove his shoes and socks to get his best footing. His barefoot shot did get him back in the fairway. Furyk's approach shot from 49 yards, his third on the hole, landed on the green, but he could not convert his par putt from eight feet, ten inches and had to settle for a bogey. Furyk's bad lie that forced him to hit one shot in that tournament without his golf shoes was the one-stroke difference in his not playing in the final round. On the PGA Tour, all shots determine the result, and any one of those shots can be looked at as the difference between the positive or negative side of one of golf's many dividing lines.

Three weeks earlier, on Sunday, January 29, 2017, another critical dividing line on the PGA Tour was crossed at Torrey Pines in La Jolla, California. Torrey Pines is most remembered for hosting the epic 2008 U.S. Open duel between Tiger Woods and Rocco Mediate. That tournament is very well detailed in Mediate's book, written with noted golf writer John Feinstein, *Are You Kidding Me? The Story of Rocco Mediate's Extraordinary Battle with Tiger Woods at the U.S. Open.* At the 2017 Farmers Insurance Open at Torrey Pines, 22-year-old Jon Rahm, in his first full regular season on the PGA Tour, crossed the dividing line by winning his first PGA tournament.

Rahm started the 2015–2016 season as an amateur. He turned professional after playing in the U.S. Open, a tournament in which he tied for 23rd. Rahm tied for third place at the 2016 Quicken Loans National tournament the week after the U.S. Open. He earned $400,200 for that performance. With the Quicken Loans National part of The Open Championship qualifying series, his result gained Rahm entrance into The Open Championship. Rahm finished tied for 59th and earned $21,035 in his first appearance in that major championship. Rahm was given a sponsor exemption into the RBC Canadian Open later in the season. That tournament was Rahm's best finish of the season when he tied for second, earning $440,533. Overall, for the 2015–2016 season, Rahm had nine starts in PGA tournaments. He made the cut on eight occasions and had six top-25 finishes to earn just over $1 million.

At the Farmers Insurance Open in 2017, Rahm's score of even par 72 in the first round placed him 77th on the leaderboard. He rebounded with consecutive scores of 69 to put him at six under par entering Sunday's final round. Rahm was tied with four other golfers who were three shots off the lead, held by Patrick Rodgers and Brandt Snedeker, the 2016 Farmers Insurance Open tournament champion. Rahm began his final round with a bogey on the first hole. After he birdied the 3rd and 5th holes and parred holes 6 through 9, Rahm finished the front nine with a 35, one under par. His score for the tournament was seven under par.

The back nine on Sunday at Torrey Pines would alter the trajectory of Rahm's young career. After a par on the 10th hole, Rahm birdied the 11th to move to eight under par. He arrived at the par-5 13th hole two shots off the lead. His tee-shot traveled 306 yards, but it was off of the fairway on the right. His second shot was from 227 yards. Rahm put that shot onto the green and when he converted the putt from 18-feet, seven-inches he scored an eagle.

Rahm was now in a four-way tie for the lead with Tony Finau, C. T. Pan, and Patrick Rodgers. The four-way tie remained when Rahm and J. J. Spaun, his playing partner, went to the par-4, 442-yard 17th hole. Spaun was also very much in contention, only one stroke behind the leaders. Putting first, Spaun made a birdie to create a five-way tie on top of the leaderboard. The logjam, however, was broken only moments later when Rahm converted his own birdie putt from five feet to give him a one-stroke lead with one hole left.

The 18th hole at Torrey Pines is a par-5, 536 yards. The Sunday pin placement was on the front, left side of a green that has a steep decline going from the back toward the front. The pin was located only a few yards behind a small water hazard that protects that part of the green. It is the tee-shot on 18 that very much determines whether a golfer can go for the green in two and give himself a chance for an eagle putt or has to lay up in the fairway and hit a pitch shot to the green for his third. Spaun, only one stroke behind Rahm, hit his tee-shot off to the right and was forced to lay up on his second shot. Spaun's third shot would come up short of the green and roll back into the water, eliminating him from contention.

Rahm's tee-shot was hit squarely in the fairway, placing him 240 yards from the green. His second shot needed 236 yards to clear the front, left water hazard. Using a 5-wood, Rahm landed his golf ball on the back of the green, 60 feet from the hole. Rahm was now in position to increase his lead. As he stood over his lengthy, downhill, left-to-right eagle putt, Dottie Pepper, CBS Sports golf analyst and 17-time tournament winner on the LPGA Tour, explained the difficulty of what she described as a "two-part putt" in which Rahm would have to correctly assess the speed as well as the angle as it traveled downhill. Struck at the perfect speed, along a perfect line, the golf ball drifted to the right side of the hole as it traveled downhill, only to turn back to the left and drop into the cup. Rahm's eagle putt secured his first PGA Tour victory. The eagle on 18 was his third of the tournament and his second in six holes. Rahm completed a back nine score of 30, six under par, to end the tournament at 13 under par. Rahm's first PGA Tour victory in only his 17th tournament start earned him more than $1.2 million.

The CBS broadcast team provided an explanation of the meaning of Rahm's victory beyond the financial award. A graphic on the television screen showed all of the tournament opportunities that Rahm secured with the win: 500 FedEx Cup points, which moved him from 67th place in the season-long FedEx Cup points standings to sixth place, entrance into all PGA Tour regular season tournaments through the 2018–2019 season, and invitations to the Masters, the Arnold Palmer Invitational, The Players Championship, the Memorial, the Dean & Deluca Invitational, and the PGA Championship in the current season. During the CBS broadcast, legendary golf announcer Jim Nantz rhetorically asked lead golf analyst and six-time major tournament winner Nick Faldo of Rahm's victory, "life-changing moment, isn't it?"

Although the tournament winner at Torrey Pines in 2017 was decided, there were meaningful outcomes still to be determined as other golfers finished their final rounds. Each week on the PGA Tour is not just about determining that tournament's champion. Other golfers are continuing on their quest to earn prize money and accumulate points toward the season-long FedEx Cup standings.

J. J. Spaun completed the 18th hole with a double-bogey, finishing in a five-way tie for ninth place. Spaun earned $167,500 and 70 FedEx Cup points. Tony Finau was nine under par for the tournament when he stood over a lengthy birdie putt on the 18th hole that, if made, would put him into a tie for second place. Nantz described the putt as one "that could be worth a whole lot." Finau's putt ended up a few revolutions of the golf ball short of the hole. Moments later, Patrick Rodgers, at eight under par, would sink his own birdie putt on 18 to join Finau, Justin Rose, Keegan Bradley, and Pat Perez in fourth place. Each was awarded $252,590 and 104 FedEx Cup points. Second-place finishers Charles Howell III and C. T. Pan each earned $589,600 and 245 FedEx Cup points at Torrey Pines.

As the results of the 2017 AT&T Pebble Beach Pro-Am and the 2017 Farmers Open at Torrey Pines demonstrate, every position where a golfer finishes on the leaderboard matters. Those who do not win the tournament championship still have the opportunity to earn prize money or move higher in the FedEx Cup points standings. These tournament results also demonstrate how each golfer is on his own unique path in navigating the PGA Tour system and his quest for career-changing moments.

1

Getting to the Tee

A moment can only be created if an opportunity presents itself. The opportunity simply to put a tee in the ground at a PGA tournament is earned through a golfer's performance in relation to every other competitor. The PGA Tour system is one where past performance has a profound future opportunity carryover. A team winning the Super Bowl does not automatically get to participate in the following season's NFL playoffs. In all other sports, the teams start their season with a record of 0–0. On the PGA Tour, one win creates tournament entrance opportunities for multiple seasons.

A golfer's performance determines what is referred to by the PGA Tour as his exempt status. The exempt status is granted through an elaborate qualification system that assigns each golfer to a ranking group for the season that is based on a specific achievement. The importance of the exempt status group is that it is a priority system that determines entrance into regular season tournaments. The golfers positioned in a higher priority ranking group have the right of first refusal to compete in a tournament. This simply means that there will be some golfers in a lower-ranked group who do not get to play. They need some golfers in the higher-ranked groups to decide not to play for them to have the opportunity to compete. Every time one of the PGA Tour's top golfers, such as Jordan Spieth, Rory McIlroy, Dustin Johnson, Justin Thomas, or Jason Day, choose not to play in a tournament, a spot opens up for a golfer in a lower priority ranking group. The top golfers can play as often or as little as they choose. It should, however, be noted that a golfer's sponsors have expectations and, in some instances, contractual obligations on the number of tournaments in which a golfer will compete.

The order of these priority ranking groups most rewards the golfers who won a recent tournament. All tournament winners are provided a multi-season exempt status. Different numbers of seasons of exempt status reflect the type

17

of tournament that a golfer wins. A victory in a major tournament or The Players Championship provides an exempt status in the highest priority ranking groups for the remainder of the current season and the following five seasons. Winning a major, from an historical perspective, places that golfer in the pantheon of golf's greatest champions. From a practical, financial perspective, winning a major provides job security that allows a golfer to compete in any regular season PGA tournament he desires for the following five seasons.

The winner of the Tour Championship, a World Golf Championships tournament, the Arnold Palmer Invitational, or the Memorial Tournament becomes exempt for the remainder of the current season and the following three seasons. The winner of a regular season tournament receives an exempt status for the remainder of the current season and the following two seasons. These tournament winners' priority ranking groups accounted for 69 active golfers entering the 2016–2017 season.

A five-season exempt status has also been granted to a golfer who leads a season's final FedEx Cup points standings or leads from a season's final PGA Tour money list. Beginning with the 2017–2018 season, the PGA Tour money list will no longer be used for a golfer's exempt status, and the season money list leader ranking group will eventually be phased out. Moving forward, only FedEx Cup points will be considered in the creation of an exempt status group.

In some instances, there are not any names in these cumulative season accomplishment groups as a golfer may qualify in an even higher priority ranking group. After all, the highest earnings and FedEx Cup points are accumulated by winning golf's most elite tournaments. For example, Dustin Johnson was the PGA Tour money list leader in 2015–2016. Johnson earned just under $9.4 million for the 22 tournaments that he played. However, he had his exempt status for the 2016–2017 season through the top priority ranking group for having won the 2016 U.S. Open. Similarly, Rory McIlroy was the leader of the final FedEx Cup point standings in 2015–2016. McIlroy is part of the highest priority ranking group for his victory at the 2014 PGA Championship, the major tournament that he also won in 2012. Brandt Snedeker is the one golfer who for the 2016–2017 season had his exempt status for being the final FedEx Cup points standings leader in 2012.

In 2016–2017, Justin Thomas earned the most prize money, winning more than $9.2 million in 25 tournaments. Thomas also won the FedEx Cup season-long championship in that season. Thomas began a five-season exempt status, through 2021–2022, in the top priority group for winning the 2017 PGA Championship. Billy Horschel is the one golfer who for the 2017–2018 season earned his exempt status by being the final FedEx Cup points standings leader, winning in 2014.

All other exemptions, except life member status, are for one season. Career performance is next in the tournament player priority selection process, with golfers who are in the top 50 or top 25 in career prize money earnings. These golfers have the choice to exercise a one-time, one-season exempt status. A golfer can use both his top-50 and top-25 career earnings for exempt status in different seasons if he qualifies to do so. In the 2016–2017 season, three golfers used their top-50 career earnings exemption and one golfer used his top-25 career earnings exemption.

Each individual tournament also has its own entrances that are provided for that specific event. These are the golfers who are given sponsor exemptions, chosen as the international commissioner picks, the PGA sectional qualifying champion, the winners of that specific tournament in the last five seasons, and the top four finishers in the one-day Monday qualifying tournament. The exemptions for the individual tournaments could produce between 15 and 19 golfers who are granted entrance into the event.

Career performance is again recognized with a group consisting of what the PGA Tour refers to as its life members. These are golfers "who have been active members of the PGA Tour for 15 years and have won at least 20 co-sponsored events." Being a life member is a permanent accomplishment and status. In the 2016–2017 season, two golfers applied their accomplishment as a life member for their exempt status.

Performance in PGA tournaments allows for the accumulation of FedEx Cup points. A golfer's position in the FedEx Cup points standings at the end of the regular season determines if he qualifies for the FedEx Cup Playoffs. To qualify for the first round of the FedEx Cup Playoffs, a golfer must place among the top 125 in the standings. If a golfer is playing in the FedEx Cup Playoffs, he is already guaranteed an exempt status for next season of no lower than the priority ranking group of the top 125 golfers in the FedEx Cup standings. This exempt status group is high enough in the tournament priority selection process to ensure that a golfer will gain entrance into any regular season tournament that he chooses to play. These golfers are ordered within the group based on their position in the final FedEx Cup points standings that is determined after the playoff tournaments are held. The top 125 in the FedEx standings group represented the largest number of exempted golfers, with 65 for the 2016–2017 season.

There are obviously golfers who qualify for the FedEx Cup Playoffs who are in higher priority ranking groups for the following season due to their past tour victories. For example, Phil Mickelson has his exempt status through the 2017–2018 season for his win at The Open Championship in 2013. Although Mickelson did not win a tournament from the 2013–2014 through the 2016–2017 season, he qualified for the FedEx Cup Playoffs in each of those seasons.

After the top 125 FedEx Cup points standings group, in 2016–2017 there was a separate group for being in the top 125 of the official PGA Tour money list at the end of the previous season. These golfers did not win a tournament, nor were they in the top 125 of the FedEx Cup standings in the previous season. In 2016–2017, six golfers qualified for this group. The 2016–2017 season represented the last time that a separate exempt group for those in the top 125 of prize money was used.

A separate group exists of the golfers who were non-members of the PGA Tour, but through their performances in their limited appearances in PGA Tour events accumulated either enough FedEx Cup points or earned enough prize money to qualify in the top 125 of either list. These non-members are ordered within the group based on their previous season's FedEx Cup points. There were four golfers in this group entering the 2016–2017 season.

The top 125 PGA Tour non-member group was the exempt status of Jon Rahm entering the 2016–2017 season. Rahm received special temporary member status on the PGA Tour in the 2015–2016 season when he reached a FedEx Cup points total that would have surpassed the 150th position in the standings. As he continued to play well in that season, Rahm accumulated the FedEx Cup points and prize money to rank amongst the top 125. Starting in 2017–2018, only the non-members achieving enough points to have finished in the top 125 in the FedEx Cup standings will comprise this group. The non-members will be placed in the priority order immediately after the FedEx Cup Playoff qualifiers group.

Golfers who were injured in the previous season are put into their own group with a designation of a major medical extension. They are placed next in the priority order. The PGA Tour gives these medical extension golfers a certain number of tournaments to earn a certain amount of prize money or FedEx Cup points to regain their full Tour exempt status. The medical exemption calculation is based on a golfer's recent history of tournament participation and the prize money or FedEx Cup points that would have been needed to reach the top 125. Again, only FedEx Cup points will be used in this calculation beginning with the 2017–2018 season. There were 14 golfers starting the 2016–2017 PGA Tour season with a medical extension.

Next in the tournament priority selection process are the professional golfers who finished in the top ten, including ties, in the most recent PGA tournament, earning entrance into the next regular season tournament. The number of golfers getting exempt into a tournament through this provision will vary on a weekly basis. Finishing in the top ten does create another critical dividing line of golf tournament outcomes and offers a significant opportunity to those who would not have otherwise qualified for entrance into the next PGA Tour event.

As explained in the PGA Tour media guide, the Web.com Tour is the "path to the PGA Tour." The golfers who graduate from the Web.com Tour onto the PGA Tour are placed in their own group, the top finishers of the Web.com Tour. PGA Tour cards achieved through the Web.com Tour qualifying process are only for the following season. There are 50 PGA Tour cards annually granted through the Web.com Tour. PGA Tour cards are awarded to the golfers who finish in the top 25 on the Web.com Tour's regular season money list. The other 25 PGA Tour card recipients emerge from the golfers who earn the most prize money in the four tournaments that comprise the Web.com Tour Finals.

The fields for the Web.com Tour Finals tournaments consist of the top 75 golfers on the Web.com Tour regular season money list, the PGA Tour golfers who are ranked 126 through 200 in the FedEx Cup points standings at the end of the PGA Tour regular season, and the non–PGA Tour members who, had they been members of the Tour, would have accumulated enough FedEx Cup points to be in the 126th through 200th position in the standings.

The 25 golfers who earned their PGA Tour card through the Web.com Tour regular season play in the Finals tournaments to determine their priority position within the top finishers of the Web.com Tour group for the following PGA season. These golfers essentially compete against each other with the prize money earned for the Finals tournaments added to the prize money that they earned in the regular season to create their position.

The ordering of the golfers within the top finishers of the Web.com Tour priority group is done on an alternating basis. A position first goes to a golfer from the combined regular season and Finals money list. He is followed by a golfer from only the Finals tournaments money list. The final golfer of the 50 within the Web.com ranking group is, thus, the 25th finisher on the Finals money list.

A golfer's performance on the Web.com Tour in the previous season can very well be the difference in determining his number of tournament starts in the current PGA Tour season. To illustrate, in the 2016 Web.com Tour season, Wesley Bryan accumulated the most prize money in the combined regular season and Finals tournaments. Grayson Murray earned the top prize money in the four Finals tournaments. Bryan played in 25 regular season events and Murray in 27 in the 2016–2017 PGA Tour season. Both won a tournament in their rookie season on the PGA Tour. They each would compete in three FedEx Cup Playoff tournaments. Cameron Percy and Tim Wilkinson held the last two positions in the top finishers of the Web.com Tour group. Percy played in 23 PGA Tour events and Wilkinson in 22. Neither qualified for the FedEx Cup Playoffs.

Troy Merritt played in 29 PGA Tour events in 2010 and 23 PGA Tour events in 2011 before having to spend the 2012 and 2013 seasons on the Web.com Tour. He made it back to the PGA Tour and played in 19 regular season tournaments in the 2013–2014 season as the number 30 ranked golfer in the top finishers of the Web.com Tour group. Merritt explains that when playing out of the Web.com Tour group, "you can do some planning, but you can't play in everything [tournaments] you want to play."

The last of the Web.com Tour's roles in the tournament priority selection process is the golfers who are granted a Web.com Tour medical extension. These golfers are placed in the group following the top finishers of the Web.com Tour group. There were 11 golfers given a Web.com Tour medical extension for the 2016–2017 season.

The Web.com Tour groups are followed by the golfers who finished 126 through 150 in the FedEx Cup points standings in the previous season. These golfers were unable to improve their exempt status by being in the top 25 in prize money earned in the Web.com Tour Finals tournaments. There were ten golfers in this exempt status group for the 2016–2017 season. Qualifying for the FedEx Cup Playoffs, therefore, represents one of the most important and consequential dividing lines on the PGA Tour because of the opportunity to continue earning in the current season, as well as setting up tournament entrance opportunities in the following season. For the 2016–2017 season, the difference in the tournament priority selection process between the final golfer in the top 125 finishers in the FedEx Cup standings group and the first golfer in the 126 through 150 finishers in the standings group was 85 golfers.

The next priority group consists of past tournament champions. These golfers are previous PGA tournament winners who were not able to qualify into a higher ranking group for that season. There were 53 golfers in the past champions group in 2016–2017. The past champions are ranked within the group by their combined earnings on the PGA Tour and Web.com Tour in the previous season.

Finally, veteran members comprise the last group. These are the golfers who have made a minimum of 150 tournament cuts in their career. These veteran members are prioritized within the group based on their placement on the career PGA Tour money list.

It is necessary to note that the golfers in certain groups are reordered within those groups at various points during the PGA Tour season. The golfers in the top finishers of the Web.com Tour group and the Web.com Tour medical extensions group are reordered. The golfers in the 126 through 150 in the FedEx Cup point standings group and the golfers who have a non-exempt, major medical or family crisis status are reordered. Finally, the past champions group and the veteran members group are reordered. In the 2016–2017 season, the reordering took place after the RSM Classic in November, the seventh tournament of the season, the Genesis Open in February, the 14th tournament of the season, and on the Mondays after the Masters, The Players Championship, the U.S. Open, and The Open Championship.

The priority selection process is used for the PGA Tour regular season tournaments. In 2016–2017, the PGA Tour's regular season began in October and consisted of 43 tournaments, including the four major championships. The regular season tournaments were played over 39 weekends. There were four weekends when the PGA held simultaneous tournaments. PGA tournaments were held opposite three of the World Golf Championships tournaments and a fourth the weekend of The Open Championship.

For the 2016–2017 regular season, in October, when the World Golf Championships—HSBC Champions tournament was being held in Shanghai, China, the PGA Tour hosted the Sanderson Farms Championship tournament in Jackson, Mississippi. In March, on the same weekend that the World Golf Championships—Dell Match Play tournament was held in Austin, Texas, the PGA Tour held the Puerto Rico Open. When The Open Championship was played in July in Great Britain, the PGA Tour held the Barbasol Championship in Auburn, Alabama. Finally, when the World Golf Championships—Bridgestone Invitational in Akron, Ohio, was held in August, the PGA Tour had the Barracuda Championship, contested in Reno, Nevada.

The 2016–2017 regular season schedule opened with seven tournaments played over six weekends in the autumn. The season began on Thursday, October 13, 2016, with the Safeway Open in Napa, California. The autumn portion of the season concluded on Sunday, November 20 with the RSM Classic from St. Simons Island, Georgia.

The golfers then had their longest break from PGA Tour events, as the Tour does not resume until January. It is important to note that there are other tournaments during this time period, such as the Australian Open and the Australian PGA Championship, the Hero World Challenge tournament in the Bahamas, and the QBE Shootout, a two-player team tournament. The participants can earn prize money in these tournaments, but their outcomes have no impact on the FedEx Cup points standings.

The PGA Tour resumed its 2016–2017 regular season schedule on Thursday, January 5, 2017, with the Tournament of Champions in Hawaii. Every week from that point in the season, there was a PGA tournament. The regular season concluded on August 20, 2017, with the final round of the Wyndham Championship. One week later, the four tournaments that comprise the FedEx Cup Playoffs began. Once the FedEx Cup Playoffs end with the Tour Championship as the final tournament, the next regular season begins immediately. When the Tour Championship concluded on Sunday, September 25, 2016, the 2016–2017 regular season commenced only 18 days later. The break between the 2016–2017 and 2017–2018 seasons was even shorter with only 11 days spanning the two seasons.

Setting the playing schedule has other unique challenges. The PGA Tour schedule needs to be coordinated with the Ryder Cup or the Presidents Cup. The Presidents Cup at Liberty National Golf Club in Jersey City, New Jersey, in 2017 was held on the weekend in between the Tour Championship and the first tournament of the 2017–2018 season. In 2016, another scheduling challenge was created when golf was introduced to the Olympics.

In August 2017, the PGA of America announced that beginning in 2019, it will move the PGA Championship from August to May. In addition to the PGA Championship schedule change, The Players Championship will move from May to March. This change provides professional golf with a signature event for five consecutive months prior to the FedEx Cup Playoffs, which will then conclude by Labor Day to avoid competition from the NFL, college football, and Major League Baseball pennant races. Peter Bevacqua, PGA of America Chief Executive Officer, stated of the schedule change, as quoted in the *Wall Street Journal*, "it provides our PGA Championship a strong landing spot on the calendar and a consistent major-championship rhythm that golf fans can embrace." These changes demonstrate that the tournament schedule is a tool designed to increase interest in the PGA Tour.

With the right of first refusal given to the golfers in the higher groups in the priority selection process, learning who is competing in a tournament and where a golfer is on a tournament entrance list is important to communicate. Every Friday at 5:00 p.m. Eastern becomes one of the most important times in golf. As the cut line and playing on Saturday and Sunday are being finalized for that week's tournament, the field for the following week's tournament is being determined. Golfers have until 5:00 p.m. on Friday to contact the PGA Tour office to communicate their entrance to or rescind their commitment from the following week's tournament.

There is an online system that golfers can use to commit to a tournament. The golfers, however, have to call the PGA Tour to withdraw from a tournament. Tour officials then call the golfer who is next in line in the priority process and inform him that he is now part of the tournament field. The Tour officials also call the next couple of golfers who are on the priority list to communicate to them that they moved up in the selection order. The entrance of golfers into the PGA Tour event has a domino effect on the field of the Web.com Tour event. A golfer may have thought that he was going to play in the Web.com

Tour event based on the initial commitments of higher ranked golfers, but the priority process could reach his position on the entrance list, and he is now part of the PGA Tour event field. This then opens up a spot in the Web.com Tour event.

Three other late variables play a role in the final formation of a tournament field. The golfers chosen as the sponsor exemptions are provided to the PGA Tour before the Friday 5:00 p.m. deadline. The second variable is that weekend's PGA Tour event, with the golfers who finish in the top ten on the leaderboard, including ties, granted entrance into the next PGA Tour regular season event. Finally, the Monday qualifying round produces four golfers who will join a tournament field.

It is because of this week-to-week schedule that attaining placement in a higher priority group is so vital. A higher position in the priority order allows these golfers to set their own tournament schedule. These golfers are picking the tournaments that they want to compete in on the golf courses they like and feel comfortable on rather than only playing in tournaments when they are given the opportunity. The advantage of setting your own schedule amplifies the benefits of winning a tournament. D. A. Points, the winner of three PGA Tour events, explains that with a win, "confidence is way up, pressure is off. Your shoulders hang a little bit softer to know I am going to play in the tournaments that I want to play in."

Kevin Kisner, winner of the RSM Classic in 2015 and the Dean & DeLuca Invitational in 2017, offers one reason why certain golfers prefer certain courses: they feel confident that they can consistently get the ball into the fairway off the tee. Kisner speaks to the value of winning and the relief of having two full seasons of status. He contends that while playing out of the top 125 in the FedEx Cup standings group does allow for choice of regular season tournament participation, it is still challenging because that status is for only one season. Kisner claims that a golfer in the top 125 in the FedEx Cup standings status is "still never comfortable" and that there is a feeling that, "I got to play all of the time."

Kisner points out that when on a one-season exempt status any golfer is capable of having a bad season, and there is always the fear of going back to the Web.com Tour. Kisner experienced that setback prior to winning a tournament. Kisner appeared in 24 PGA tournaments in both the 2011 and 2012 seasons before having to play 22 tournaments in 2013 on the Web.com Tour. He had only one PGA Tour start in that season. After finishing 13th in prize money in his 2013 season on the Web.com Tour, Kisner returned to playing 26 tournaments on the PGA Tour in 2013–2014.

Chesson Hadley won the Puerto Rico Open in 2014, but he had to return to the Web.com Tour for 2017 to obtain his PGA Tour card for the 2017–2018 season. He explains that upon returning to the PGA Tour, playing often early in the season will be important to once again "get used to the Tour." Hadley points out that on the PGA Tour, "it is easy to get distracted." There are many more fans watching at PGA Tour events than Web.com Tour events, including when the golfers are on the practice range or the putting green. Golf is unique in that a player is practicing next to his competitors with fans only a few yards away. There are also more demands from the media. Hadley says that his goal upon returning to the PGA Tour is to "keep it simple. The golf ball is the same size [on the PGA Tour as it is on the Web.com Tour]. The fact that there are other great players does not change certain things."

For Cody Gribble, a PGA Tour rookie in 2016–2017, his victory in the Sanderson Farms Championship, played the third week of that season, allowed him to set his tournament schedule for the remainder of the season. Being a rookie, Gribble indicates that one important aspect of the win and picking his schedule is that he can play as many tournaments as possible to learn the various golf courses that host the PGA tournaments.

Mackenzie Hughes, a PGA Tour rookie, was the winner of the RSM Classic, held the sixth weekend of the 2016–2017 regular season. Hughes explains that with the victory, he was afforded an amazing opportunity to "pick a schedule around the best tournaments and the best golf courses in the world." Hughes also describes it as a luxury to be able to take breaks from competing in tournaments during the season. The physical and mental grind of the PGA Tour's schedule is certainly a factor in strategically deciding when to play.

Golfers have to address the question of how many tournaments they are capable of competing in a row without becoming physically and mentally compromised. Kevin Kisner simply explains, "it is hard to play four tournaments in a row." Brendan Steele, who began playing regularly on the PGA Tour in 2011, points out, "you are always going to play in the big events [majors, World Golf Championships]." For the golfers who can pick which tournaments they choose to compete in, Steele describes the remainder of the schedule as a "balance between rest and events that you like to play." He contends that "you need time off to regroup not only physically, but you need a mental break too." Steele says that he likes to "get a couple of weeks off to miss it, and then be excited to go back out and play."

It is important to note that a golfer's week entails more than the four days of the tournament. There are Pro-Am events on Monday and Wednesday. The golfers are not required to play on Monday, but they are required to participate in a certain number of Wednesday Pro-Am events over the course of the season. Imagine that the day before an NFL game, Aaron Rodgers is told by the league that he has to play in a scrimmage flag-football game with executives of corporate partners.

In terms of the physical demand and the travel involved, golfers on the PGA Tour might or might not choose to participate in a tournament based on its geographic location. For example, there are two tournaments on consecutive weeks in January in Hawaii. The first is the Tournament of Champions, which a golfer only qualifies for if he won a tournament in the previous calendar year. If a golfer did not qualify for the Tournament of Champions, he will have to travel a considerable distance to play in only one tournament. There is also the point in the season when the Tour shifts from its West Coast swing with a tournament in California ending on Sunday to its Florida swing, with a tournament beginning the following Thursday.

Tournament location could have a personal connection that influences participation, such as a hometown or where a golfer played in college. Among the many examples, as an Arizona State alum, Jon Rahm pointed out that one of the early thrills in his golf career was playing the 16th hole at the Waste Management Phoenix Open held in Scottsdale, Arizona, with many Sun Devil fans rooting for him. The par-3 16th hole is known for its raucous gallery that surrounds the entire hole in a stadium setting. Billy Hurley III explained at the press conference for the 2017 Quicken Loans National tournament held at TPC Potomac at Avenel Farm in Potomac, Maryland that he played on that course while in high school. He was inspired by the professional golfers while serving as a caddie at the golf course when it was host to the Kemper Open on the PGA Tour. For Wesley Bryan, as a native of South Carolina, it was extra special that his first win on the PGA Tour occurred at the RBC Heritage played on Hilton Head Island. Bryan became the first South Carolinian to win that tournament.

The final variable of the priority selection process is that the number of golfers who participate in each tournament is capped. The majority of regular season tournaments begin with 156 golfers. Some regular season tournaments in the autumn have fields of only 144 golfers. Other tournaments that are invitation-only have even smaller fields, with qualifying for these tournaments based on a specific achievement. Entrance into the World Golf Championships tournaments, for example, is based on a golfer's Official World Golf ranking. In 2017, the World Golf Championships—Mexico Championship had only 77 golfers. The World Golf Championships—Dell Match Play is an event that invites only 64 golfers.

In other examples, in 2017, the Arnold Palmer Invitational at the Bay Hill Golf Club in Orlando, Florida, and the Memorial Tournament from the Muirfield Village Golf Club in Dublin, Ohio, had 120 players. The Dean & DeLuca

Invitational at the Colonial Country Club in Fort Worth, Texas, the longest-running host course for a non-major tournament on the PGA Tour, dating back to 1946, had 121 players. With the cut line for an invitational tournament the same as it is for any other regular season tournament that might have a field of 156 golfers, playing in these events offers less competition to make the cut and earn prize money and FedEx Cup points.

2

The FedEx Cup

Regardless of a golfer's exempt status priority ranking group entering the season, it is his performance during the current season that determines if he qualifies for the FedEx Cup Playoffs. In the quest to qualify for the FedEx Cup Playoffs, every golfer begins the season at zero. Moving up and down the FedEx Cup points standings is a week-to-week battle, with participation in the playoffs representing one of the most critical dividing lines of opportunity.

For each tournament that a golfer plays and makes the cut at, he accumulates points based on his performance. Just as a golfer's finish in a tournament has a dollar value assigned to it, each tournament finishing position has a certain amount of points. For 30 regular season tournaments, the winner receives 500 FedEx Cup points, which increases to 550 for the four World Golf Championships events. The winner of The Players Championship and each of the four major tournaments earns 600 points. The winner receives 300 FedEx Cup points in the four opposite tournaments. The winners of the Zurich Classic of New Orleans team event earn 400 points each.

The points scale for all positions on the leaderboard follows the similar pattern, based on the tournament prestige. For example, a tenth-place finish in the 30 regular season tournaments earns a golfer 75 points, 82 points for The Players Championship and the majors tournaments, 78 points for the World Golf Championships events, and 40 points for the opposite tournaments. For the FedEx Cup Playoff tournaments, points values for performance are greatly increased. The winner of a playoff tournament receives 2000 points.

The field for each of the FedEx Cup Playoff tournaments gets smaller as the playoffs progress. A golfer's placement in the FedEx Cup points standings determines his advancement to further tournaments in the playoffs. The top 125 golfers in the FedEx Cup points standings qualify for the first tournament of the playoffs, the Northern Trust (formally the Barclays), held in the New

York region. The field of 125 golfers in the first playoff tournament drops to 100 for the second playoff tournament, the Dell Technologies Championship (formally the Deutsche Bank Championship), played in the Boston region. In this tournament, the first round of the tournament is on Friday, instead of the customary Thursday, and the tournament concludes on Labor Day Monday.

There is a week off during the playoffs. In 2017, the break was between the second and third playoff tournaments, which eliminated the quick turnaround of completing one tournament on Monday and starting the next on Thursday. The third playoff tournament, the BMW Championship, in the Chicago region (played in Philadelphia for only the 2018 season), features 70 golfers. Finally, only 30 golfers tee off at the final tournament of the FedEx Cup Playoffs, the Tour Championship, held in Atlanta. The BMW Championship and the Tour Championship are no-cut, guaranteed prize money events. With a purse of $8.75 million spread out over 30 golfers, participating in the Tour Championship represents a lucrative capstone to a golfer's very successful season.

Each position in the final FedEx Cup points standings provides a golfer a playoff bonus. The winner of the FedEx Cup receives $10 million, with the runner-up being awarded $3 million. Payments of $2 million, $1.5 million, and $1 million round out bonuses for the top five finishers. On the bottom end of playoff qualifiers, the golfers in positions number 101 through 125 earn a bonus of $70,000. Even those golfers in positions number 126 through 150 in the FedEx Cup points standings, despite missing the playoffs, receive a bonus payment of $32,000.

In 2007, the PGA Tour landscape changed with the introduction of the season-long points race that would culminate in an end-of-season, four-tournament playoff. The belief among PGA executives at the time was that fans were losing interest in golf once the PGA Championship concluded in August. Even the Tour Championship, then played in November, did not garner significant interest from casual sports fans. The main objective of the season-long points race and the playoff format was to make golf relevant into the autumn by providing tournaments that featured the best players, even if that meant competing against football and the end of the Major League Baseball season. The final event of the four playoff tournaments would be the Tour Championship.

The season-long points race lends itself to each regular season tournament having more meaning. Upon announcing the new system at his State of the Tour address in November 2005, PGA Tour Commissioner Tim Finchem explained, "we're the only major sport that doesn't have a stronger finish than our regular season, a playoff system, if you will, that balances what's happening during the course of the year with what's happening week-to-week."

While conceived as a strategy to increase year-round interest in golf, creating a season-long points race and playoff system was certainly designed for revenue generation through television network and sponsorship interest. Finchem also announced that Federal Express agreed to serve as the title sponsor of the points series, creating the FedEx Cup. FedEx had been the title sponsor of the FedEx St. Jude Classic since 1986, the PGA Tour event held in Memphis, Tennessee, home of FedEx corporate headquarters. FedEx also became a sponsor of the PGA Tour in 2002.

In January 2006, the PGA Tour announced that it reached six-year television deals with CBS and NBC, as well as making the Golf Channel the exclusive cable television partner of the Tour for the next 15 years. For NBC, which did not televise the NFL on Sunday afternoon and had only Notre Dame home football games on Saturday, the FedEx Cup would provide valuable programming at that time of the year. The creation of the FedEx Cup was credited with stabilizing the broadcast rights fees paid by the networks to the PGA Tour.

The timing of the launch of the FedEx Cup playoff system was certainly opportunistic, as it gave the PGA Tour another chance to capitalize on one of the greatest assets that it has ever known—Tiger Woods. In 2007, Woods was at the height of his excellence and popularity. Prior to 2007, Woods won 12 majors and was the PGA Tour "Player of the Year" eight times between 1997 and 2006, with only Mark O'Meara in 1998 and Vijay Singh in 2006 interrupting his streak. Woods ended the 2006 season by winning his last six PGA Tour events, including The Open Championship and the PGA Championship. When Woods won the first tournament that he played in 2007, he completed a stretch from July through January in which he won every PGA Tour event that he entered.

With the total playoff bonus prize money for the FedEx Cup at $35 million and the winner receiving $10 million, the FedEx Cup Playoff tournaments would mean more opportunities to put Woods and the Tour's other premier players on television in events that would now be viewed as significant.

Finchem summarized his vision in detail:

> We think every one of our events is going to be strengthened. We think players are going to be motivated and incentivized to actually play more. Our television, we think is going to be not only more impactful, but more balanced because we'll have a better number of huge profile events at the end of the season which can tie to our different television packages. We think overall field strength will be supported, as well, and we think fan interest and some of the other things we're going to do, different platforms, can bring fans to be related to FedEx Cup competition during the course of the year.

The championship series benefits obviously give us what we've wanted for a long time, a culminating end to our season. We think that in and of itself, if you look at all of our sports, if we do anything approaching any other sports, it's a huge impact on our overall television position, and it helps carry our audience into the fall.

The reaction of the golfers was mixed. Davis Love III was quoted in the *Dallas Morning News*, stating, "changing the format is a great idea, having a new product is a great idea, and ending it in a playoff is a great idea." Vijay Singh was quoted in *USA Today*, commenting, "this is going to bring the whole game of golf to a different level. All the top guys are going to be there toward the end of the year. I think this is going to do very well for the spectators and for the Tour." Paul Azinger, however, was quoted in the *Toronto Globe & Mail* on January 18, 2006, saying, "you're not going to make history winning some kind of FedEx Cup."

Members of the media were skeptical of the new playoff format and the perceived manufactured relevance, particularly in relation to the major championships. Ron Kroichick wrote in the *San Francisco Chronicle*, the day after the announced changes, that Finchem "made it sound as if fans breathlessly will follow the points race from January through September…. Sorry, Tim, but that's a stretch. Many people tune in only for the majors—history matters—and for the final round of tournaments in which big-name players are chasing victory." Tod Leonard wrote in the *San Diego Union-Tribune*, "professional golf is defined by its major championships. It always has been, and hopefully, always will be."

The early years of the FedEx Cup format brought several obstacles. Golfers were critical that the playoff bonus was a deferred payment (a structure that was changed after the first season to one where the golfers received 90 percent of their playoff bonus immediately). There was some confusion about how the points system worked, despite the PGA's efforts to get the standings published in newspapers and to have the announcers during golf broadcasts attempt to better educate the fans.

Golfers were also concerned about their playing schedule and the possibility of having to compete for many consecutive weeks. When some golfers did skip playoff tournaments in the first year, the criticism then became that these events could not be that important. Tiger Woods missed the first tournament, Ernie Els skipped the second tournament, and Phil Mickelson and Padraig Harrington did not participate in the third tournament in the first year of the playoffs. Dave Perkins wrote in the *Toronto Star*, "no problem here with the stars doing their own thing," but he added, "please don't tell us tell us how important the FedEx Cup is, either." Mike Downey similarly commented in the *Chicago Tribune*, "if the golfers don't treat it like a major, it's a minor."

Woods won the inaugural FedEx Cup and the $10 million bonus. After his victory at the Tour Championship, another criticism became that a golfer could miss a playoff tournament, yet still win the season-long championship. After skipping the first playoff tournament and falling out of first place in the FedEx Cup points standings, in the three remaining playoff tournaments, Woods finished in a tie for second and won both the third tournament and the Tour Championship. For some, there was a sense of justification in Woods winning the FedEx Cup, as in 2007 he also won the PGA Championship and the PGA "Player of the Year." Had a golfer other than Woods won the FedEx Cup in 2007, there would have been criticism regarding how valid a FedEx Cup Championship is when the best golfer in the sport is not the winner.

There were some early signs of success for the new playoff system. Steve Stricker won the first FedEx Cup Playoff tournament in 2007 with a birdie on each of the last three holes to claim a two-stroke victory over K. J. Choi. Tod Leonard, one of the early skeptics of the FedEx Cup format, wrote in the *San Diego Union-Tribune* about that first playoff tournament, "I was actually caring what the results were going to be in a PGA Tour event. I hadn't really expected to be intrigued much at all, given all of my reservations about the worthiness of the new FedEx Cup playoffs."

The second playoff tournament featured Tiger Woods and Phil Mickelson battling for the championship. Paired together for the final round, Mickelson birdied the 16th and 18th holes to help secure a two-stroke victory over Woods, who birdied 14, 16, and 18. Brett Wetterich, who birdied 16 and 18, and Aaron Oberholser, who birdied 16, were also only two strokes behind Mickelson.

Despite an occasional skipping of a tournament by a couple of golfers, it quickly became evident that one goal of the FedEx Cup was being accomplished: these playoff tournaments were getting many of the top players to compete. Steve Stricker was quoted on ESPN.com, stating, "we saw in every tournament the great fields." He added, "I think that shows you right there that it's working." Bill Nichols wrote in the *Dallas Morning News* that the FedEx Cup "accomplished what it set out to do by getting the top players together more often." Ron Kroichick, another columnist who expressed some skepticism of the FedEx Cup format, stated in the *San Francisco Chronicle*, "don't call the FedEx Cup Playoffs boring or irrelevant. No way. This has been absolutely compelling. In other words, three of the best tournaments of the season, no question. The debut of the FedEx Cup still seems like a rousing competitive success."

There were also some positive fan behavior metrics that the PGA Tour noted to indicate the success of the FedEx Cup Playoff tournaments. In 2006,

Tiger Woods did not even compete in the November PGA Tour Championship. In 2007, with the Tour Championship now played in September as the culminating event of the FedEx Cup and with Woods winning the tournament, as reported in *Street & Smith's Sports Business Journal*, television ratings increased 87 percent on Saturday and 200 percent for Sunday's final round. *Street & Smith's Sports Business Journal* also reported that traffic on the pgatour.com web site increased an estimated 200 percent for the FedEx Cup Playoffs, with the Tour Championship seeing a 300 percent increase. *New York Times* sports editor Tom Jolley commented that his newspaper increased its golf coverage and sent reporters to all four playoff tournaments. Jolley told *Street & Smith's Sports Business Journal*, "I don't think we would've [done that] if the FedEx Cup hadn't been created."

The early years of the FedEx Cup continued with adjustments in how the points were awarded. One change was to respond to the criticism that the winner of the FedEx Cup was essentially determined before the Tour Championship. In 2008, after winning the first two tournaments of the FedEx Cup Playoffs, all Vijay Singh had to do to win the FedEx Cup was make it through all four rounds of the Tour Championship. Even Camilo Villegas winning the final two playoff tournaments could not overcome the lead that Singh amassed.

The 2008 season was one of only three in which the winner of the season-long FedEx Cup Championship was not the winner of the Tour Championship. In 2009, Tiger Woods won the FedEx Cup Championship despite not winning the Tour Championship. In that season, Woods had six PGA Tour wins, including the third tournament of the playoffs. He also had three second-place finishes, including the first tournament of the playoffs and the Tour Championship, where he lost to Phil Mickelson by three strokes.

From 2010 through 2016, every winner of the Tour Championship was the FedEx Cup Champion. In 2017, Justin Thomas won the FedEx Cup Championship despite not winning the Tour Championship. Thomas won five tournaments during the season, including the PGA Championship and the Dell Technologies Championship, the second tournament of the FedEx Cup Playoffs. Thomas also finished tied for sixth at the Northern Trust tournament that began the FedEx Cup Playoffs. Finally, Thomas came in second at the Tour Championship, losing to Xander Schauffele by one stroke.

Another issue was raised when some of the top golfers did not qualify for FedEx Cup Playoff tournaments, particularly the Tour Championship. In 2008, Padraig Harrington won The Open Championship and the PGA Championship, but he did not qualify for the Tour Championship. In 2010, Tiger Woods would not defend his 2009 FedEx Cup Championship when he did not qualify for the Tour Championship. John Feinstein stated on the Golf Channel, "you certainly don't exempt anybody into an event where you have to be in the top 30 for the year to qualify. That means you qualify, you don't get a sponsor exemption or Tour exemption because you help TV ratings." Steve Elling posted on cbssports.com, "it was Woods' decision not to play more tournaments over the summer to increase his chances of adding points." An adjustment, however, was made as to how points were awarded, with an emphasis placed on winning a major or other elite events by allocating more FedEx Cup points for those tournaments.

For the sport's top golfers, the bonus money increase through the FedEx Cup Playoff tournaments has been significant. Despite not competing in the playoffs from 2014 through 2017, Tiger Woods earned more than $25 million in FedEx Cup Playoff bonuses. In addition to the $10 million playoff champion bonus, the PGA Tour recognizes winning the FedEx Cup Championship as significant by awarding the winner a five-season exempt status. More than the season-long champion, it is undeniable that the FedEx Cup benefited all golfers by providing them with another opportunity to earn.

For all of its critiques and format iterations in its early years, the FedEx Cup achieved two of its most fundamental goals. The first is making the PGA Tour regular season more relevant. The broadcasters even emphasize this importance at the beginning of a PGA Tour telecast by announcing that the tournament is part of the "season-long race for the FedEx Cup." The second goal is making the PGA Tour more relevant at the end of the season. Even if not viewed in the same manner as the major tournaments, the FedEx Cup Playoffs continue to provide more tournaments that bring together the best golfers in the world. In that light, the comparison to the major tournaments is a bit irrelevant. The FedEx Cup Playoffs can produce exciting competition among the game's best golfers, with significant consequences based on the outcome.

The sponsors and television networks have responded positively to the FedEx Cup. According to a January 2012, article in *Street and Smith's Sports Business Journal*, FedEx renewed its title sponsorship at a cost of an estimated $30 to $35 million per year. In May 2017, FedEx extended its naming-rights agreement with the PGA Tour for the playoff series for an additional ten years, through 2027. The PGA Tour also signed television deals with CBS and NBC that began in the 2012–2013 season and run through 2020–2021.

Much of the criticism of the FedEx Cup subsided, and after a decade in existence, being a part of the FedEx Cup Playoffs is a goal for every golfer on the Tour. As Phil Mickelson stated in 2012 in *Golf World*, "there was a lot of skepticism when it first came out. We were not sure how it was going to evolve, but now it's really become a staple of the PGA Tour and something that the players really look forward to and strive for."

3

The Next Opportunity

The priority system for tournament entries creates vastly different experiences amongst the PGA players. Again, all of these opportunities are based on performance—they are earned. There are those golfers who have earned a spot on the PGA Tour, where their tournament participation consists of the majors, the World Golf Championships events, The Players Championship, and any regular season tournaments that they choose to participate in.

It is the elite tournaments that have higher prize money and FedEx Cup points, and in some instances smaller fields. For the major tournaments in 2016–2017, The Open Championship total prize money was $8.45 million, the Masters and the U.S. Open had $10 million, with $1.8 million awarded to the winner, and the PGA Championship had $10.5 million, with $1.89 million awarded to the winner. The Players Championship also awarded $10.5 million, with $1.89 million to the winner. For the four World Golf Championships, the HSBC Champions tournament in China had total prize money of $9.5 million, with $1.4 million awarded to the winner. The other three World Golf Championships events had total prize money of $9.75 million, with $1.755 million awarded to the winner. Each FedEx Cup Playoff tournament in 2017 had total prize money of $8.75 million, with a winner's share of $1.575 million.

There is a subset of golfers who are exempt into any regular season tournament, but have not qualified for all of the majors or World Golf Championships tournaments. Finally, there is a third subset of golfers who are in the lower priority ranking groups and are hoping the priority selection process reaches their position for entrance into regular season tournaments. This group of golfers may be splitting time between PGA Tour and Web.com Tour events. They may also be hoping for sponsor exemptions or participate in Monday qualifiers to try to obtain entrance into a PGA tournament.

Every golfer is, thus, competing for his own individual next set of opportunities. Brendan Steele, two-time winner on the PGA Tour at the conclusion of the 2016–2017 season, spoke with excitement about 2017 being the first time in his career he was able to play in all four majors in the same season, as well as compete in three World Golf Championships tournaments. Steele secured his entrance into the 2017 Masters upon winning the Safeway Open in the autumn of 2016. It was the first time that he qualified for the Masters since 2012, when he missed the cut. Steele shot three over par and finished tied for 27th at the 2017 Masters. He earned $78,100.

Trying to break into a higher status of the golfers who consistently play in the majors and World Golf Championships is not easy because the golfers already in those status positions have some advantages in staying there. Kevin Kisner began 2016–2017 in the regular season tournament winners group. He explains that by winning a tournament, a golfer has a big advantage to maintain status because he is going to get into the higher prize money, more FedEx Cup points events.

To illustrate, in the 2013–2014 season, the only major that Kisner appeared in was the U.S. Open. He did qualify for the FedEx Cup Playoffs, but his season ended after missing the cut at the first playoff tournament. In 2014–2015, Kisner appeared in three majors, but not the Masters. Since his win at the RSM Classic in the autumn portion of the 2015–2016 season, Kisner appeared in every major tournament, and he reached the Tour Championship from the 2015 through 2017 seasons.

Kisner was part of the 121-golfer field at the 2017 Dean & DeLuca Invitational at Colonial Country Club. He entered the final round three strokes behind tournament leader Webb Simpson. Kisner made up the deficit when he scored consecutive birdies on the 10th through 12th holes. The birdie on 10 was the result of Kisner draining a 40-foot putt. Kisner became the tournament leader when he birdied the 15th hole. A bogey by Kisner on the 16th hole and a birdie by Jon Rahm on the 17th hole tightened the lead to one stroke. Kisner missed the green in regulation on 18 to create an opening for Rahm. After Rahm missed his birdie putt, Kisner dropped his five-foot par putt that completed a back-nine 32 and gave him his second PGA tournament championship. Kisner extended his exempt status in the tournament winners group through the 2018–2019 season.

Other examples speak to the opportunities for a golfer to maintain his status. Participating in the World Golf Championships tournaments is significant not only because of the smaller fields, but because these tournaments are no-cut, guaranteed prize money and FedEx Cup points events. In another example, the Tournament of Champions consists only of the golfers who won a tournament in the previous calendar year. In 2017, the field was made up of

32 golfers. With no cut administered in this tournament, these golfers are obtaining prize money and FedEx Cup points on a weekend when no other golfers are competing.

Participation in the Tour Championship also exemplifies the advantaged starting point to maintaining high status. There are only 30 golfers in the no-cut, guaranteed prize money event with one of the largest purses on the Tour. Moving forward, all of the golfers who participate in the Tour Championship will have an exempt status that is no worse than being in the highest finishers in the top 125 of the FedEx Cup points standings group. Many golfers participating in the Tour Championship won a tournament recently and are in an even higher priority ranking group. Simply put, all of the golfers playing in the Tour Championship know that they will get into any regular season tournament they choose in the following season.

Of the 30 golfers in the 2016 Tour Championship, 21 won a tournament during the 2015–2016 season. As for how the 30 Tour Championship participants in 2016 entered the season, 11 had their exempt status for winning a major, World Golf Championships tournament, or The Players Championship. There was one golfer whose status was as a former FedEx Cup Champion. Another four golfers played out of the regular season tournament winners group. Ten golfers in the Tour Championship emerged from the top 125 in the FedEx Cup standings in the previous season group. There were three golfers in the Tour Championship who began the 2015–2016 season in the top finishers of the Web.com Tour group. Finally, there was one golfer who began the season in the past champion group and qualified for the Tour Championship. The high exempt group advantage is also demonstrated in the consistency in the Tour Championship field year-to-year. Of the 30 golfers in the 2016 tournament, 15 played in that event the previous season.

Similar dynamics played out in the 2016–2017 season. Of the 30 golfers in the 2017 Tour Championship, 20 won a tournament during the 2016–2017 season. As for how the 30 Tour Championship participants in 2017 entered the season, nine had their exempt status for winning a major, World Golf Championships tournament, or The Players Championship. Another nine golfers played out of the regular season tournament winners group. Eight golfers in the Tour Championship emerged from the top 125 in the FedEx Cup standings in the previous season group. There was one golfer who made the Tour Championship who started the season on a PGA Tour medical exemption and one golfer who started the season on a Web.com Tour medical exemption. One golfer made the Tour Championship playing out of the top finishers of the Web.com Tour group. Finally, one golfer who started the season as the non-member of the PGA Tour who would have been in the top 125 of FedEx Cup points or prize money group was able to play his way into the Tour Championship. Of the 30 golfers in the 2017 Tour Championship, 14 played in that event the previous season.

Being in the Tour Championship offers a significant added benefit, entrance into the following year's Masters tournament. As a major, the Masters offers golfers higher prize money and more FedEx Cup points. Certainly, winning the Masters, or any major, will secure entrance into that season's FedEx Cup Playoffs. Danny Willett plays many tournaments in Europe and comes to the United States mostly to play in the majors and World Golf Championships. In the 2015–2016 season, Willett played in only nine PGA Tour events, while playing in 12 European tournaments. Willett's win at the Masters in 2016 gave him 600 FedEx Cup points. He finished the regular season with only 695 points, ranking him 75th in the standings. Without the Masters performance, Willett would not have qualified for the FedEx Cup Playoffs. Although Willett chose not to compete in the FedEx Cup Playoffs, instead playing in tournaments in Europe, he still finished in 93rd place in the final FedEx Cup standings to earn a playoff bonus of $75,000.

While each major tournament has its own unique qualifying standards, the reverence that professional golfers have for the Masters cannot be overstated. Playing Augusta National is always one of the significant goals that a golfer has for the season as well as a meaningful career achievement. The golfers who are in the top 50 on the leaderboard or are within ten strokes of the lead after the second round of the tournament make the cut at the Masters.

The criteria for participation at the Masters begin with honoring its past champions, as all former winners of the Green Jacket are given entrance. Masters' entrances are also provided to the winners of the other major tournaments for the past five years. The winner of The Players Championship gets admittance into the Masters for the next three years.

One of the storylines at the 2017 tournament was the possibility of Ernie Els participating in his last Masters. Els, a four-time major champion, was part of the Augusta National field every year since 1994 except one, 2012. Els finished second at the Masters on two occasions, 2000 and 2004. He qualified for the 2017 Masters by winning The Open Championship in 2012. With a five-season exemption for winning that major, it made 2017 the final year that Els qualified through that path. Els finished 53rd in the 2017 Masters to earn $27,060.

Tournament performance at Augusta National is recognized with the top 12 finishers, including ties, from the previous year's Masters granted entrance. In the 2017 Masters, Brooks Koepka, Hideki Matsuyama, Russell Henley, Rickie Fowler, and Jordan Spieth finished tied for the 11th and final position to qualify for the 2018 Masters (the next finisher on the leaderboard is considered then to be in 16th place). Fowler and Spieth already had their entrances for the 2018 tournament secure, Fowler as the winner of The Players Championship in 2015, Spieth as the 2015 Masters champion. Other past Masters champions who finished in the top 12 in 2017, Charl Schwartzel and Adam Scott, had their entrances for the 2018 tournament for winning a past Masters, Schwartzel in 2011 and Scott in 2013. Of course, one other top 12 finisher in 2017 now had a permanent spot in the Masters field, tournament winner Sergio Garcia.

In the 2017 Masters, Martin Kaymer and Steve Stricker finished in a tie for 16th place, one stroke short of being in the top 12. Kaymer opened the Masters with a 78 on Thursday that included a six-over-par performance on the back nine. He also bogeyed the 18th hole in the final round to just miss being a part of the quintet who tied for 11th place. Kaymer, a two-time major winner with his most recent win coming at the U.S. Open in 2014, already had his trip back to the 2018 Masters secure for that victory at Pinehurst. Stricker rallied with three birdies on the back nine to finish even par in the final round. Although Stricker would now have to find another path back to the 2018 Masters, he did earn $181,500 for his performance at the 2017 tournament.

The top four finishers, including ties, in each of the previous season's major tournaments are invited to the Masters. While most golfers qualify for the Masters through multiple criteria, the interesting storylines belong to the golfers who earned their trip to Augusta through a singular method. Stricker achieved his entrance into the 2017 Masters due to a fourth-place finish at The Open Championship in 2016, when he played the final 31 holes at six under par.

Daniel Summerhays also qualified for the 2017 Masters due to a top performance in a major, a third-place finish at the 2016 PGA Championship. He birdied the 15th, 16th, and 18th holes in the final round to get into third place. At the 2017 Masters, Summerhays finished in a tie for 46th to earn $36,300.

Similarly, Summerhays qualified for the 2017 U.S. Open due to his performance at the 2016 U.S. Open. One of the entrance criteria for the U.S. Open is finishing in the top ten, including ties, at the previous year's tournament. Summerhays had a final round 74, four over par, but his birdie on the 17th put him into a tie for eighth place with three other players at the 2016 U.S. Open. An additional stroke would have dropped Summerhays to 11th place. Summerhays would not have been part of the 2017 U.S. Open field through any other entrance qualification. He finished 65th at the 2017 U.S. Open to earn $23,454.

The Masters continues its tradition of inviting amateur champions. The U.S. amateur champion and runner-up, the British amateur champion, the Latin

America amateur champion, and the U.S. mid-amateur champion all receive entrance.

The winners of PGA tournaments since the previous year's Masters in which full FedEx Cup points are awarded qualify for the Masters (the winners of the opposite tournaments are not invited to the Masters simply on the basis of winning those events). Sergio Garcia, the 2017 Masters champion, earned his entrance into that year's tournament by winning the AT&T Byron Nelson in May 2016. The winner of the RBC Heritage, the tournament played the week after the Masters, already knows that he will be spending a week playing golf at Augusta National the following April.

Again, the participants from the previous autumn's Tour Championship are given entrance into the Masters. Brendan Steele describes one aspect of his season's goals in terms of thinking of two of the paths to get to the Masters— win a tournament or qualify for the Tour Championship. An elite tournament such as the Masters, with more FedEx Cup points, gives those golfers who qualify a tremendous opportunity to improve their positioning for that current season's FedEx Cup Playoffs. Then, once back in the playoffs, the cycle can continue. If a golfer can advance all the way to the Tour Championship, it means that he is heading back to Augusta.

For Sean O'Hair and Roberto Castro, being in the Tour Championship in 2016 became the only way that either player would qualify for the 2017 Masters. O'Hair began the FedEx Cup Playoffs in the 108th position, but he played his way into the Tour Championship largely on the strength of a tie for second in the Barclays, the first playoff tournament. He tied for 53rd in the Deutsche Bank Championship and tied for 52nd in the BMW Championship. It would be O'Hair's seventh time playing in the Masters and his first appearance since 2012.

Castro entered the FedEx Cup Playoffs in the 53rd position and remained in that spot heading into the BMW Championship. Castro missed the cut in the Barclays before finishing tied for 24th in the Deutsche Bank Championship. At the BMW Championship, Castro shared the lead with Dustin Johnson at 14 under par at the conclusion of the second round. Castro recorded 15 birdies and only one bogey over the first two rounds of the tournament. In the third round, a two over par 74, in which he did not score a birdie, put Castro's season in jeopardy.

Castro rose to the occasion in the final round. He shot a five under par 67 that featured an eagle on the par-4 7th hole when his shot from 160 yards found the bottom of the cup. His four additional birdies offset the lone bogey on his scorecard. Castro finished the BMW Championship alone in third place to earn the requisite number of points to qualify for the 2016 Tour Championship and the 2017 Masters. It was Castro's first trip back to Augusta since playing in the 2014 tournament. Neither Castro nor O'Hair made the cut at the Masters in 2017.

The final entrants into the Masters occur through the Official World Golf rankings. The top 50 from the final world ranking in 2016 and the top 50 from the world ranking on March 26, 2017, qualify. Ross Fisher of England became the last qualifier for the 2017 Masters through the Official World Golf rankings. Fisher ended the 2016 season at number 65 in the rankings. Fisher's late rally into the Masters began with a tie for third at the World Golf Championships–Mexico Championship that concluded on March 5. He was two strokes behind tournament winner Dustin Johnson. Fisher's final-round 65 featured five birdies on the back nine, including birdies on the 16th, 17th, and 18th holes.

Fisher found himself in the 53rd position in the rankings on March 12. That position still was not good enough for entrance into the Masters, but it was good enough to get him into the World Golf Championships–Dell Match Play that would conclude on March 26. The World Golf Championships—Dell Match Play invites only 64 golfers, using the Official World Golf rankings to set the field of participants. Prior to 2015, the Match Play used a single-elimination tournament competition. In the revised tournament format, the 16 top-seeded golfers are spread out over 16 groups, with each group consisting of four golfers. The golfers play a round-robin within their group over the first three days of the tournament that begins on Wednesday. In these Wednesday through Friday matches, the winners are awarded one point, and one-half point is awarded for a halved match. If there is a tie within a group after all of the preliminary matches, a sudden-death playoff is conducted. The winners of each group advance to the round of 16 to begin the single-elimination portion of the event.

Fisher was placed in a group with Hideki Matsuyama, the number four seed for the entire event, Louis Oosthuizen, and Jim Furyk. Fisher lost his first match to Oosthuizen, 4 and 3 (trailing by four holes with three holes left to play). Victories over Matsuyama, 2 and 1 (up two holes with one hole left to play), and then Furyk, 4 and 2, created a tie for the group winner with Oosthuizen, who dropped his match to Furyk. Fisher and Oosthuizen would have to break the tie in a sudden-death playoff. Both found the fairway on their tee-shots on the second hole of the playoff, with only 12 yards separating the two. Fisher lying 159 yards from the green placed his shot to 14 feet, nine inches from the cup. Oosthuizen, from 147 yards out, left himself 45 feet for his birdie. Fisher made his birdie putt and Oosthuizen did not. Fisher advanced out of the group stage.

In the round of 16, Fisher defeated Bubba Watson, 4 and 3. Fisher's run in the World Golf Championships—Dell Match Play ended in the round of eight when he lost to Hideto Tanihara, 4 and 2. Fisher's performance did allow him to leap into the top 50 of the Official World Golf rankings calculated on March 26, 2017, settling in at number 49. For Fisher, it was his fifth trip to the Masters and his first appearance since 2012. Fisher shot seven over par at the Masters, which tied him for 41st place. He earned $46,200.

4

Making the Cut

Once a golfer gains entrance into a tournament, the initial objective is to make the cut and continue to play in the third and fourth rounds. The beginning of a tournament is the one time on the PGA Tour where past performance does not matter. Every golfer puts a tee in the ground at his first hole of the first round starting at zero. Upon making the cut, it guarantees a golfer that some prize money will be earned and some FedEx Cup points will be accumulated.

If a golfer does not make the tournament cut, he does not earn any prize money or FedEx Cup points for that week's effort. Multiple weeks of not making the cut can be devastating, considering a golfer's cost structure to participate in a tournament. Golfers on the PGA Tour have to pay for their own travel to tournaments, although the Tour does provide a hotel room at a reduced rate and a free rental car for the week. Golfers also have to pay their caddies and other support staff (swing coach, agent). Nick Taylor, a graduate from the Web.com Tour in 2014 and the winner of the Sanderson Farms Championship in the 2014–2015 PGA Tour season, was quoted by Jim Caple on espn.com in 2016, stating, "it's hard to explain to people sometimes. The majority of athletes in every other sport, they might be paid less than what golfers make but all of their expenses are taken care of, so they don't have to worry about that. If a golfer makes 50 grand in a year, he's at least spending that amount for traveling and caddies."

D. A. Points, PGA Tour member since 2005, contends that two of the greatest pressure situations for a golfer are on Sunday if he is near the tournament lead and on Friday if he is sitting near the cut line with a couple of holes left to play. He adds that for the golfers in the ranking groups that are reordered during the season, it is incredibly important that they consistently make tournament cuts to improve their positioning. Roberto Diaz, who played regularly on the Web.com Tour starting in 2014 before earning his PGA Tour card for the first time at the conclusion of the 2017 season, considers that if he makes the cut, "it is a good week." Diaz says that his next benchmark is "hoping to have a chance to win the tournament with nine holes to go."

The cut line for all tournaments, except the AT&T Pebble Beach Pro-Am, is after the second round. The top 70 golfers on the leaderboard, including ties, advance to the final two rounds. If 78 golfers or more make the cut after the second round due to ties, there is another tournament cut administered after the third round to bring the total number of golfers as close to 70 as possible. The golfers who made the second round cut, but do not survive the third round cut are given a result of MDF: made the cut, did not finish. They do earn prize money and FedEx Cup points.

The golfers who just clear the top 70 second round cut line are hoping that there are not enough golfers tied to exceed the 78-golfer threshold that will force a cut after the third round. If there are not 78 golfers, those who made the second round cut are guaranteed to play in both the third and fourth rounds. However, if there are 78 golfers or more remaining, the pressure returns to all golfers to play well in the third round or risk being eliminated after that round's cut. Having an outcome that results in missing the cut in round three not only significantly reduces earnings and FedEx Cup points for that week, it also eliminates the possibility of playing well in the fourth round to move up on the leaderboard to increase earnings and FedEx Cup points. When crossing the dividing line of making the tournament cut, significant opportunities remain.

The Players Championship from TPC Sawgrass in Florida in 2017 offers a unique example. There were 17 golfers tied for 66th after the second round with a score of 146, two over par. All of these golfers made the cut by one stroke and got to compete in round three. All of the golfers who finished ahead of the group tied for 66th place now had to play well enough to make the tournament cut that was going to take place after the third round.

The results of round three at The Players Championship dramatically altered who got to compete in the fourth round. Of the 17 golfers who were tied for 66th place, 14 played well enough in the third round to once again make the cut and play in round four. Some of those golfers turned in spectacular performances in round three, and subsequently round four, to dramatically move up the leaderboard. Three golfers who were tied for 66th place after the second round made it into the top 20 on the tournament's final leaderboard.

Blayne Barber birdied the 13th and 16th holes in the second round to move to two under par with seemingly no concerns about making the cut.

However, double-bogey on both the 17th and 18th holes put his score right at the cut line of 146. Barber's third-round score of even par 72 got him to survive the 54-hole cut, tied for 44th. Barber's fourth-round score of three under par 69 put him into a tie for 16th place on the tournament's final leaderboard. Barber earned $152,250 and 54 FedEx Cup points for his performance at The Players Championship.

Chris Kirk and Bernd Wiesberger also found themselves with scores of 146 after the second round. Kirk shot two under par on the back nine of the second round with a birdie on the 11th and 12th holes to achieve the score needed to make that day's cut. Starting his second round on the 10th hole, Wiesberger scored a birdie on his final hole of the day, the 9th hole, on his way to making the tournament cut. Both players would end The Players Championship in a tie for 12th place. Kirk carded a 69 in the third round and posted a 71 in the fourth round. Wiesberger shot a 68 in the third round and an even par 72 in the final round. Both players took home $212,625 and 66 FedEx Cup points in a tournament when two days earlier it was questionable whether they would even continue playing.

Conversely, other golfers who were safely above the cut line after round two of The Players Championship were eliminated after the third round cut. Justin Thomas had a two-round total of 144, two strokes within the cut line. However, a third round 79, seven over par, put him on the wrong side of the cut line and out of the tournament's final round. In an example of a golfer seemingly much safer within a cut line, Jon Rahm had a two-round total of 140, four under par. He then turned in his worst single round of the 2016–2017 season when he carded an 82 to eliminate himself from competing in the fourth round of The Players Championship. Thomas earned $19,635 and Rahm earned $20,370 for the MDF performance. They both were awarded three FedEx Cup points.

The Players Championship in 2017 demonstrates that by hanging on to make the cut, a good third or fourth round could equate to a meaningful tournament finish. The chance to move up the leaderboard and earn greater prize money and FedEx Cup points is the true opportunity that those not making the cut are missing. Cody Gribble, winner of the Sanderson Farms Championship in the autumn of his rookie season in 2016, explains that even when you are playing poorly, and you are working hard at just grinding through the round "you never know when it is going to turn."

While The Players Championship cut was a setback for Justin Thomas, earlier in the season he exhibited the opportunity that could emerge when squeaking by the cut line. Thomas scored an uncharacteristic four over par on his final nine holes of the day, including two triple-bogeys, in the first round of the season-opening Safeway Open. He ended the day with a 75 at the par 72 golf course. The cut line for the tournament was 142. Thomas started round two having to play the same stretch of nine holes that produced his four over par. This time, in round two, Thomas rebounded and shot four under par over those nine holes. Thomas still needed to make a 15-foot, 11-inch birdie putt on 17 and another birdie putt on 18 to post 141 to make the cut. In round three, Thomas posted his second consecutive round of 66, with four birdies on the back nine. He ended the tournament by shooting a 67 in the final round, again four under par on the nine-hole stretch that put him in a precarious position in round one. Thomas finished the tournament in a tie for eighth place to earn $162,000 and 75 FedEx Cup points.

The prize money and FedEx Cup points earned by just surviving tournament cuts add up and have great relevance in the final season calculations. Conversely, one missed cut could be the difference in not crossing over to the positive side of a PGA Tour dividing line. Matt Jones won the 2014 Shell Houston Open to give him an exempt status as a tournament winner through the 2015–2016 season. Jones played in 27 regular season tournaments in his final season with that status. He made the cut on 15 occasions, with three top ten finishes. Jones was in the 124th position in the FedEx Cup standings after he received 41 points for his tie for 27th at the John Deere Classic, the second-to-last tournament of the 2016 regular season. Jones did not make the cut at the regular season-ending Wyndham Championship, missing by a distant six strokes. With that outcome, Jones dropped back to 126th in the FedEx Cup standings with 445 points. Jones was nine points short of Seung-Yul Noh's 125th and final position total of 454 points.

Missing the cut at the Wyndham Championship and just missing out on the FedEx Cup Playoffs was compounded for Jones by his finishing 126th on the PGA Tour money list in that season. Jones earned $712,723 in 2015–2016. He was $5,167 behind Morgan Hoffmann, who finished 125th on the strength of his performance in the John Deere Classic. Hoffmann finished that tournament in a tie for third to earn $278,400 of his season total $717,890. Although he made the top 125 money list, Hoffmann did not qualify for the FedEx Cup Playoffs. He finished 133rd in the FedEx Cup standings, 30 points behind Seung-Yul Noh. Hoffmann would still have an exempt status going into the following season, in the top 125 on the PGA Tour prize money list.

As for Jones, instead of having an exempt status in the 2016–2017 season through being in the top 125 golfers in the FedEx Cup points standings or the top 125 on the PGA Tour's regular-season money list, he was placed in the FedEx Cup standings 126 through 150 finishers priority group. This exempt status group placed Jones 79 golfers lower in the tournament player priority selection process than he would have been had he made it onto the top 125 money list, and 85 golfers lower than if he achieved the final playoff spot.

Overall, in the 2015–2016 season, Jones played 80 rounds of golf in PGA Tour events and participated in the World Golf Championships—Dell Match Play. Considering that finishing one spot higher in a tournament would generally net the additional $5,167 to break into the top 125 on the PGA Tour money list or generate the additional ten points that he needed to qualify for the FedEx Cup Playoffs, one stroke less by Jones or one stroke more by any number of golfers who finished just ahead of him in any of those tournaments that he played became the difference.

It should also be noted, independent of Jones, that one lower finish in a tournament by any of the golfers who nudged him out of the top 125 in the FedEx Cup points standings or the top 125 on the PGA Tour money list also could have been the difference. For example, while Morgan Hoffmann earned $278,400 for finishing tied for third in the John Deere Classic, the golfers who were tied for fifth place, two shots behind Hoffmann, earned $175,200. Two strokes more by Hoffmann at the John Deere would have easily put his earnings below Jones' prize money total for the season.

Furthermore, in four tournaments, Jones missed the cut by one stroke. Simply making the cut in any of these tournaments could have easily been the difference in acquiring the additional points to qualify for the FedEx Cup Playoffs. For Seung-Yul Noh, his finish in the 125th position in the 2015–2016 FedEx Cup points standings could be traced back to his barely making the cut on two occasions. In November 2015, at the OHL Classic, Noh posted first- and second-round scores of 70. His 140 was one stroke better than the cut line of 141. Propelled by a third-round 67, Noh ended the OHL Classic in a tie for 40th and earned 29 FedEx Cup points.

At the Travelers Championship in August, Noh would once again barely survive the cut line at 139, one stroke better than the cut line of 140, a result shared by 14 players. Noh took advantage of his opportunity to continue playing on the weekend as his third- and fourth-round scores of 68 moved him into a tie for 38th place. He claimed 29 FedEx Cup points at the Travelers Championship. Noh needed all of these points as he ended the regular season by withdrawing from the John Deere Classic and missing the cut at the Wyndham Championship. Noh did not make the cut at the Barclays, but he did receive the $70,000 bonus for making the playoffs.

In that same season, Derek Fathauer earned 491 FedEx Cup points, which was good for the 118th position in the standings. Fathauer was 46 points ahead of Matt Jones' non-qualifying playoff total of 445. Fathauer on six occasions made the tournament cut by one stroke. His continuing to play in these six tournaments accounted for 67 FedEx Cup points. Three of the tournaments equated to 57 points, creating the eventual 46-point difference between him and Jones. At the Sanderson Farms Championship, third- and fourth-round scores of two under par 70 moved Fathauer into 50th place and awarded him 12 FedEx Cup points. At the Barbasol Championship, Fathauer's third-round 68 was followed by a fourth-round 66 to end the tournament at ten under par for a 35th-place finish. Fathauer earned 19 FedEx Cup points for that outcome. Finally, one week later at the RBC Canadian Open, Fathauer posted a third-round 65, with seven birdies and no bogeys, to withstand a fourth-round three over par 75. He finished in a tie for 43rd to earn 26 FedEx Cup points.

Fathauer parlayed his entrance in the FedEx Cup Playoffs by shooting even par at the Barclays, good for a tie for 31st. He earned $45,220 for this performance and advanced to the Deutsche Bank Championship. The season would end for Fathauer at the second playoff tournament as he would not make the cut after an opening-round 69 was paired with a second-round 76. Fathauer did receive a $75,000 playoff bonus for finishing at position number 100 in the final FedEx Cup points standings.

Sometimes a player barely making the cut can turn things around so quickly that he wins the tournament. Such was the case at the Shriners Hospitals for Children Open in October 2015. Smylie Kaufman was playing in his fifth career PGA Tour event and only his second tournament as a member of the PGA Tour. In the 2014–2015 season, Kaufman played in two PGA Tour events. He made the field at the Shell Houston Open when his performance in the Monday qualifier earned him entrance. He missed the cut in that tournament. Kaufman was given a sponsor exemption at the Barbasol Championship. He completed that tournament in a tie for 66th place to earn $7,210. In 2015, Kaufman played in 20 tournaments on the Web.com Tour. He won a tournament, had a second-place finish, and overall had five top-ten finishes. Kaufman finished the Web.com Tour regular season in sixth place on the prize money list to achieve graduation onto the PGA Tour.

Kaufman opened the 2015–2016 season with a tie for tenth at the Frys. com Open. One week later, Kaufman's 139 over the first two rounds of the Shriners Hospitals for Children Open was only two strokes better than the 141 of golfers who missed the cut. In the first round Kaufman had a birdie at the 10th hole, and he had a stretch of four consecutive birdies from holes 12 through 15 to score a 67 at the par-71 course. Kaufman's second-round 72 left him seven strokes behind the four leaders, who were at ten under par. In round three, Kaufman scored a double-bogey on the 7th hole to drop to one under par. He did begin to heat up as a birdie on the 9th hole and four birdies on the back nine moved him to six under par for the tournament. However, he remained seven strokes off the lead.

The beginning of the fourth round did not appear to be anything extraordinary for Kaufman in terms of challenging for the tournament championship, as he shot one under par through the first seven holes. Kaufman then had his second stretch in the tournament of four consecutive birdies as he connected on holes 8 through 11. He added another birdie at the par-5 13th hole. Now playing the round at six under par, 12 under for the tournament, Kaufman arrived at the par-4 15th hole, which had a distance of only 295 yards. Kaufman's tee-shot stopped on the green, 13 feet from the flagstick. Kaufman dropped in the eagle putt. On the par-5 16th, he just missed another eagle putt from 40 feet, eight inches, but a tap-in birdie gave him the tournament lead. Kaufman added one more birdie for the day on 18. His fourth-round 61, ten under par, with a 29 on the back nine, combined with his five under par over the last ten holes in round three, added up to 15 under par over the final 28 holes of the tournament.

Kaufman took his 16 under par, tournament-leading score to the clubhouse, where he waited for two and a half hours for the other golfers to complete their rounds. Five golfers would have tied for the lead if they birdied the 18th hole, but none did. Six golfers ended up one stroke behind Kaufman. The making up of seven strokes entering the fourth round was the largest final-round deficit to win a tournament in the 2015–2016 season.

Kaufman played in 28 PGA tournaments in the 2015–2016 season. He made the cut on 18 occasions, with ten top-25 finishes and four in the top ten. He qualified for the FedEx Cup Playoffs and advanced to the third playoff tournament before falling short of making the Tour Championship. Kaufman finished the season at number 43 in the final FedEx Cup points standings to earn a bonus of $132,000. In addition, Kaufman ended the season earning more than $2.5 million in prize money, a substantial increase from the $255,928 in prize money that he earned in 2015.

Moving forward, Kaufman would reap all of the benefits of winning a tournament. Winning any tournament is, thus, not only about that victory and the prize money and the FedEx Cup points earned from that week's effort, it is very much about the future. Brendan Steele, winner of two PGA Tour events by the conclusion of the 2016–2017 season, explains that winning a tournament "is the beginning of what could be several opportunities." Kevin Kisner, who also had two PGA Tour tournament victories after the 2016–2017 season, simply states, "any victory opens up a whole new world."

5

Winning a Tournament

Because a priority system determines playing opportunities, golfers on the PGA Tour are always cognizant of their ranking group position and are working to improve that exempt status. Golfers are obviously trying to achieve the ultimate prize, a tournament win that provides the job security of a multi-season exempt status. It does not matter which group a golfer was in previously or how he plays for the duration of the season, having four magical days and claiming a tournament championship moves him into a status that allows for entrance into all regular season tournaments, among other opportunities.

Again, it is the major tournament winners who gain status for the remainder of the current season and the following five seasons. The ranking group for winning the PGA Championship or the U.S. Open is one where, ironically, many of the golfers have long since retired. In addition to winners of those tournaments in the last five seasons and the current season, this group recognizes PGA Championship and U.S. Open winners prior to 1970. As a way to honor the great champions of these tournaments, this rule means that the top priority ranking is still given to legendary players, such as Jack Nicklaus, Lee Trevino, and Gary Player, along with other living PGA Championship and U.S. Open winners, including those whose victories were in the 1950s: Jack Burke, Jr., winner of the 1956 PGA Championship, and Dow Finsterwald, whose 1958 PGA Championship occurred when for the first time the tournament was decided by stroke play instead of match play. As implausible, and silly, as it obviously is, Nicklaus and the 11 retired players who were part of this group entering the 2016–2017 season are all still eligible to play in any regular season tournament they wish.

Although it is not recognized as a major, considering the prize money, the number of FedEx Cup points, the five seasons of exempt status, and the entrance into all of the majors for the next three years, the importance of The

Players Championship is well-known by all golfers. The winner of The Players Championship receives $1.89 million and 600 FedEx Cup points. In the 2016–2017 season, only the PGA Championship offered the same prize money, and only the major tournaments offered the same number of FedEx Cup points. The points accumulated for The Players Championship tournament win alone not only essentially guarantees entrance into the FedEx Cup Playoffs, but for 2016–2017 it was good enough for 75th in the points standings for the regular season, already high enough to get a golfer into the second playoff tournament and only a few spots away from the 70th position that qualifies him for the third playoff tournament.

To further illustrate, in the FedEx Cup era, the only golfer who won The Players Championship but did not qualify for the Tour Championship was Si Woo Kim in 2017. Kim made the cut in 11 of the 27 tournaments that he played in the 2016–2017 regular season, with one other top-ten finish. Kim ended the regular season in 41st place in the FedEx Cup points standings. He made the cut in the first three playoff tournaments, but he finished no better than in a tie for 40th place. Kim was 54th in the FedEx Cup standings after the third playoff tournament. He collected more than $2.68 million in tournament prize money on the season and a bonus of $113,000.

At The Players Championship in 2017, 147 golfers competed at the 7,189-yard Stadium Course at TPC Sawgrass in Ponte Vedra Beach, Florida. Kim started the final round at seven under par, one stroke behind Louis Oosthuizen and two strokes behind tournament leaders Kyle Stanley and J. B. Holmes. The leaderboard was quickly reshuffled as a birdie by Kim and a bogey by both Stanley and Holmes created a four-way tie along with Ian Poulter, who birdied the 2nd and 6th holes. All shared the lead at some point on the front nine in the final round of The Players Championship.

Kim began to separate himself from the field at the 7th hole when he connected on a 24-foot, six-inch, left-to-right birdie putt to take sole possession of the lead. He would never relinquish the top position on the leaderboard. An 18-foot, two-inch birdie putt on the 9th hole pushed Kim's score to ten under par and his lead to two strokes. Poulter pulled to within one stroke with a birdie on 11.

Golf courses get redesigned to make them more challenging, especially for the most elite tournaments. These changes force the golfers to make difficult decisions about how to approach the playing of a hole. Redesigns could include changing the tee-box locations to bring water, trees, or bunkers into play, adding length to a hole, or, in the case of the 12th hole of the Stadium Course at TPC Sawgrass, making the hole shorter. The 12th hole used to be a par-4, 358 yards. For The Players Championship in 2017, the length was reduced to 302 yards.

Golfers now had to decide whether to try to reach the green on their tee-shot and set up an eagle putt opportunity, or hit their tee-shot and set up what they hoped would be a comfortable approach shot to the green. To add to the complexity of the hole and a golfer's decision about how it should be played, if going for the green on the tee-shot, any ball that drifted left of the green could easily land in the water. To hit the tee-shot in the narrow fairway, the golfers had to contend with a bunker along the left side and a downslope on the right. Of course, whatever the strategy decision, a golfer needs to execute.

Ian Poulter arrived at the 12th hole in the final round at nine under par. He chose not to go for the green as he hit his tee-shot 186 yards on the right side of the fairway. Poulter's second shot, however, left him short of the green on the left side of the fairway. Poulter chipped onto the green, but he could not drop the six-foot, eight-inch putt for par. It was Poulter's first bogey since the eighth hole in the second round, a 39-hole stretch of bogey-free golf. Poulter was now two strokes behind Kim.

There are occasions in a final round of a golf tournament when heroics are not necessary to capture the championship, when steady, consistent play is all that is required. Kim was the epitome of that approach on the back nine at The Players Championship. At the 12th hole, Kim hit his tee-shot 221 yards on the right side of the fairway. His approach shot landed on the green, 30 feet from the hole. The birdie putt left him one foot from the cup, and he safely made a par.

The par-5, 519-yard 16th hole was also illustrative of Kim's approach. For the first three rounds of the tournament, Kim made eagle-birdie-bogey on the hole. Still up two strokes, Kim's drive landed in the rough on the right side of the fairway. Any slight pause for concern was easily and quickly resolved when his second shot found the fairway, 118 yards from the hole. Kim's third-shot sand wedge landed on the green at just over 25 feet from the hole to help him complete another par.

The Players Championship cannot be decided until the 17th hole of the Stadium Course at TPC Sawgrass is conquered. With its island green, the signature hole of the course is one of the most famous in golf and can easily alter a leaderboard. Kim made par-bogey-birdie on the 17th hole in the first three rounds. Kim's tee-shot safely landed on the green at the 129-yard, 17th in the final round to set up another flawlessly executed par. Kim was the only golfer in the final round to make his way around the challenging Stadium Course without a bogey. On the back nine, Kim had a stretch of six straight holes where his par putt was less than two feet. With a final-round 69 and a tournament score of ten under par, 278, the 21-year-old Kim became the youngest golfer to win The Players Championship. Kim has exempt status through the 2021–2022 season for The Players Championship win.

Ian Poulter started the 18th hole down two strokes, with faint hopes of making a birdie and putting some pressure on Kim. After his tee-shot missed the fairway, Poulter's second shot from the rough at the par-4 went far to the right, banking off a hospitality tent, bouncing off a cart path, and settling into a bush. Poulter was forced to take a penalty stroke. He now had to hit his fourth shot off of the pine straw. Poulter's shot from that difficult lie miraculously carried through the trees to leave him only inches from the cup. His bogey ended his tournament at seven under par to finish in a tie for second place, along with Louis Oosthuizen.

There is an exempt status for the remainder of the current season and the next three seasons for winning the Tour Championship, a World Golf Championships event, the Arnold Palmer Invitational, or the Memorial Tournament. For the 2016–2017 season, seven golfers on the PGA Tour accounted for their exempt status through winning these tournaments. One of those golfers was William McGirt.

McGirt arrived at the 2016 Memorial Tournament making his 165th career start on the PGA Tour. McGirt began playing regularly on the PGA Tour in 2011 and earned qualification for the FedEx Cup Playoffs in every season. He amassed more than $4.9 million in career earnings prior to the 2015–2016 season. McGirt's best season at that point of his career was in 2013–2014, when he earned just under $1.3 million. He made the cut in 19 of the 29 tournaments that he played in that season, with eight top-25 finishes and four in the top ten. Entering the 2015–2016 season, McGirt's highest tournament result was a tie for second, which he accomplished at both the 2012 and 2013 RBC Canadian Open. The 2012 finish was only one stroke behind Scott Piercy, while the 2013 effort left McGirt three strokes behind tournament winner Brandt Snedeker.

In the autumn of the 2015–2016 season, McGirt recorded the third second-place finish of his career when he and David Toms finished one stroke in back of Peter Malnati at the Sanderson Farms Championship. In the weeks leading up to the Memorial Tournament in 2016, McGirt made the cut in five consecutive tournaments, highlighted by a tie for ninth place at the RBC Heritage and a tie for 17th at the Wells Fargo Championship.

McGirt posted a two under par 70 in round one of the 2016 Memorial. He was six strokes behind leader Dustin Johnson, who made ten birdies and two bogeys on his way to an eight under par 64. McGirt's second-round 68 still left him six strokes behind the tournament lead, now held by Matt Kuchar and Brendan Steele. Johnson posted a second-round 71 to put him three strokes off the pace.

The start of the third round began McGirt's move up the leaderboard. McGirt was five under par on the first five holes of the day after he birdied the

1st, 3rd, and 4th holes and eagled the 5th. His front nine score of 31 was paired with a 33 on the back nine where he scored four more birdies. A bogey on the 16th hole was the only blemish on McGirt's scorecard. That bogey was his last of the tournament. After his eight under par 64, McGirt ended round three in a tie for the lead with Kuchar and Gary Woodland at 14 under par. They were one stroke ahead of the quartet of Jon Curran, Emiliano Grillo, Adam Hadwin, and Dustin Johnson.

In round four of the Memorial, McGirt scored a birdie on the 5th hole and parred every other hole to shoot a 71. He ended the Memorial tournament at 15 under par. Other contenders would falter. Woodland bogeyed holes 9 through 11 on his way to a final-round 73. Kuchar also shot 73 after a bogey on 12, a double-bogey on 13, and a bogey on 15 dimmed his tournament championship aspirations. Hadwin shot one over par on both the front and back nine to finish with a final-round 74. Grillo appeared to be well-positioned on the leaderboard after shooting three under par on the front nine in the final round. However, four consecutive bogeys on the 10th through 13th holes and a double-bogey on the 17th hole gave Grillo a final-round 74 and removed him from championship contention. After three birdies on the front nine, Johnson shot two over par on the back nine with four bogeys and two birdies. Johnson's back nine score of 38 left him with a final-round 71 to remain one stroke shy of McGirt.

Curran, 29 years old, also had not won a PGA tournament. He started the final round of the Memorial by bogeying the 1st hole. Curran recovered with a birdie on the 2nd, 5th, and 8th holes to get to 15 under par. He bogeyed the 12th hole before making a par on holes 13 through 16. Curran, 14 under par, came to the par-4, 477-yard 17th hole one stroke behind McGirt. His tee-shot on 17 placed him in the fairway bunker on the right, 185 yards from the flagstick. Curran placed his second shot seven feet, four inches away from the cup. When Curran sank that birdie putt, he completed the miraculous up-and-down to tie for the lead. A par by Curran on the 18th hole would lead to a playoff with McGirt.

McGirt displayed his own bunker magic on the first playoff hole. Just off of the green and needing to get up-and-down to save par, McGirt's sand shot landed well past the hole, but with the proper amount of backspin, the ball rolled back past the cup and left him in a position to make the par putt and continue the playoff. Curran missed the green in regulation on the second playoff hole. After his lengthy putt to save par came up short, the door was open for McGirt. Resting on the fringe of the green for his third shot, McGirt chipped on and made his 19th par putt in 20 holes played that day. With only seven bogeys over the four rounds, and only one in rounds three and four, McGirt claimed his first PGA tournament victory only a couple of weeks before his 37th birthday. The win earned McGirt more than $1.5 million, the single highest tournament earning for his career. McGirt received an exempt status for three seasons as a Memorial Tournament champion, through 2018–2019.

The win at the Memorial propelled McGirt to many other prominent tournament opportunities. He got to play in the U.S. Open and The Open Championship for the first time in his career, although he did not make the cut in either. McGirt earned his first trip to the World Golf Championships—Bridgestone Invitational, which resulted in a tie for seventh. He earned $233,333 in prize money and 89 FedEx Cup points in that tournament. McGirt also qualified to play in the PGA Championship for the first time since 2012. He capitalized on that opportunity as well when he finished in a tie for tenth to earn $233,000 and 77 FedEx Cup points.

The 500 FedEx Cup points earned for his win at the Memorial and the 166 combined points accumulated at the World Golf Championships—Bridgestone Invitational and the PGA Championship led to his finishing the regular season 16th in the FedEx Cup standings with 1360 points. That position was well within the top 30 spots needed to qualify McGirt for the Tour Championship for the first time in his career.

In the playoffs, McGirt's 41st-place finish in the Barclays tournament and 20th-place finish in the BMW Championship offset his missing the cut in the Deutsche Bank Championship to maintain his qualifying position for the Tour Championship, where McGirt finished 17th to earn $166,600. McGirt won $295,375 in the four playoff tournaments and by finishing 24th in the final FedEx Cup standings, he earned a $205,000 bonus.

Regular season tournament victories provide an exempt status for the remainder of the current season and the following two seasons. The regular season tournament winners group obviously represents a large number of golfers, as there are many different tournament winners in a given season. In the 2015–2016 season, six golfers won multiple tournaments. Dustin Johnson and Jason Day won three tournaments, with Adam Scott, Rory McIlroy, Jordan Spieth, and Russell Knox winning two tournaments. In 2016–2017, again six golfers won multiple tournaments. Justin Thomas won five tournaments, Dustin Johnson won four, Jordan Spieth and Hideki Matsuyama won three, and Marc Leishman and Xander Schauffele won two tournaments.

If a golfer already has an exempt status for having won a tournament and is victorious in another event, his placement in the tournament winners group is extended for an additional season. For example, Chris Kirk won the McGladrey Classic in November 2013 and the Duetsche Bank Championship in September 2014, both part of the 2013–2014 PGA season. The first win gave him exempt status for the 2014–2015 and 2015–2016 seasons. The second tournament victory extended this exempt status for the 2016–2017 season. In May 2015, Kirk added a tournament win at the Crowne Plaza Invitational at Colonial Country Club (now called the Dean & DeLuca Invitational). This victory added an additional season in the tournament winners priority ranking group, where he enjoyed status as a multiple tournament winner through the 2017–2018 season.

Because of the points totals, winning one regular season tournament is the easiest way to accumulate the requisite points to qualify for the FedEx Cup Playoffs. Greg Chalmers is an example of a rare golfer who did not qualify for the FedEx Cup Playoffs in 2016 despite having won a tournament. In 2016, Chalmers won the Barracuda Championship, an opposite tournament that allocates only 300 FedEx Cup points to the winner. Moving forward, of course, Chalmers still has two seasons of exempt status in the tournament winners priority ranking group.

It should also be noted that a golfer does not automatically qualify for the FedEx Cup Playoffs because of his exempt status due to a victory in the previous season. The FedEx Cup is a season-by-season achievement. A recent tournament win does allow for entrance into many tournaments, so a golfer will have the opportunities to compete, but now he has to play well enough to be in the top 125 in the points standings.

It is the final season in the tournament winners group that brings additional pressure. If a golfer does not win a tournament in that season to renew his exempt status, he will be relegated to another ranking group that is lower in the priority order, with that status for only one season. Entering the 2016–2017 season, of the 44 golfers who comprised the regular season tournament winners group, 19 were in their final season. Of those 19 golfers, only Brooks Koepka won a tournament.

The other 18 golfers entered lower-ranked groups for the 2017–2018 season. Nine were able to maintain a high status by finishing in the top 125 in the FedEx Cup points standings. Three golfers were forced to drop to the past champions group. There were two golfers who reclaimed their PGA Tour card through the Web.com Tour Finals and became a part of the top finishers of the Web.com Tour group. Two golfers received medical extensions. One golfer fell into the 126 through 150 FedEx Cup standings finishers group. Finally, one golfer returned to life member status.

If a golfer in the regular season tournament winner group has a win that occurs in a major, World Golf Championships, The Players Championship, the Arnold Palmer Invitational, the Memorial, or the Tour Championship, he advances into that higher priority ranking group. All group advancement is significant.

Brooks Koepka had his exempt status as a regular season tournament winner through 2016–2017 for his 2015 victory at the Waste Management Phoenix Open. His victory at the U.S. Open in 2017 now places him in the highest priority ranking group with that exempt status for five seasons, through 2021–2022.

With an exemption gained for the remainder of the current season, the tournaments early in the season have additional value as they essentially provide a full extra season of status in the tournament winners group. The winner of the first tournament of the season gains this priority entrance status for as many as an additional 34 regular season tournaments compared to the golfer winning the final tournament of the regular season (the 34 tournaments do not include the four major tournaments that have their own qualifying standards, but do take into account the four weekends where tournaments are played simultaneously).

Winning a tournament is the only way for a golfer to advance his exempt status group during the season. The win can significantly shift a golfer's tournament schedule for that season, including providing a pathway into elite events. For example, William McGirt played in the first two opposite tournaments in the earlier part of the 2015–2016 season: the Sanderson Farms Championship and the Puerto Rico Open. After winning the Memorial Tournament that concluded on June 5, 2016, McGirt participated in the World Golf Championships—Bridgestone Invitational and The Open Championship instead of the opposite tournaments played on those same weekends.

By contrast, Jon Curran, who lost to McGirt in a playoff, did not compete in either the World Golf Championships—Bridgestone Invitational or The Open Championship. Curran elected not to play in the opposite tournaments on those weekends, having already made 13 cuts in the 22 tournaments that he played in that season, with two other top-ten finishes. Curran was ranked 36th in the FedEx Cup standings, having moved up from 84th after his second-place performance in the Memorial. Curran ended up advancing as far as the third tournament of the FedEx Cup Playoffs.

There are some significant opportunities that only a win can provide. A victory in any PGA Tour event provides a golfer entrance into the following January's Tournament of Champions, played in Hawaii. The Tournament of Champions is the first PGA Tour event of the calendar year. A golfer's position on the exempt status priority rankings has no consideration in qualifying for the Tournament of Champions. This strict qualification leaves out some of the top golfers in the world who are in a high priority ranking group. For example, golfers such as Justin Rose, Webb Simpson, and Phil Mickelson, who have a high exempt status for their recent wins in a major, did not qualify for the 2017

Tournament of Champions because they did not win a tournament in the 2016 calendar year. Other top players who also have a high priority ranking for winning recent major tournaments, such as Dustin Johnson, Jason Day, and Jordan Spieth, all won tournaments in 2016 and therefore qualified for the Tournament of Champions played in 2017.

Brandt Snedeker had his exempt status entering the 2016–2017 regular season for winning the FedEx Cup Championship in 2012. It was his win at the Farmers Insurance Open at Torrey Pines in January 2016, that qualified him for the 2017 Tournament of Champions tournament. Without that one-stroke victory over K. J. Choi, Snedeker would not have been eligible for the Tournament of Champions. Snedeker finished in a tie for 14th, earning $122,000 and 55 FedEx Cup points at the Tournament of Champions.

A golfer's position in the final FedEx Cup standings has no consideration in obtaining entrance into the Tournament of Champions. Kevin Chappell finished eighth in the final FedEx Cup standings in the 2015–2016 season, but without a tournament victory he was not eligible for the 2017 Tournament of Champions. Conversely, Greg Chalmers finished 142nd in the FedEx Cup standings, but he did qualify for the Tournament of Champions for his win at the Barracuda Championship. At the Tournament of Champions, Chalmers earned $66,000 and 31 FedEx Cup points for his five under par, 28th-place finish.

The Tournament of Champions represents an opportunity to move up in the season's FedEx Cup points standings while most golfers are not playing. In 2017, only 32 golfers comprised the Tournament of Champions field. The Tournament of Champions is also a no-cut, guaranteed prize money and FedEx Cup points event. Brendan Grace, who qualified for the Tournament of Champions with his win at the RBC Heritage, ended up shooting the highest score in the 2017 Tournament of Champions to finish 32nd. He still earned $61,000 in prize money and 25 FedEx Cup points.

Kevin Kisner notes another advantage of playing in the Tournament of Champions is that after not playing competitive golf for a few weeks, there is an opportunity to knock off some of the tournament rust before full-field tournaments commence. The week after the Tournament of Champions is the Sony Open, also in Hawaii. This is the first full-field tournament of the calendar year. Fabian Gomez's playoff victory over Brandt Snedeker in the 2016 Sony Open qualified him to play in the Tournament of Champions that would not begin for another 51 weeks. Gomez's 20th-place performance in the 2017 Tournament of Champions earned him $88,000.

To further illustrate, in addition to all of the benefits for the remainder of the 2015–2016 season after he won the Memorial Tournament, William McGirt's victory at that event opened the door for opportunities in the following season.

At the 2017 Tournament of Champions, a tie for ninth earned McGirt $172,333. Finally, a win in a tournament that offers full FedEx Cup points means an instant invitation to the Masters. It was the first time in his career that McGirt got to play in the Masters. At Augusta National in 2017, McGirt tied for 22nd and earned $105,600. In these two tournaments combined, McGirt also accumulated 107 FedEx Cup points. All McGirt needed to create these additional tournament opportunities was four magical days.

6

Playing Great
Even When Not Winning

Having four magical days and winning a tournament is, of course, not so easy. Actually, it cannot be overstated how difficult it is to claim a PGA tournament championship. There are 47 tournaments in a season, including the four FedEx Cup playoff tournaments. It may seem as if there is ample opportunity to win one tournament, but there can be at most only 48 different tournament winners, with the Zurich Classic of New Orleans becoming a two-player team event in the 2016–2017 season. Although many different golfers are going to win tournaments in a given season, obviously most will go the entire season without claiming a title.

Winning a tournament is difficult because of the elite competition. Kevin Kisner, two-time winner on the PGA Tour, offers that "if you take the best 150 in the world in any field, who is to say who is going to be the best on that day? It is a going to be a combination of timing, confidence, and luck." Kisner says that when he is near the top of the leaderboard going into the final round, his approach is to keep it simple and get off to a fast start. Then he "looks at the leaderboard at the tenth tee and starts to figure out what it might take to win the tournament." Kisner adds that he has won tournaments, and certainly played well in those events, but good things still have to happen. Kisner feels that on other occasions he played well enough to win, but a couple of small things did not go his way.

There is little margin for error in winning a tournament. To win, a golfer needs to maintain a high degree of excellence relative to the competition over all four rounds, and possibly into extra playoff holes. It may take only one bad round to eliminate a golfer from championship contention. At the 2017 Puerto Rico Open, J. J. Henry, three-time PGA tournament champion, played the par-72 course at three under par and seven under par in the first two rounds of the tournament. He was one stroke behind the leaders. However, a third-round 75 ended Henry's hopes of winning the tournament. He dropped to eight strokes off the pace. Henry rebounded in the fourth round by shooting a 29 on the front nine, with an eagle on the 2nd hole and five birdies. He ended the day with a nine under par 63. Henry's brilliance in round four placed him at 16 under par and tied for eighth on the final leaderboard. If the tournament consisted of only rounds one, two and four, Henry's total score of 197 was better than any other golfer in the field.

Conversely, one great round is not enough to secure a tournament championship. In the 2015–2016 season, no golfer had a lower score in a single round than Jim Furyk. At the 2016 Travelers Championship, Furyk shot a fourth-round 58 at the par-70 course. It is the first time in an official PGA Tour event that a golfer scored a 58. Furyk had been one of only six golfers to shoot a 59 in a PGA Tour event. In the Travelers final round, Furyk's 27 on the front nine featured an eagle on the 3rd hole and six birdies. Furyk had a stretch of seven consecutive birdies from holes 6 through 12. Furyk entered the final round in 71st place at one over par after scores of 73–66–72. With his 12 under par final round performance, Furyk advanced into a tie for fifth place, three strokes behind tournament champion Russell Knox. Furyk earned $231,825 at the Travelers.

It certainly takes more than a spectacular 18 holes to win a major, even when that golfer is setting a record for the lowest round of golf in the 157 years of major championships being played. Brendan Grace made the cut at The Open Championship in 2017, held at Royal Birkdale, by only one stroke. He entered the third round at four over par after shooting 70 and 74 at the par-70 course. Grace proceeded to shoot a 62. He eclipsed the 31 golfers who posted a round of 63 in a major. Justin Thomas shot a 63 in a major earlier in the 2017 season in the third round of the U.S. Open at Erin Hills in Wisconsin. Grace shot a 29 on the front nine with five birdies. He added three more birdies on his back nine score of 33. Grace's 62 moved him to four under par for the tournament and into a tie for fifth place. He was still seven strokes behind tournament leader Jordan Spieth. In the final round, Grace shot an even par 70, with two birdies and two bogeys. Grace was one of five golfers who tied for sixth place, each earning $281,000.

When playing great, someone might simply play better to swipe a championship. Even a legend such as Phil Mickelson can be a victim of another golfer's greatness on a given day or for a given tournament. Mickelson shot an opening round 63 at The Open Championship in 2016, played at Royal Troon in Scotland. After he birdied 16 and 17, Mickelson came to the 18th needing a birdie to become the first golfer in major tournament history to shoot a 62. His birdie putt from 18 feet rolled around the cup before lipping out. He ended the day at eight under par with a three stroke lead. After Mickelson's second-round 69, his lead slimmed to one stroke over Henrik Stenson, who posted scores of 68 and 65 in his first two rounds. Stenson moved past Mickelson after his third-round 68 was two strokes better than Mickelson's 70. Stenson had a one-stroke lead heading into the remaining 18 holes.

The final round provided a suspenseful duel of excellence. Mickelson posted a six under par 65, with an eagle and four birdies. He finished the tournament at 17 under par. On many days, the final-round 65 would have been more than enough to secure the championship. Stenson, however, became only the second player to shoot a 63 in the final round as part of a major tournament victory, equaling Johnny Miller's performance at the 1973 U.S. Open. After bogeying the first hole, the rest of Stenson's eight under par 63 featured ten birdies and one other bogey. He secured the championship with a birdie on four of the last five holes to complete a back nine 31. Stenson finished the tournament at 20 under par. John Huggan and Dave Shedloski wrote in *Golf Digest* that Stenson and Mickelson put on "perhaps the finest head-to-head final-round matchup in the game's history." Bob Harig, espn.com senior golf writer, commented on the performance of Stenson and Mickelson, "it was simply superb, just a mind-boggling display of excellent golf."

To further put Stenson's performance in perspective, his 264 broke the record for the lowest total score in a major. It also tied him for the lowest total score in a major in relation to par with Jason Day, 20 under par at the 2015 PGA Championship. Stenson's score did set The Open Championship record, surpassing Tiger Woods' 19 under par at St. Andrews in 2000. Stenson became only the fourth player in the history of The Open Championship to win while posting all four rounds under 70. Jordan Spieth would repeat that achievement in 2017 with rounds of 65–69–65–69.

Considering how difficult it is to win a tournament, fortunately for all of the golfers on the PGA Tour, the system is set up to reward those who play well despite not winning. These performances are recognized with entrance into the FedEx Cup Playoffs. While there is a premium placed on winning, consistently finishing high in tournaments can also provide some of the biggest opportunities. In the 2015–2016 regular season, Kevin Chappell had three second-place finishes. He lost out to Kevin Kisner by six strokes at the RSM Classic and twice came up short against Jason Day, losing by one stroke at the Arnold Palmer Invitational and by four strokes at The Players Championship. In those performances alone, Chappell earned $2.43 million and generated 930 FedEx Cup points of his season total of 1422. Chappell also finished in a tie for third at the World Golf Championships—Bridgestone Invitational and a tie for fourth at the Valero Texas Open. Chappell ended the regular season 13th in the FedEx Cup standings.

In the FedEx Cup Playoffs, after a tie for 31st at the Barclays, Chappell finished in a tie for eighth at the Deutsche Bank Championship. He finished in a tie for 61st at the BMW Championship. Chappell then had one final outstanding performance of the season when he posted rounds of 66–68–68–66 to get into a playoff at the Tour Championship. He and Ryan Moore would eventually lose to Rory McIlroy. Chappell earned more than $4.5 million for the entire season. He finished eighth in the final FedEx Cup standings to claim a playoff bonus of $600,000.

Many other golfers have gotten into the Tour Championship without a win in the current season or recent seasons. Matt Kuchar is a seven-time tournament champion on the PGA Tour. Kuchar's tournament wins include The Players Championship in 2012, the World Golf Championships—Match Play and the Memorial in 2013, and the RBC Heritage in 2014, his most recent tournament victory.

Despite not winning a tournament, Kuchar still qualified for the Tour Championship in 2015, 2016, and 2017. Kuchar remains one of the most consistent golfers on the PGA Tour. He played in 77 tournaments and made the cut in 70 in those three seasons. Kuchar is not only making a high number of tournament cuts, but he often finds himself near the top of the leaderboard. Kuchar finished in the top 25 of a tournament on 37 occasions in the three seasons between 2015 and 2017. Of those 37 tournaments, Kuchar had 22 top-ten finishes, including four third-place finishes and two second-place finishes.

Kuchar ended the regular season in the top 30 of the FedEx Cup standings, the threshold for the Tour Championship, in the 2015, 2016, and 2017 seasons. Kuchar improved his final position in the standings through his performance in the playoffs in two of those seasons, while maintaining the same position in the other. He made the cut in all of the playoff tournaments over those three seasons.

In 2015, Kuchar had two top-ten playoff finishes, including a tie for tenth at the Tour Championship. He moved from the 26th to the 19th position in the standings. In 2016, Kuchar finished the BMW Championship in a tie for fourth. He was in the 18th position in the FedEx Cup standings after the regular season, and he stayed in that position after the playoffs. Kuchar entered the playoffs in 15th place in 2017 and posted three top ten performances in the playoffs. He finished tied for tenth at the Northern Trust. Following a tie for 56th at the Dell Technologies Championship, Kuchar tied for fifth at the BMW Championship and tied for tenth at the Tour Championship. He ended the final season standings in the 14th position. Overall, between 2015 and 2017, Kuchar earned more than $10.8 million in prize money, of which more than $1.8 million was accumulated in the FedEx Cup Playoff tournaments. In addition, his bonus payments in those three seasons totaled $735,000.

The only PGA Tour victory for Paul Casey occurred at the Shell Houston Open in 2009. Casey still qualified for the Tour Championship in the 2015, 2016, and 2017 seasons. He reached the final playoff tournament through different paths. In 2015 and 2017, Casey's path to the Tour Championship was well set up by his performance in the regular season. In 2015, Casey ended the regular season 19th in the standings. He would improve his final position in the standings to number 13 based on his playoff performances that included a tie for fifth at the Tour Championship. He collected $302,500 of his season total of more than $3.48 million at the Tour Championship. His bonus payment was $280,000.

In 2017, Casey entered the playoffs in the 18th position and had three top-five finishes in the playoffs. He was fifth in the Northern Trust and tied for fourth in the Dell Technologies Championship. After a tie for 33rd at the BMW Championship, Casey finished fifth at the Tour Championship. In the playoffs, he earned more than $1.13 million of his season total of more than $3.9 million. Casey finished the playoffs 11th in the standings to claim a bonus of $300,000.

Casey entered the 2016 FedEx Cup Playoffs 68th in the final regular season standings. His best finish that season was fourth place at the Masters. He also finished seventh at the World Golf Championships—Cadillac Championship at Trump National Doral, and tenth at the PGA Championship. These three tournaments accounted for 299 of his 710 FedEx Cup points in his 18 regular season starts.

A poor performance in the first two FedEx Cup playoff tournaments could have easily had golfers leap over Casey into the top 70 in the standings and into the BMW Championship. Casey finished in a tie for 31st at the Barclays but had stellar performances in the remaining FedEx Cup Playoff tournaments. Casey posted consecutive second-place finishes at the Deutsche Bank Championship and the BMW Championship. The Deutsche Bank Championship performance was two strokes behind tournament winner Rory McIlroy. In the BMW Championship, Casey shot 20 under par, only to be outdone by Dustin Johnson setting a new record as his 23 under par surpassed Tiger Woods' and Jason Day's record of 22 under par. The performances by Casey moved him into fifth place in the standings entering the Tour Championship.

At the Tour Championship, a final-round 64 helped Casey finish fourth. The FedEx Cup Playoff performances for Casey earned him the fifth position in the final FedEx Cup standings. In 2016, for the FedEx Cup Playoff tournaments

Casey earned just under $2.3 million of his season total of more than $3.85 million. He also received a $1 million bonus for his placement in the final standings.

Many golfers who qualify for the Tour Championship enter the season with a high enough exempt status to gain entrance into all regular season tournaments they choose, as well as some of the majors and the World Golf Championships. For example, Matt Kuchar is in a high-exempt status group for winning The Players Championship in 2012. Two golfers did recently make their way into the Tour Championship from the Web.com priority ranking group without winning a tournament in that season, Daniel Berger in the 2014–2015 season and Roberto Castro in the 2015–2016 season.

Berger quickly made his way through the Web.com Tour. After playing in only four Web.com Tour events in 2013, he competed in 21 tournaments in 2014. Berger made the cut in 15 of those starts. He had ten finishes in the top 25, five top-ten finishes, one third place, and one second-place performance. Berger ended the regular season at 15th on the Web.com Tour money list to earn his PGA Tour card for the 2014–2015 season.

The meteoric start to Berger's professional career continued on the PGA Tour. Berger made 14 cuts in 27 tournaments in his first full regular season on the PGA Tour. He had five top-ten finishes, highlighted by two seconds, one at the Honda Classic. Berger entered the final round in a tie for 12th, nine strokes behind tournament leader Ian Poulter and six strokes behind Padraig Harrington and Patrick Reed, who shared second place. Berger shot a 64 in the final round with a birdie on 17 and 18 to force a playoff with Harrington, as Reed faltered with a 73 and Poulter posted a 74. Harrington made par for the tournament victory on the second playoff hole. Despite missing the cut in his last seven regular season tournaments, including The Open Championship and the PGA Championship that were his only two major tournament appearances of the season, Berger entered the FedEx Cup Playoffs in the 46th position.

Berger missed the cut at the Barclays, but he responded with a tie for 12th at the Deutsche Bank Championship, followed by his other second-place finish of the season at the BMW Championship, a distant six strokes behind Jason Day. Berger earned $891,000 for that performance. He also played his way into the Tour Championship, where he finished in a tie for 12th to earn $196,350. Berger earned just over $3 million for the season, finishing 11th in the final FedEx Cup standings in 2014–2015 and earning a bonus of $300,000. Berger was named the PGA Tour Rookie of the Year. He would enter the 2015–2016 season with an exempt status for being in the top 125 in the FedEx Cup points standings.

Roberto Castro missed the FedEx Cup Playoffs for the second consecutive season in 2014–2015. He reclaimed his PGA Tour card through his performance in the Web.com Finals. Castro played in 23 PGA Tour regular season tournaments in 2015–2016 and made the cut in 19. He had four tournament finishes in the top 25, with three outcomes in the top ten. The highlight of his season was advancing to a playoff at the Wells Fargo Championship played at Quail Hollow in Charlotte, North Carolina, where he came up short to James Hahn. Castro appeared in only one major that season. He finished in a tie for 66th at the PGA Championship held at the Baltursol Golf Club in New Jersey. Castro made the cut in his last ten tournaments in the regular season. He was 53rd in the FedEx Cup points standings at the conclusion of the regular season. Through his performance in the playoffs, Castro advanced to the Tour Championship, where he tied for 17th and earned $166,600. Castro ended the playoffs at the 22nd position in the FedEx Cup standings to receive a bonus of $215,000.

As demonstrated, even if not winning, playing great in a few tournaments will result in a golfer having a very successful season. In the 2015–2016 season, Phil Mickelson played in only 18 regular season tournaments. He made the cut in 13 with six finishes in the top five and three second-place finishes, including his remarkable performance at The Open Championship. Mickelson finished eighth in the regular season FedEx Cup points standings. After playoff performances with results of one missed cut, a tie for 13th, a tie for 24th, and a 22nd-place finish, Mickelson dropped to the 16th position in the final FedEx Cup standings. He earned a playoff bonus of $245,000 in addition to the more than $4 million he won in prize money during that season.

Two golfers competed in fewer than 15 regular season PGA tournaments in 2015–2016, but were still able to compete in three FedEx Cup Playoff tournaments. Louis Oosthuizen, who is an active participant on the European Tour, played in only 14 regular season PGA Tour events. He made the cut in ten, with eight performances in the top 25. The other two results were 28th and 44th. His season was highlighted by a second-place finish in the World Golf Championships—Dell Match Play, where he lost the final match to Jason Day. Oosthuizen ended the regular season 56th in the FedEx Cup standings. Despite playoff finishes of a tie for 18th, a tie for eighth, and a tie for 17th place, he did not qualify for the Tour Championship. Oosthuizen did improve his final position to 38th in the standings to earn a $137,000 playoff bonus. He won prize money of more than $2.42 million.

Justin Rose played in 15 PGA tournaments in the 2015–2016 regular season, making the cut in 12. Rose had ten tournament finishes in the top 25 and five in the top ten, including a tie for tenth at the Masters (Rose also won the

Gold Medal at the Rio Olympic Games). Rose ended the regular season 51st in the FedEx Cup points standings. He remained in that spot after competing in the first three FedEx Cup Playoff tournaments to claim a bonus payment of $120,000. Rose collected more than $2.08 million in tournament prize money for the season. It can be surmised that if golfers with the talent of Oosthuizen and Rose participated in more regular season PGA tournaments, they would have gotten into the top 30 in FedEx Cup points to qualify for the Tour Championship.

Neither Oosthuizen nor Rose won a tournament in the 2016–2017 season. Again, both did not appear in many PGA Tour events, but they both repeated their outstanding seasons. Oosthuizen played in 15 regular season tournaments plus three playoff tournaments, making the cut in 17, with nine finishes in the top 25 and four in the top ten. Oosthuizen had a third-place finish in The Players Championship, earning $924,000, and a tie for second at the PGA Championship, winning $784,000.

Oosthuizen entered the playoffs in 35th place in the FedEx Cup standings. He finished in a tie for tenth at the Northern Trust and won $187,500. He ended the Dell Technologies Championship in a tie for 30th to move up to 31st in the standings. However, at the BMW Championship, an opening-round 77 and a second-round 74 led to a tie for 63rd. Oosthuizen remained in 31st place and did not make the Tour Championship. He earned more than $3.1 million for the 2016–2017 season and collected an additional playoff bonus of $165,000.

Rose played in 14 regular season tournaments in the 2016–2017 season. He produced three second-place finishes: the Sony Open, earning $648,000; the Masters, winning more than $1.18 million; and the BMW Championship, collecting $770,000. He also finished in a tie for fourth at the Farmers Insurance Open and the Genesis Open. In 18 starts, including the playoffs, Rose made 15 cuts, with ten top-25 finishes and eight in the top ten. Rose played spectacular golf in the playoffs. He had a runner-up finish at the BMW Championship and completed the other three playoff tournaments all in a tie for tenth place. He earned more than $1.42 million in the four FedEx Cup Playoff tournaments out of his season total prize money of more than $4.24 million. Rose began the playoffs in the 32nd spot in the standings and ended in ninth place. He was awarded a bonus of $550,000.

7

Playing Often

Many golfers achieve a successful season simply by playing often. Playing in a tournament cannot hurt a golfer in that he cannot reduce his total money earnings or lose FedEx Cup points. With a poor performance, however, other golfers will leap ahead in the FedEx Cup standings, a result that, of course, would have happened if a golfer did not play in that tournament at all. Some golfers are, thus, showing up week after week and being rewarded for competing by grinding out rounds and making tournament cuts. Playing often is of necessity as these golfers know what is at stake on two measures. First, they are aware of the opportunities remaining in the current season by qualifying for the FedEx Cup Playoffs. Second, they fully understand how different the prospects for the following season will be if they have to play out of a lower priority ranking group.

One prominent challenge for the golfers who play so often is that they can certainly become fatigued both physically and mentally. They will also be competing against other golfers whose playoff status is secure and may have been able to rest leading into that tournament. In the 2015–2016 season, ten golfers did not win a tournament despite having more than 30 tournament starts, including their appearances in the FedEx Cup Playoffs. In the 2016–2017 season, 14 golfers had at least 30 tournament starts, including their appearances in the FedEx Cup Playoffs, but did not win a tournament.

Spencer Levin began playing regularly on the PGA Tour in 2009. He has yet to win a tournament, with his best result being a second-place finish in a playoff loss to Johnson Wagner at the 2011 Mayakoba Golf Classic. That season resulted in Levin's highest prize money earnings, more than $2.32 million. In the 2014–2015 regular season, Levin played in 29 tournaments, making the cut in 16. He had six tournament outcomes in the top 25, with one top-ten finish. Levin ended the regular season 115th in the FedEx Cup points standings. He finished in a tie for 16th in the Barclays to advance in the playoffs. He did make the cut at the second playoff tournament to improve to 82nd in the final standings and claim a bonus of $75,000. Levin collected $836,698 in tournament prize money.

Levin had the same active scheduling approach for the 2015–2016 regular season. He competed in 30 PGA tournaments, with eight top-25 performances and two top-ten finishes. He ended the regular season 90th in the FedEx Cup standings. His season would again come to a conclusion after the second tournament of the FedEx Cup Playoffs. Levin missed the cut in the Barclays before finishing in a tie for 57th at the Deutsche Bank Championship. Levin received another $75,000 playoff bonus for finishing 94th in the final FedEx Cup points standings. He earned more than $1.17 million. It was Levin's fourth season earning more than $1 million.

Zac Blair joined the Tour in the 2014–2015 season, but he has yet to win a PGA tournament. Blair played in 31 tournaments in that season. After making the cut in 17, with seven top-25 finishes and one top ten, he ended the regular season 106th in the FedEx Cup standings. He improved his position greatly when he finished in a tie for fourth at the Barclays. After a tie for 60th at the Deutsche Bank Championship, Blair advanced to the BMW Championship, where a tie for 53rd ended his season. Blair finished 59th in the final FedEx Cup standings to receive a playoff bonus of $110,000. Blair collected more than $1.24 million in prize money for the season.

Blair competed in 30 tournaments in the 2015–2016 regular season. The highlight of the season was the best tournament result of his career, a third-place finish at the Sony Open in Hawaii. Blair entered the FedEx Cup Playoffs in the 103rd position. He would only compete in the opening playoff tournament. His tie for 74th at the Barclays dropped him back to the 110th position. Blair did claim a $70,000 playoff bonus as well as prize money of $903,459.

Levin and Blair continued to be very active on the PGA Tour in the 2016–2017 season, but it did not yield participation in the FedEx Cup Playoffs. Levin played in 31 tournaments and made the cut in 13. He had two top-25 finishes, with only one of those getting him into the top ten. Levin ended the season 163rd in the standings. He won $469,730 in tournament prize money. Blair participated in 32 PGA tournaments and made the cut in 21. He had two top-25 performances and one top-ten finish, a tie for eighth at the Shell Houston Open. He ended the regular season 126th in the standings. Blair earned $788,352 in prize money. Levin and Blair participated in the Web.com Tour Finals, but neither made it into the top 25 in Finals prize money. While Blair was able to begin the 2017–2018 season in the 126 through 150 finishers in the FedEx Cup points standings group, Levin began the season with conditional status on the Web.com Tour.

Some golfers with tournament wins in recent seasons were very active in 2016–2017. Danny Lee started 2016–2017 in his final season in the tournament winners group for his victory at the Greenbrier Classic in 2015. Lee played in 29 regular season tournaments and made the cut in 19, with nine top-25 and four top-ten finishes. His season was highlighted by a tie for third at the Travelers Championship. Lee went into the playoffs 56th but missed the cut in the first two playoff tournaments and had to withdraw from the BMW Championship. Lee finished 70th in the final standings to claim a bonus of $110,000. Lee won more than $1.61 million in prize money for the season.

Charley Hoffman entered 2016–2017 in the regular season tournament winners group. He won the OHL Classic at Mayakoba in the autumn of the 2014–2015 season and the Valero Texas Open in the 2015–2016 season. His status lasts through the 2017–2018 season. Hoffman had 27 regular season starts in 2016–2017 and made the cut in 20. Thirteen of those results were in the top 25, with seven finishes in the top ten. Hoffman finished in second place on two occasions, in a tie along with Kevin Kisner, one stroke behind Marc Leishman at the Arnold Palmer Invitational, and losing in a playoff to Jhonattan Vegas at the RBC Canadian Open. Hoffman entered the playoffs 11th in the standings. He made the cut in all four tournaments, but with his best showing as a tie for 17th at the Northern Trust, he slid to 20th in the final FedEx Cup standings. Hoffman won more than $4.16 million in prize money for the season and added a bonus of $225,000.

Some golfers play more often near the end of the regular season to accumulate the needed points to gain entrance into the FedEx Cup Playoffs, on some occasions without a top finish. Troy Merritt had his exempt status for the 2016–2017 season secure for winning the 2015 Quicken Loans National. However, even the golfers who have the following season's exempt status secure group are cognizant of what they need to do to qualify for the FedEx Cup playoffs. Merritt's playoff quest in the 2015–2016 season was still to be determined after missing the cut at the Quicken Loans National tournament at the end of June. Merritt was in 111th place in the FedEx Cup standings. Merritt's record at the conclusion of the Quicken Loans was 19 tournaments played, with eight made cuts. His season was highlighted by a tie for third at the Arnold Palmer Invitational. Merritt did not play in the two weeks following the Quicken Loans before playing six consecutive weeks at the end of the 2015–2016 season.

Merritt's stretch started at the Barbasol Championship that began on Thursday, July 14, and concluded with the Wyndham Championship that ended on August 21. Merritt earned 26 FedEx Cup points when he finished tied for 20th at the Barbasol Championship. It was his highest finish during this stretch of tournaments. He was awarded 37 points for finishing in a tie for

32nd at the following week's RBC Canadian Open. After missing the cut at the PGA Championship and the Travelers Championship, Merritt added 13 points at the John Deere Classic and one point at the Wyndham Championship. These six tournaments accounted for 77 of the 482 FedEx Cup points that Merritt accumulated for the season. Merritt ended the regular season in the 120th position in the FedEx Cup standings, 37 points ahead of Matt Jones in the non-playoff qualifying position of number 126. Although Merritt missed the cut at the first playoff tournament, by qualifying for the FedEx Cup Playoffs he earned a $70,000 playoff bonus, instead of a $32,000 bonus awarded to the golfers ranked 126 through 150 in the standings.

While some golfers are trying to qualify for the FedEx Cup Playoffs, others are playing often in an attempt to solidify their position within the top 100, top 70, or top 30 thresholds needed to advance to the further tournaments of the playoffs. Heading into July of 2016, Daniel Summerhays looked to the end of the regular season more to advance his position in the FedEx Cup points standings. At that point in the season, Summerhays played in 20 tournaments and made the cut on 17 occasions. His best performance was an eighth-place finish at the U.S. Open, which earned him 85 FedEx Cup points. Four other top-15 finishes by July earned him an additional 217 points of his total of 681.

Summerhays then played in tournaments on five consecutive weeks. He earned 11 points at The Open Championship. He missed the cut at the RBC Canadian Open the following week. At the PGA Championship, Summerhays improved his FedEx Cup positioning dramatically when his ten under par performance was good for a tie for third place. He accumulated 210 FedEx Cup points for that effort. The following week, he added 61 points with an 11th-place finish at the Travelers Championship. Summerhays ended his regular season by missing the cut at the John Deere Classic. Summerhays added 282 points of his season total of 963 at the tournaments over these five weeks at the end of the season. Summerhays was 37th entering the FedEx Cup Playoffs.

Although Summerhays missed the cut at both of the first two playoff tournaments, he remained high enough in the standings to qualify for the third playoff tournament. At the no-cut, guaranteed prize money BMW Championship, despite finishing in last place, Summerhays won $17,340. Summerhays could point to his late-season performances as the reason that he solidified his position enough to participate in three playoff tournaments. Summerhays finished 65th in the final FedEx Cup standings. He earned a playoff bonus payment of $110,000 and prize money of more than $2.04 million.

Ryan Moore was another golfer who made a late-season charge to improve his FedEx Cup Playoff position in the 2015–2016 season. Moore already had a tournament winners exempt status through the 2016–2017 season for winning the CIMB Classic in the autumn portion of the 2014–2015 season. Moore made 12 cuts with four top-ten finishes after his 16th tournament start in 2015–2016. He amassed 667 FedEx Cup points. Moore was having what many would consider a very successful season and was well on his way to qualifying for the FedEx Cup Playoffs. After finishing in a tie for 70th in the PGA Championship, Moore was 68th in the FedEx Cup standings. Moore still decided to participate in the final three tournaments of the regular season. This meant that if Moore was successful in advancing in the FedEx Cup Playoffs, he would play seven consecutive weeks prior to the week off before the Tour Championship.

At the Travelers Championship, Moore earned 51 FedEx Cup points when he tied for 17th. The following week at the John Deere Classic, Moore posted three consecutive rounds of 65 and a final-round 67, playing the final 46 holes of the tournament without a bogey. He finished at 22 under par and delivered a two-stroke win over Ben Martin. Moore earned 500 FedEx Cup points for his victory and extended his exempt status through the 2017–2018 season. Moore added 17 points at the regular season-ending Wyndham Championship. The last three tournaments of the regular season accounted for 568 of Moore's season total of 1235 FedEx Cup points. Moore entered the playoffs in 23rd place.

The significance of being near the top of the FedEx Cup standings heading into the playoffs toward reaching the goal of being in the Tour Championship field has been demonstrated. In 2015, all of the golfers in the top 20 in the final regular season FedEx Cup points standings participated in the Tour Championship. In 2016, the top 13 golfers and 17 of the top 20 golfers in the final regular season standings all reached the Tour Championship. In 2017, the top 15 golfers and 19 of the top 20 golfers in the final regular season standings participated in the Tour Championship.

Already having the inside track to get to the Tour Championship, Moore continued with strong performances in the 2016 playoffs. Moore finished the Barclays in a tie for seventh and the Deutsche Bank Championship in a tie for eighth. He placed 64th at the BMW Championship. Moore made it to the play-off at the Tour Championship, along with Rory McIlroy and Kevin Chappell. Moore extended the playoff to four extra holes before McIlroy prevailed. Moore earned $752,250 for his performance in the Tour Championship. His combined prize money for the four FedEx Cup Playoff tournaments was more than $1.2 million. His season total was more than $3.7 million. Moore also earned a $700,000 playoff bonus for finishing seventh in the final FedEx Cup points standings. Moore received one final distinction: he was named to the Ryder Cup team as the final pick by captain Davis Love III.

Richy Werenski entered the 2016–2017 season as the sixth-ranked golfer in the top finishers of the Web.com Tour group. From the Valero Texas Open that concluded on April 23, 2017, through the Greenbrier Classic which ended on July 9, 2017, Werenski played in seven tournaments and missed the cut in six. His lone made cut was at the Zurich Classic of New Orleans team event, when he and his partner, Ollie Schniederjans, finished in a tie for 39th place. Werenski was in 160th place in the FedEx Cup standings after the Greenbrier. There were six weeks left of the regular season schedule.

For Werenski, the Greenbrier Classic began a stretch of playing five consecutive weeks. The week after he missed the cut at the Greenbrier, Werenski finished in a tie for 25th at the John Deere Classic to earn 26 FedEx Cup points. He climbed to the 154th position in the standings. Despite adding 25 points with a tie for 18th at the Barbasol Championship, one of the opposite tournaments, he slipped one spot to number 155 (keeping in mind that golfers were adding points on that same weekend at The Open Championship). Werenski moved up to number 154 after a tie for 42nd at the RBC Canadian Open gave him 12 points.

Werenski then played the Barracuda Championship, where a tie for second place was the season-altering result that he needed. He accumulated 135 FedEx Cup points and was now 121st in the standings. He did not play the following week at the PGA Championship. Werenski strengthened his position with a tie for tenth at the Wyndham Championship, the regular season finale, that moved him up to 108th in the standings and into the playoffs. Werenski's season ended after a tie for 49th at the Northern Trust. He earned $21,595 for that playoff tournament, and by finishing 106th in the final standings, he was awarded a bonus of $70,000. His total prize money for the season was $890,262. Werenski also gained his exempt status for the 2017–2018 season.

8

Career Earnings

Two priority groups have been created to recognize career prize money winnings. A golfer whose earnings place him in the top 50 or top 25 on the PGA Tour career money list at the end of the previous season is given the opportunity to exercise a one-time, one-season exemption. A golfer can use both the top 50 and the top 25 career money list exemptions in separate seasons if he meets the qualifications. This gives a golfer two seasons of high priority status based on his career accomplishments. Tiger Woods was the career money list leader at the conclusion of the 2016–2017 season with more than $110 million in PGA Tour earnings. Phil Mickelson was second on the list, earning more than $83.5 million. Vijay Singh at $70.8 million, Jim Furyk at $67.7 million, and Ernie Els at $48.9 million completed the top five in career earnings.

For some veteran players, continuing to be in the top 50 or top 25 of the PGA career money list represents their excellence, considering that a large portion of their careers occurred at a time when prize money was not as lucrative as it is today. For example, Justin Leonard entered the 2016–2017 season ranked 20th on the PGA career money list with earnings of more than $33.8 million. Leonard may be best known for sinking a 45-foot birdie putt at the 17th hole on the final day of the 1999 Ryder Cup in Brookline, Massachusetts, that completed the comeback win for the United States team.

For his career, Leonard has 12 PGA Tour victories that span from 1996 through 2008. Leonard's tournament championships are highlighted by his winning The Open Championship in 1997, for which he earned $418,000. In contrast, Jordan Spieth's victory at The Open Championship in 2017 paid him more than $1.84 million. For further perspective, Spieth did not start competing regularly on the PGA Tour until 2013, yet entering the 2016–2017 season with his eight career wins, Spieth was already 35th on the career earnings list with more than $25.7 million in tournament earnings. In the 2016–2017 season,

Spieth won more than $9.43 million. His career total surpassed $35.2 million and placed him at number 20 on the all-time career money list entering the 2017–2018 season.

The golfers who use their one-time exemption based on career earnings are in a precarious position because, as stipulated by the PGA Tour rules, they know for sure that they will be in another priority ranking group for the following season. Unless a golfer wins a tournament in that season, the ranking group will be lower in the priority selection process. Qualifying for the FedEx Cup Playoffs certainly becomes the second goal of a season using a career earnings exemption.

Chad Campbell's first full regular season on the PGA Tour was in 2002, when he had 34 tournament starts. Campbell is a four-time PGA tournament winner, including the 2003 Tour Championship. Campbell finished 136th in the final 2012–2013 FedEx Cup points standings and 137th on the money list. It was the first time in Campbell's career that he did not qualify for the FedEx Cup Playoffs and the first season since 2001 that he was not in the top 125 on the money list.

In the 2013–2014 season, the 39-year-old Campbell had an exempt status for being one of the 126 through 150 finishers in the FedEx Cup points standings. Campbell appeared in 18 tournaments and made the cut on nine occasions. The highlight of Campbell's season was a tie for seventh at the Travelers Championship, his only top-ten finish of the season. He earned $186,775 for that tournament. Campbell had one other top-25 finish in 2013–2014, a tie for 13th at the John Deere Classic that included a third-round 62. He earned $470,798 in that season to place him 149th on the PGA Tour money list. Campbell finished 152nd in the FedEx Cup standings with 317 points. He missed the 150th position that would have provided a bonus and an improved priority rank group by only six points as Johnson Wagner held that spot with 323 points.

Competing in the Web.com Tour Finals in 2014 did not improve Campbell's exempt status group. He missed the cut in two tournaments and amassed $18,330 in the other two events, with a tie for 17th and a tie for 50th. Campbell earned $17,982 less than Eric Axley's $36,312 amount that secured him the final PGA Tour card. Rather than dropping to the past champions group, Campbell chose to use the top 50 career earnings exemption for the 2014–2015 season. Entering that season, Campbell had career earnings of more than $22.26 million.

Campbell did not squander this opportunity. With a much higher exempt status priority group than the previous season, and certainly much higher than if he decided to compete out of the past champions group, Campbell was able to be more active in the 2014–2015 season. He played in 28 PGA tournaments.

After missing the cut in five of his first seven tournaments, Campbell made the cut in five straight events. Campbell ended the regular season by making the cut in eight consecutive starts, including a tie for eighth at both the FedEx St. Jude Classic and the Zurich Classic of New Orleans. He also had consecutive ties for 11th place, in the RBC Canadian Open and the Quicken Loans National.

Overall, in 2014–2015, Campbell made the cut in 18 of his 28 starts, with seven top-25 finishes and two in the top ten. Campbell ended the regular season 100th on the money list, earning more than $1 million. He finished at number 73 in the FedEx Cup points standings. Although he did not make the cut in either of the first two tournaments of the FedEx Cup Playoffs, his finish at the 96th position earned him a playoff bonus of $75,000. Equally important, Campbell would have an exempt status as part of the top 125 in the FedEx Cup points standings ranking group heading into the 2015–2016 season.

Campbell again took advantage of the opportunity to be exempt into any regular season tournament that he chose to enter. He remained active by playing in 26 regular season tournaments in 2015–2016. Buoyed by another late-season run in which he made the cut in seven of his final eight tournaments, for the second consecutive year Campbell qualified for the FedEx Cup Playoffs. Campbell made the cut in 16 regular season tournaments, with seven top-25 finishes and three top-ten performances. He ended the regular season 85th in the FedEx Cup points standings.

Campbell missed the cut in the Barclays. A final-round score of 67 at the Deutsche Bank Championship got him a tie for 21st, but it did not allow for further advancement in the playoffs. Campbell totaled more than $1.16 million for the season. He earned a playoff bonus of $80,000 by finishing 73rd in the final FedEx Cup points standings. Campbell once again secured his exempt status for the 2016–2017 season.

The consistent play of Campbell continued in 2016–2017. He started the season by making the cut in his first seven tournaments, including his season-best performance of a tie for sixth at the CareerBuilder Challenge. Campbell won $201,550 and 95 FedEx Cup points for that finish. For the season, Campbell appeared in 29 tournaments and made the cut in 20. He had eight top-25 and three top-ten finishes on his way to winning more than $1.32 million. With that finish, since 2003, Campbell has 11 seasons in which he earned over $1 million, with four seasons over $2 million and one season over $3 million.

Campbell ended the regular season 73rd in the FedEx Cup standings. In the playoffs, Campbell finished in a tie for 67th in the Northern Trust and was awarded $17,938. When Campbell missed the cut at the Dell Technologies Championship, his season concluded. Campbell finished 83rd in the final standings to earn a playoff bonus of $75,000. He entered 2017–2018 again with a status in the top 125 of the FedEx Cup standings. Campbell was 39th in career prize money at the end of the 2016–2017 season, with a total of more than $25.7 million.

Obviously, using the career earnings exemption does not always lead to a successful season and an improved status moving forward. Robert Allenby was a four-time winner on the PGA Tour with career earnings of just under $27.4 million at the conclusion of the 2014–2015 season. Allenby had a 12-year stretch from 2000 through 2011 in which he finished no lower than 63rd on that season's PGA Tour money list. His best season was in 2008, when he earned more than $3.6 million. He was 11th in prize money in that season after making the cut in 27 of 28 tournaments, with 17 top-25 finishes and nine top-ten performances.

Allenby was the 125th and final player to qualify for the FedEx Cup Playoffs in the 2013–2014 season. Allenby finished one point higher in the standings than Nicholas Thompson. With that exempt status in the 2014–2015 season, Allenby competed in 25 PGA tournaments, but he made the cut in only eight. He had one top-ten and no additional top-25 performances. Allenby ended the season at 179th on the money list, earning almost $272,000, and 187th in the FedEx Cup points standings. Allenby's post-season was spent in the Web.com Tour Finals, but he played in only two tournaments. Allenby withdrew from one tournament, and the $6,360 that he earned for a tie for 30th at the Web.com Tour Championship left him far below the prize money needed to qualify for the PGA Tour through that path.

Allenby, 44 years old at the time, decided to use his top 50 career earnings exemption for the 2015–2016 season. Allenby competed in 23 PGA tournaments in that season, but he could muster only two made cuts, a tie for 63rd and a tie for 68th. He earned $25,271. Allenby entered the 2016–2017 season 34th in the past champions priority group.

Allenby played in only four tournaments on the PGA Tour in 2016–2017. He missed the cut at the Shell Houston Open and the Barracuda Championship. He finished tied for 27th at the Barbasol Championship and tied for 68th at the Sanderson Farms Championship. His PGA Tour prize money winnings totaled $32,851. Allenby instead played the majority of his tournaments on the Web.com Tour. He earned $35,514 by making the cut on six occasions in 16 Web.com Tour events. Allenby had two top-25 finishes and one top-ten outcome. He ranked number 111 on the Web.com Tour regular season prize money list, below the top 75 dividing line needed to qualify for the Finals. The 46-year-old Allenby was once again in the past champions group for the 2017–2018 season.

Some players use the career earnings exemption in an attempt to extend their career on the PGA Tour before they transition to the senior Champions Tour. In the 2014–2015 season when Chad Campbell used his career earnings exemption, so did Kenny Perry. Then 54 years old, Perry used his top 25 in PGA Tour career earnings status. Perry earned just under $32 million and was 15th on the career prize money list. Perry is the winner of 14 PGA tournaments, the first in 1991 and the last in 2009.

Campbell's and Perry's careers intertwined at the 2009 Masters. The two found themselves in a playoff along with Angel Cabrera. At the first extra hole, Campbell was eliminated when he made a bogey. After a poor tee-shot, Cabrera's second shot hit a tree but bounced into the fairway, leaving him 114 yards from the hole. Cabrera hit his approach shot six feet from the cup. When Cabrera made that putt, he matched Perry's par to force a second extra hole. There, Cabrera captured the green jacket as his par topped Perry's bogey. The 2009 Masters ended up being the second time that Campbell and Perry completed a major tournament in the runner-up position.

In the 2014–2015 season, Perry appeared in only nine PGA Tour events, making the cut in three. Perry played in his last PGA Tour event in June 2015, at the Memorial, a tournament that he won on three occasions. Perry instead spent his playing time on the Champions Tour. He earned his first win on the Champions Tour at the 3M Championship in August 2015, one week before he turned 55, with a four-stroke victory over Bernhard Langer. Perry's second-round score of 61, 11 under par, at the 3M Championship included a hole-in-one, an eagle, and seven birdies. He earned $262,500 for the win.

Perry remained active on the Champions Tour in 2017. He won the U.S. Senior Open when he posted rounds of 65–64–67–68 for a two-stroke win over Kirk Triplett. He won $720,000 for that tournament. In 2017, Perry made the cut in all 22 Champions Tour events that he played. He had 16 top-25 finishes, with nine of those performances resulting in a top ten effort. In addition to his win, Perry had two second-place and one third-place performance. He won more than $1.5 million in prize money.

For the 2016–2017 season, three players exercised their special one-time exemption for being among the top 50 in career earnings: Bo Van Pelt, Carl Pettersson, and Geoff Ogilvy. Van Pelt, the winner of the 2009 U.S. Bank Championship in Milwaukee, actually exercised his career earnings exemption for the 2015–2016 season, but he played in only five tournaments before having surgery to repair a torn labrum in his left arm. Van Pelt received an extension to once again use his career earnings exemption for the 2016–2017 season. Van Pelt, however, was unable to play in any PGA Tour event during that season. The extension was once again applied for the 2017–2018 season.

Carl Pettersson had an exempt status for being in the top 125 FedEx Cup points standings entering the 2015–2016 season. He played in 22 tournaments but made the cut on only five occasions in that season. His best finish was a tie for 39th at the Sanderson Farms Championship. For the season he earned $66,986. Pettersson was number 214 in the FedEx Cup standings.

The 40-year-old Pettersson is a five-time winner on the PGA Tour, with his most recent being the 2012 RBC Heritage. Pettersson decided to use his career earnings exemption for the 2016–2017 season. He played in 27 tournaments that season, making the cut in six. His top finish was a tie for 16th at the Valero Texas Open. He earned $102,300 and 52 FedEx Cup points for that tournament. Aside from a tie for 35th at the Sanderson Farms Championship, all other made cuts were no better than a tie for 62nd place. Pettersson's prize money total for 2016–2017 was $164,621. He was 205th in the FedEx Cup points standings, not high enough to participate in the Web.com Tour Finals had he chosen that path. Pettersson entered the 2017–2018 season in the past champions group.

Geoff Ogilvy is an eight-time champion on the PGA Tour. He won the U.S. Open in 2006, played at Winged Foot Golf Club in New York, with a one-stroke victory over Phil Mickelson, Jim Furyk, and Colin Montgomerie. Ogilvy has seven other top-ten finishes in major tournaments. He is also the winner of three World Golf Championships tournaments. For the 2015–2016 season, Ogilvy was in the final season of an exempt status as a regular season tournament winner for his victory at the 2014 Barracuda Championship. In 2015–2016, Ogilvy got off to a slow start when he missed the cut in his first five tournaments and eight of the first nine. Ogilvy's only made cut was a tie for 51st at the Waste Management Phoenix Open. He earned $15,392 and 18 FedEx Cup points for that performance. Ogilvy competed in only one major, missing the cut at the U.S. Open, and no World Golf Championships tournaments in that season.

Ogilvy made a late-season rally by making the cut in four of his last five tournaments, with three top-25 finishes. These performances were highlighted by a tie for ninth at the RBC Canadian Open, for which he earned $159,300 and 73 FedEx Cup points. Overall, however, in his 22 tournaments, Ogilvy made the cut in only nine. He amassed $397,595 in prize money for the season, which put him in 167th place on the PGA Tour money list. He finished the season 161st in the FedEx Cup standings.

Rather than trying to improve his exempt status through the Web.com Tour Finals or play the following season from the past champions group, Ogilvy chose to use the one-time exemption for being in the top 50 of career earnings. Ogilvy earned more than $29.4 million in PGA Tour career prize money entering the 2016–2017 season.

Upon being near the top of the leaderboard after the second round of the Quicken Loans National tournament, played just two weeks after his 40th birthday, Ogilvy provided a detailed explanation of his decision to use the career earnings exemption for the 2016–2017 season. "I just thought it was a good time to use it. I could have gone to the Web.com Playoffs [the previous season]. You can't come out of that with a better card than my career money was going to be. I just kind of figured that's what it was for. Everyone kind of thinks it's when you're 48, 49, just to get ready for the Champions Tour. But I wouldn't want to play a full season when I'm 48, but now I wanted to play a full season, so I took it." Ogilvy also spoke of the pressure of playing with a one-time career earnings exemption, stating, "when you've always been fully exempt you sit down and start the year and play whatever you want to play. When you've always got it in the bank [the career earnings exemption], like say the last few years if I lost my card, it didn't matter because I always had one or two of those. But now I don't have one unless I get back in the top 25 [of career earnings]."

Ogilvy was able to take advantage of his career earnings exemption. He made 13 cuts in 25 tournaments, highlighted by a tie for fourth at the Shriners Hospitals for Children Open. For the season, Ogilvy had six top-25 finishes. He claimed the 116th position in the regular season FedEx Cup standings. In the playoffs, a tie for 40th at the Northern Trust earned Ogilvy $35,875 of his season total of $867,249 in prize money. Although he did not advance past the first tournament in the 2016–2017 playoffs, Ogilvy did play well enough to place in the top 125 of the FedEx Cup standings group for the 2017–2018 season. Ogilvy accomplished what he intended to do at the outset of the season.

Stewart Cink was the only player in 2016–2017 who exercised his one-time exemption for being in the top 25 of PGA Tour career earnings. Cink finished 147th in the regular season FedEx Cup standings in the 2015–2016 season. Had Cink obtained another 123 points, he would have qualified for the playoffs and could have saved his one-time exemption for another season. Cink had career earnings of just below $34 million entering the 2016–2017 season.

Cink would join Ogilvy in parlaying his decision to use his career earnings into a very successful season. After missing the cut at the season-opening Safeway Open, Cink made the cut in 11 of his next 12 tournaments. Cink made 19 cuts in 25 starts for the season. He tied for tenth in three tournaments and overall had ten top-25 performances. Cink played in two major tournaments: the U.S. Open, where he finished tied for 46th, and The Open Championship, where he missed the cut. It is The Open Championship where Cink won his only major championship. Cink defeated 59-year-old Tom Watson in a playoff in the 2009 tournament at Turnberry, Scotland. Cink birdied the 18th hole, while Watson bogeyed 18 to create the playoff.

Cink entered the 2016–2017 FedEx Cup Playoffs 76th in the standings. He missed the cut at the Northern Trust, but he finished 12th in the Dell Technologies Championship. That performance earned Cink $201,250 of his season total of more than $1.46 million and got him into the third playoff tournament. He finished in a tie for 27th at the BMW Championship. Cink was awarded a playoff bonus of $114,000 for finishing 53rd in the final FedEx Cup standings. Cink, 44 years old, entered the 2017–2018 season in the top 125 of the FedEx Cup points standings exempt group.

A golfer's career achievements are once again recognized with the priority ranking group designation of life members, defined by the PGA Tour as those "who have been active members of the PGA Tour for 15 years and have won at least 20 co-sponsored events." This exempt status will get these golfers into the regular season tournaments of their choice. However, these golfers are veterans who are likely looking to play a very limited PGA tournament schedule. For the 2016–2017 season, Tom Watson and Vijay Singh held life member status.

Watson, who turned 68 in September of 2017, last played in a PGA tournament in 2016, when for the 43rd and final time he participated in the Masters. Watson did play a limited schedule on the Champions Tour in 2017. Watson appeared in eight tournaments and made the cut in seven. Watson had two finishes in the top-25 and earned $73,613.

Singh is a three-time major champion. He split time between the PGA Tour and the Champions Tour in 2016–2017. Singh played in 18 tournaments on the PGA Tour and made the cut in six. His PGA Tour season was highlighted by a tie for 14th at the RBC Canadian Open, winning $102,000, and a tie for 16th at The Players Championship, collecting $152,250. Singh, the 2000 Masters champion, did play at Augusta in 2017, but he missed the cut. His other major tournament appearance for the season occurred in the PGA Championship, where he tied for 66th. For the season on the PGA Tour, Singh finished 178th in the FedEx Cup points standings and earned $337,305 in prize money.

Singh was active and highly successful on the Champions Tour in 2017. He and Carlos Franco won the Bass Pro Shops Legends of Golf team event. He had three second-place finishes, including the Charles Schwab Cup Championship, where he lost to Kevin Sutherland by one stroke, and the Senior PGA Championship, where he was one stroke behind Bernhard Langer. For his Champions Tour season, Singh made the cut in all 12 tournaments that he played, with nine top-25 and seven top-ten finishes. Singh won more than $1.33 million on the Champions Tour.

Davis Love III is one player who turned using his life member status entering the 2014–2015 season into a tournament winner status when he won the

2015 Wyndham Championship. Love would have that tournament winner exempt status for the 2015–2016 and 2016–2017 seasons. Love could make only 15 starts in 2015–2016 before his season was cut short in late June when he underwent surgery to repair a torn labrum in his left hip. He made the cut in 11 tournaments and earned $222,422. Love had one other significant achievement in 2016 when he captained the United States team to a victory in the Ryder Cup. It was the first victory for the United States since 2008.

In the 2016–2017 season, Love played in 13 PGA tournaments and made the cut in seven. His only top-25 performance of the season was a tie for tenth at the Wyndham Championship. Love earned $257,270 on the season. He ended up 185th in the FedEx Cup standings. For the 2017–2018 season, Love returned to his life member status. Moving forward, Love could also choose to be more active on the Champions Tour. He played in the Bass Pro Shops Legends of Golf team event in 2017, where he and partner Scott Verplank tied for eighth. In September 2017, Love also played in the Champions Tour's Pure Insurance Open, where he finished in a tie for tenth place.

9

Individual Tournament Exemptions

There are multiple tournament entrances for each singular event, rather than part of the priority ranking group selection process that is applied for all regular season tournaments. For these tournaments, some entrances are earned through a golfer's performance, others are at the discretion of the PGA Tour, while others are selected by each individual tournament's organizing committee.

A maximum of eight sponsor exemptions is provided for each specific tournament. It is the organizing committee, chaired by a tournament director, that has the responsibility of offering the sponsor exemption. These decisions are critical, considering that a golfer's opportunity to compete and earn is at stake.

There are conditions placed on who can receive a tournament entrance through the sponsor exemption path. At least two sponsor exemptions must be granted to golfers who are PGA Tour members, but otherwise would not have received entrance into the tournament. At least two must be granted to golfers who are in the top finishers of the Web.com Tour group if all of the golfers in that group have not yet gained entrance into the tournament. The PGA Tour members can receive an unlimited number of sponsor exemptions in a given season. Non-PGA Tour members, including those playing regularly on the Web.com Tour, can receive a maximum of only seven sponsor exemptions per season. Amateur golfers can receive a sponsor exemption if they have a handicap of zero or less. The rules that dictate two entrances for PGA Tour members and two entrances for golfers in the top finishers of the Web.com Tour group essentially leave each tournament organizing committee with the selection of four unrestricted sponsor exemptions.

The selection of sponsor exemptions is designed to increase the interest in that tournament, for both the short-term and the long-term. Within that general mandate, each tournament organizing committee has its own specific criteria for sponsor exemptions. Performance can certainly be a factor, as a tournament wants to form the strongest field of golfers possible. This could include objective measures such as a golfer's rank in the current season's FedEx Cup points standings, Official World Golf rankings, the Web.com Tour, or performance in the Web.com Tour Finals from the previous season. For amateur golfers, objective measures could include their world amateur ranking, whether they were an NCAA All-American, or a member of a Walker Cup team, the amateur equivalent of the Ryder Cup between the United States and a team of golfers from Great Britain and Ireland that is held every other year. Performance variables could also include how a golfer played in that specific tournament in the past.

Loyalty can be a variable in the sponsor exemption decision, as the organizing committee may reward a golfer who frequently played that tournament. The desire to participate in the tournament might even be demonstrated, if need be, by a willingness to play in the Monday qualifier. On the point of loyalty toward an event, a tournament organizing committee might specifically aim to offer sponsor exemptions to young, talented players, knowing that soon they very well might be exempt into the tournament on their own merits by being part of a high priority ranking group. The tournament organizing committee hope is that the sponsor exemption invitation will be remembered later in a golfer's career when he is successful, that he will recall having a great experience at the tournament and will want to come back and play in that event.

Golfers indicated that the decision to make a certain tournament part of their playing schedule was often due to a past sponsor exemption that they received for the event. After his victory at the John Deere Classic in 2017, while being interviewed on the CBS broadcast, Bryson DeChambeau acknowledged tournament director Clair Peterson and recognized that the sponsor exemption that he received early in his career into the John Deere Classic made his first PGA Tour win extra special.

Golfers often appeal to an organizing committee for a sponsor exemption. Golfers will call and send hand-written notes to the committee members to express their desire to play in the tournament. Rod Pampling finished 124th on the PGA Tour money list in the 2011 season, earning $668,768. By finishing just inside the top 125 threshold, Pampling retained his PGA Tour card for the 2012 season. Pampling contacted all of the tournament directors who provided him with a sponsor exemption to thank them for entrance into their tournaments. Greg McLaughlin, former director for the AT&T National Tournament, was quoted by the *Associated Press*, a comment included in Pampling's PGA Tour biography, stating, "I've been doing this 25 years. I'm not saying I've never had a guy call me and thank me for doing that, but it's the first in a long time." McLaughlin added, "It's very rare. All the other guys are thankful and appreciative. But rarely do I get one after the season when a guy gets his card and calls you to thank you. As far as I'm concerned, he can play in one of my tournaments if he ever needs a spot. He's set for life."

In trying to create interest in the tournament, organizing committees might look to a local geographic angle in making the decision about who receives a sponsor exemption. For example, at the Puerto Rico Open in 2017, native Rafael Campos was provided with a sponsor exemption. Campos walked up the 18th fairway in the tournament's final round waving the flag of Puerto Rico. He finished the tournament in a tie for tenth place.

Billy Hurley III received a sponsor exemption into the 2016 Quicken Loans National tournament played at the Congressional Country Club in Bethesda, Maryland. As a native of Leesburg, Virginia, and still residing in Annapolis, Maryland, Hurley provided a local angle to his selection. The Quicken Loans National tournament, with its proximity to Washington, D.C., is the PGA Tour event that most recognizes and honors the United States Military. At the 2017 tournament, military members introduced the golfers as they teed off to begin their rounds, and they operated the flagstick on the 16th hole that had an American flag instead of the customary tournament flag. As the golfers completed the 16th hole, they removed their caps to shake the hands of the military members who were working the hole.

Hurley's background provided an even more impressive reason for his sponsor exemption entrance into the Washington, D.C., area tournament. Hurley graduated from the United States Naval Academy in 2004 and was commissioned as a Surface Warfare Officer in the Navy until 2009. His Naval tours included time in the Persian Gulf, from 2007 through 2009, the Red Sea, and the South China Sea. Hurley also taught economics at the Naval Academy during his five years of active duty. Having Hurley receive a sponsor exemption for the Quicken Loans National tournament was a natural choice.

In the 2014–2015 season, Hurley played in 28 tournaments, making the cut in 14. He had four top-25 finishes and one top-ten finish, a tie for eighth at the CIMB Classic. Hurley ended the regular season 136th in the FedEx Cup standings, 38 points short of qualifying for the FedEx Cup playoffs. Hurley participated in the Web.com Tour Finals tournaments to try to improve his exempt status. He made the cut in three tournaments, including a tie for ninth, but his total of $31,812 put him behind Rob Oppenheim, who finished 25th on the Finals prize money list with $32,206. Hurley entered the 2015–2016 season with the exempt status of the golfers in positions 126 through 150 in the previous season's FedEx Cup points standings.

Hurley had 11 starts on the PGA Tour in the 2015–2016 season prior to the Quicken Loans National tournament. He made the cut in five tournaments, with his best result being a tie for 41st at the AT&T Byron Nelson. He earned a total of $80,707 in prize money on the PGA Tour entering the Quicken Loans National.

Hurley also participated in four tournaments on the Web.com Tour at that point in the season. He made the cut at the Panama Claro Championship, finishing in a tie for 47th place, to claim $1,790. Hurley missed the cut in his other three Web.com Tour starts. Hurley also missed the cut in the U.S. Open the week before the Quicken Loans National tournament.

Hurley shot a five under par 66 in the first round of the 2016 Quicken Loans National tournament. Beginning the round on the tenth hole, Hurley ended the day with birdies on six of the final 12 holes. Hurley put himself into contention to win the tournament when he went without a bogey on his scorecard from his fifth hole in round two until the 2nd hole in round four. Hurley made ten birdies over that 32-hole stretch. Hurley shot a 65 in the second round to tie Jon Rahm for the tournament lead at 11 under par. He shot a 67 in the third round to end the day with sole possession of first place. Hurley's 15 under par was two strokes better than Ernie Els and three strokes better than Rahm.

Hurley secured his victory over a two-hole stretch on the back nine in the final round. At the par-4 15th hole, on his third shot using a 60-degree wedge, Hurley chipped in from 35 yards to improve his score to 16 under par. He followed by making a 27-foot, three-inch birdie putt at the par-5 16th hole. His 17 under par score was three shots better than second place finisher Vijay Singh.

For Hurley, it was his first PGA Tour victory in 104 career starts. He earned more than $1.24 million, the single highest tournament earning for his career. Hurley also became the ninth golfer on the PGA Tour since 1991 to win a tournament on a sponsor exemption. He was the first since Padraig Harrington was victorious in the Honda Classic in 2015.

After the victory, Hurley played in five regular season tournaments and made the cut in four, including a tie for 22nd at the PGA Championship. Hurley completed the regular season with 710 FedEx Cup points, 500 of which he accumulated for the win at the Quicken Loans National. He finished the regular season in 69th place in the standings. It was the second time in his career that Hurley qualified for the FedEx Cup Playoffs.

Hurley finished in a tie for 64th at the Barclays tournament. Hurley then had his best career performance in a FedEx Cup Playoff tournament when he tied for eighth at the Deutsche Bank Championship. With that performance, he was able to advance to the BMW Championship, where he finished in a tie for 42nd. Although he did not qualify for the Tour Championship, Hurley earned $260,015 of his season total of more than $1.77 million in the FedEx Cup Playoff tournaments. His playoff performances moved him up to 55th place in the final FedEx Cup standings, earning him a bonus of $110,000.

The next golfers eligible for entrance into a tournament are those who do not compete with regularity on the PGA Tour. For each tournament, the Commissioner of the PGA can designate two international golfers for entrance. Another tournament entrance could go to the current PGA Club Professional Champion, a distinction held for the 2016–2017 season by Rich Berberian, Jr. The PGA Club Professional Champion can choose to compete in up to six tournaments, however, three of the events must be opposite tournaments. This exemption also cannot be used to gain entrance into limited field tournaments. The PGA Club Professional Champion can receive a sponsor exemption to compete in additional tournaments beyond the six that he chooses.

Berberian played in seven tournaments in the 2016–2017 season, making the cut in three. He won $26,284 in prize money. Berberian participated in three opposite tournaments as well as the AT&T Pebble Beach Pro-Am, the Genesis Open from Riviera Country Club in Los Angeles, and the Shell Houston Open. He missed the cut in the Genesis Open, and the Shell Houston Open and he had a tie for 66th MDF result at the AT&T Pebble Beach Pro-Am. Berberian also qualified for the PGA Championship, but he missed the cut.

The PGA Section Champion or the Player of the Year from the section in which the PGA tournament is being held that week is granted entrance into the tournament.

The final four entrance spots are determined only a couple of days before a tournament actually begins. On Monday, an 18-hole qualifying round is played. This one-day tournament grants the four golfers with the lowest scores entrance into the main tournament. The Waste Management Phoenix Open provides only three entrances through its Monday qualifying competition. If there is a tie for the final qualifying spot, a sudden-death playoff is held to determine the entrant. Not every tournament has a Monday qualifier, and this is not a path for entrance into the major tournaments, World Golf Championships tournaments, or invitational tournaments. The fields of a Monday qualifier generally consist of PGA Tour golfers whose position in the priority selection process has not been reached, as well as those golfers who compete more frequently on the Web.com Tour and are trying to get a start in a PGA Tour event.

There is one other group of golfers who might participate in the Monday qualifying event. The field for the Monday qualifier actually begins the previous Thursday when pre-qualifying tournaments are conducted. Some golfers emerge from the pre-qualifier to compete on Monday. Dylan Dethier reported on golf.com that in the attempt to gain entrance into the Honda Classic, 444 golfers played at three different golf courses for the right to advance into the Monday qualifier. For the Honda Classic, 30 golfers from the Thursday pre-qualifiers joined 91 other golfers in the Monday field.

For Web.com tournaments, the number of golfers competing in Monday qualifying events is even greater, with two golf courses used. The top six golfers from each course get entrance into that week's Web.com Tour event.

Considering that golfers have to pay their travel expenses to get to a tournament as well as an entrance fee of approximately $400 to $500 to play in the Monday event, some qualifying fields are larger than others. For example, in 2017, the Sony Open in Hawaii had only 82 golfers in its Monday qualifier. The Valspar Championship in Palm Harbor, Florida, had 156 golfers in its Monday qualifier.

With so many participants in this one-day competition, a golfer has to shoot incredibly low to advance out of the Monday qualifier and into the main tournament. Ben Kohles played on the PGA Tour in the 2013 season, but otherwise on the Web.com Tour. Kohles earned entrance into tournaments through his performance in a Monday qualifying round. Kohles explains, "you have to go play a flawless round of golf. You can't make mistakes and you have to be aggressive." At the Shell Houston Open Monday qualifier in 2017, for example, six golfers shot 64, but that score only got them into a playoff. Another three golfers who shot a 65 in the Monday qualifier did not even get to the playoff. Jason Gore would emerge from the playoff to get into the main tournament but did not make the cut at the Shell Houston Open.

One of the 156 golfers in the Monday qualifying tournament at the 2017 Valspar Championship was Keith Mitchell. With fully exempt status on the Web.com Tour, Mitchell was hoping to play his way into his first career PGA Tour event. Starting on the 10th hole, Mitchell shot a 30, six under par, on his opening nine holes. He arrived at the final hole of his round at five under par, with the thought that four under par seemed to be the score needed to at least get him into a playoff. Mitchell hit his tee-shot into the rough on the right. However, without spotters located throughout the golf course, as is customary in a PGA Tour or Web.com Tour event, his ball could not be located. Mitchell explains, "I had to go back to the tee, now having to essentially birdie the hole." Mitchell would get his ball to the bottom of the cup in the required shots. He was now part of a group of five who would return to the golf course the next day for the playoff. Mitchell quickly ended the playoff with a birdie on the first extra hole. In two days, he would be putting a tee in the ground in a PGA tournament.

Starting on the 10th hole in round one of the Valspar Championship, Mitchell played his first five holes at three under par. Mitchell made an eagle on his first hole in a PGA Tour event when he blistered his second shot from 220 yards to within seven feet of the hole. Mitchell posted rounds of 69–70–71–68 to end the tournament at six under par. He finished in a tie for 11th place to earn $144,900.

Mitchell did just miss out on one other opportunity, as results of the other golfers at the 18th hole altered the leaderboard configuration. When Russell Henley birdied the 18th hole to complete the tournament at 277, it moved him to seven under par and into a tie for ninth. This dropped Mitchell, with 278 strokes, down to a tie for 11th. Had Mitchell finished in the top ten, he would have automatically become part of the field at the next PGA Tour event.

Because the prospects for success are so low when starting out in the Monday qualifying tournament, it makes what Patrick Reed and Arjun Atwal achieved so remarkably impressive. In 2012, Reed played in 12 tournaments on the PGA Tour. He gained entrance into six tournaments through a sponsor exemption and six through Monday qualifying rounds. Of those six Monday qualifying entrances, Reed went on to make the main tournament cut in five, highlighted by a tie for 21st at the True South Classic, for which he earned $26,700. Overall, for the 2012 season Reed made the cut in seven tournaments, had four top-25 performances, and earned $302,977.

There is the very rare occasion when a Monday qualifier produces the main tournament champion. At the Wyndham Championship in 2010, 37-year-old Arjun Atwal entered the main tournament through his performance in the Monday qualifier. Atwal shot a nine under par 61 in the first round. He then posted rounds of 67 and 65. In his final-round 67, when Atwal converted a seven-foot par putt on 18, he bested David Toms by one stroke. Atwal was 20 under par for the tournament in what remains his only win on the PGA Tour. It was the first time since 1986, when Fred Wadsworth won the Southern Open, that the tournament winner emerged from the Monday qualifying tournament.

For the final specific tournament entrances, each regular season PGA tournament provides an exemption to the golfers who have won that event in the previous five seasons. This exemption rule means that anywhere from zero to three players could move up automatically in the tournament selection process. The winners of the last two tournaments are obviously exempt through the tournament winners group. If that tournament's other winners in the previous five seasons are in a priority group higher than the tournament winners priority ranking group, zero players will gain the leap advantage. The tournament could also have the same golfer win the event multiple times within that five-season period. However, it could be the case that a golfer who otherwise would not have qualified for entrance because he is in a lower priority ranking group is exempt into that tournament due to his recent victory at that event.

The 2017 AT&T Pebble Beach Pro-Am and the 2017 Quicken Loans National offer examples of tournaments where no golfers jumped ahead in the selection process. For the 2017 AT&T Pebble Beach Pro-Am, 2016 champion Vaughn Taylor and 2015 champion Brandt Snedeker were exempt through the tournament winners group. Snedeker actually had a higher exempt status in the 2016–2017 season for his winning the FedEx Cup Championship in 2012. Snedeker also won at Pebble Beach in 2013, eliminating the possibility of another golfer moving up in the priority selection process for having won the tournament in that season. Jimmy Walker won the 2014 AT&T Pebble Beach Pro-Am, but his win at the 2016 PGA Championship placed him in the highest priority group for the next five seasons. Finally, Phil Mickelson was the Pebble Beach tournament champion in 2012. He too was in a higher priority group for his win at The Open Championship in 2013.

For the 2017 Quicken Loans National, 2016 champion Billy Hurley III and 2015 champion Troy Merritt were exempt through the tournament winners group. Justin Rose was the tournament champion in 2014, but his win at the U.S. Open in 2013 placed him in the highest priority group. Bill Haas, the 2013 winner, was exempt through the tournament winners group for his 2015 victory at the Humana Challenge. Finally, Tiger Woods was the Quicken Loans National tournament champion in 2012, but he was in a higher priority group for his win at The Players Championship in 2013.

If a specific tournament's other winners in the past five seasons are in a priority group lower than the tournament winners priority group, those golfers leap ahead in the selection process and gain an entrance into that tournament. The 2017 Genesis Open at the Riviera Country Club in Pacific Palisades, California, a tournament formerly sponsored by Northern Trust, and the 2017 Wells Fargo Championship offer examples of tournaments where a golfer did jump ahead in the priority selection process due to his victory at that specific tournament in the previous five seasons.

At the 2017 Genesis Open, three players had exempt status in a tournament winners group. The 2016 champion, Bubba Watson, and 2015 champion James Hahn were exempt through the tournament winners group. Watson also won the tournament in 2014. Bill Haas, the 2012 champion, again had his exempt status through the tournament winners group for his 2015 victory at the Humana Challenge.

In 2013, the winner of the tournament was John Merrick. Coming into the 2016–2017 season, Merrick had his exempt status as part of the past champions group. Merrick's entrance into the 2017 tournament at Riviera was still secure. Merrick did not make the cut at the 2017 Genesis Open. Merrick played in nine PGA Tour events and made the cut in four. Of those nine starts, four were in opposite tournaments. His best performance of the season was a tie for 18th at the Barbasol Championship. Merrick earned $76,648 on the PGA Tour. He ended the season ranked 216th in the FedEx Cup points standings.

Merrick did play in 11 tournaments on the Web.com Tour. He made the cut in seven. Merrick's best showing, however, was a tie for 30th place. Merrick earned $16,196 on the Web.com Tour. Upon finishing in 150th place on the Web.com Tour regular season prize money list, Merrick did not qualify for the Finals tournaments. Merrick returned to the past champions group for the 2017–2018 season.

At the 2017 Wells Fargo Championship, the 2016 champion, James Hahn, is exempt through the tournament winners group. In 2015, Rory McIlroy was the tournament winner. His exempt status was in the highest priority group for his win at the 2014 PGA Championship. J. B. Holmes claimed victory at the Wells Fargo Championship in 2014. He was exempt in the tournament winners group for his win at the 2015 Shell Houston Open. Finally, the 2012 tournament winner, Rickie Fowler, had his exempt status for his win at The Players Championship in 2015.

In 2013, Derek Ernst was the winner of the Wells Fargo Championship. Coming into the 2016–2017 season, Ernst had his exempt status as part of the past champions group, but his entrance in the 2017 Wells Fargo Championship was secure. The Wells Fargo ended up being one of three PGA Tour events that Ernst played in 2016–2017. Ernst did not make the cut in any of those tournaments.

The remainder of Ernst's tournament play occurred on the Web.com Tour, where he competed in 20 regular season events and made the cut in 13. Ernst had five top-25 finishes, with two of those in the top ten. He earned $68,032 and was 69th on the regular season Web.com Tour money list. Ernst competed in the Web.com Tour Finals, but he would make the cut in only one of the four events, a tie for 57th that netted him $2,630. Ernst returned to the past champions group for the 2017–2018 season.

10

Medical Extension

When a golfer has to miss time on the PGA Tour due to an injury, he can be granted an exempt status for the following season as a medical extension. How the extension works is that the Tour looks at a golfer's recent seasons' playing activity and then assigns a number of tournaments during which he has to earn a certain amount of prize money and/or FedEx Cup points to regain fully exempt status. For example, if a golfer played in 15 tournaments before sustaining an injury and he normally plays in 28 tournaments, he is given an exemption for 13 tournaments. In those 13 tournaments, a golfer could obviously win a tournament, or he has to earn enough prize money or points to have qualified for the top 125 of the previous season's money list or FedEx Cup standings. There were 14 players who received a major medical extension for the 2016–2017 season.

Pat Perez made only 11 starts in the 2015–2016 season after shoulder surgery to repair a torn labrum. He missed the remainder of the regular season and, for the first time since its inception, he was not part of the FedEx Cup Playoffs. Perez made the cut in three tournaments, amassing $47,840 and only 34 FedEx Cup points. He entered the 2016–2017 season on a major medical extension. From the 2002 through 2015 seasons, Perez made 365 starts on the PGA Tour, an average of 26 per season. The PGA Tour allowed Perez 15 tournaments to earn $670,050 or 420 FedEx Cup points to remain exempt for the rest of the season.

Perez quickly eclipsed the needed prize money and FedEx Cup points totals. He returned to play at the second tournament of the season, the CIMB Classic, where he finished in a tie for 33rd. He earned $36,983 and 21 FedEx Cup points. Perez finished 15 under par to tie for seventh two weeks later at the Shriners Hospitals for Children Open. He earned $205,700 and 85 FedEx Cup points.

The week after the Shriners, Perez claimed his first PGA Tour victory since the 2009 Bob Hope Classic when he won the OHL Classic at Mayakoba with a two-stroke victory over Gary Woodland. Perez opened with rounds of 68 and 66 at the par-71 course to put him in a tie for 11th, five strokes behind Woodland. Perez shot a seven under par 29 with an eagle and five birdies on the front nine in the third round. He shot a 62 in the third round to close the gap with Woodland to only one stroke. On the front nine in round four, Perez posted a 31 to complete a 27-hole stretch of 14 under par. For the entire tournament, Perez played the front nine holes at 17 under par. Despite playing the back nine in the final round at one over par 36, Perez finished the tournament at 21 under par and held off Woodland by two strokes. Perez earned $1.26 million and 500 FedEx Cup points to secure his Tour card in the tournament winners exempt status group for the remainder of the 2016–2017 season as well as the following two seasons.

The win also gained Perez entrance into the Tournament of Champions in 2017, where he finished in a tie for third. Perez won $359,000 and received 145 FedEx Cup points at that event. By the conclusion of the Tournament of Champions, his fourth event of the season, Perez already achieved the single highest season of earnings for his career.

Perez's successful season continued as he finished in a tie for fourth at the Farmers Insurance Open. Perez got to play in the Masters for the third time in his career. He finished in a tie for 18th to earn $148,500 and 52 FedEx Cup points. It was the best performance of his career at Augusta National. One month later, Perez finished in a tie for second at the Wells Fargo Championship when he and Dustin Johnson completed the tournament one stroke back of Brian Harman.

Perez would go on to end the regular season in 12th place in the FedEx Cup points standings. He continued his outstanding season in the playoffs. Perez finished the Northern Trust in a tie for 34th place. He would complete the remaining three playoff tournaments among the top 12 on the leaderboard. Perez finished in a tie for sixth at the Dell Technologies Championship and tied for 12th at the BMW Championship. Perez finished tied for sixth in his first career appearance in the Tour Championship. Perez won $699,325 in the FedEx Cup Playoff tournaments, and by finishing 12th in the final FedEx Cup standings, he won a bonus of $290,000. Overall, Perez made the cut in 22 of his 26 tournaments, with 14 finishes in the top 25 and six in the top ten. In 2016–2017, Perez won more than $4.3 million in prize money.

Nick Watney was another golfer who started the season on a medical extension that would have his season end in the FedEx Cup Playoffs. Watney had only five starts in 2015–2016 after his season was curtailed by injury, a herniated disc in his lower back. Watney was granted a medical extension in which he would have 21 tournaments to accumulate 355 FedEx Cup points or $528,010. Watney played in 23 tournaments and made the cut in 14 in the 2016–2017 season. He had five top-25 finishes, highlighted when he and his partner, Charley Hoffman, tied for fifth at the Zurich Classic of New Orleans. Watney ended the regular season 117th in the standings to qualify for the playoffs. Although he missed the cut at the Northern Trust Open, for the 2016–2017 season, Watney won $824,162 in prize money and a bonus of $70,000. He played the 2017–2018 season in the top 125 of the FedEx Cup standings group.

In 2016–2017, The Players Championship was the 27th tournament of the regular season, leaving 16 tournaments remaining on the schedule (two of those were opposite tournaments, meaning there were a maximum of 14 regular season events left for each golfer). Ian Poulter finished tied for second at The Players Championship, along with Louis Oosthuizen, but his even teeing it up at all at the Stadium Course at TPC Sawgrass seemed very much in question only a few weeks earlier. The 41-year-old Poulter entered the 2016–2017 season on a major medical extension caused by a foot injury. Overall, he competed in only 13 tournaments in the 2015–2016 season. The PGA assigned him ten tournaments in the 2016–2017 season to earn either $347,634 or 218 FedEx Cup points to obtain an exempt status for the remainder of the season.

Entering the Valero Texas Open in April, his ninth start of the season, Poulter made the cut in six tournaments, highlighted by an 11th-place finish at the RBC Heritage Classic. He earned $317,000 and 155 FedEx Cup points. After missing the cut at the Valero Texas Open, Poulter believed that he failed to fulfill the prize money and FedEx Cup points requirements set forth by the PGA.

Brian Gay, 45 years old, found himself in a similar position to Poulter's as he too had a major medical extension entering the 2016–2017 season after suffering a back injury. The PGA Tour allotted Gay 14 starts to earn $461,851 or 309 FedEx Cup points. After his 12th tournament, the Wells Fargo Championship, held the week after the Valero Texas Open and the week before The Players Championship, Gay made eight cuts to earn $463,509 and 284 FedEx Cup points. Gay's season was highlighted by a tie for sixth place in consecutive weeks at the RBC Heritage Classic, where he earned $217,750 and 92 FedEx Cup points, and the Valero Texas Open, where he earned $200,725 and 89 FedEx Cup points. It still appeared that Gay missed qualifying for The Players Championship.

For the 2016–2017 season, the PGA Tour, however, decided to alter how it calculated FedEx Cup points when it determined that the money list would no longer be a part of the exempt qualification process. Golfers who finished 15th through 68th in a tournament now received fewer FedEx Cup points.

In looking deeper into the issue, Gay figured out that if using the previous season's calculation, he met the criteria to be in the field at The Players Championship. Gay brought the discrepancy to the attention of Andy Pazder, PGA Tour Executive Vice President and COO. After discussions with his staff, Pazder recommended to PGA Tour Commissioner Jay Monahan that the previous season's calculation be used. Monahan agreed. Ian Poulter would benefit from the same re-calculation. Poulter, who spent five days thinking he no longer had his PGA Tour card, was quoted by Bob Harig on espn.com on May 1, stating, "for the Tour to unanimously decide that was the fair thing to do today puts me in a very different situation for playing my schedule and playing all the remaining events I'd like to play to keep going in the right direction."

Both Gay and Poulter became eligible for The Players Championship, where Poulter earned $924,000 and 270 FedEx Cup points. Poulter would send a Waldorf Astoria spa gift card to Gay and his wife for finding the calculation error that allowed him entrance into The Players Championship. Gay missed the cut at The Players Championship.

Poulter and Gay joined Pat Perez and Nick Watney as the four golfers whose 2016–2017 season began on a PGA Tour medical extension and ended with an improved exempt status group for the 2017–2018 season. Overall, Gay appeared in 25 tournaments and made the cut in 16. He had four top-25 performances and three finishes in the top ten. His season was highlighted by a tie for third at the Barbasol Championship. Gay made the playoffs, but his season concluded after he missed the cut at the Northern Trust. Gay earned $942,372 in prize money and took home a $70,000 bonus.

Poulter's tie for second at The Players Championship was part of a season in which he earned more than $2 million. Poulter had 20 starts and made the cut in 16. He had seven top-25 performances, including a third-place result at the RBC Canadian Open. Poulter entered the playoffs in 48th place. Although he made the cut in his first three playoff starts, he finished 66th, tied for 23rd, and tied for 40th and slid back to 52nd in the standings. Poulter earned a playoff bonus of $115,000.

One other golfer on a medical extension had a significant comeback to his career. Patrick Cantlay began the 2016–2017 season on a Web.com Tour medical extension. Cantlay was a highly-regarded amateur in 2011 when he made the cut in all five of his PGA Tour starts. Cantlay had four top-25 finishes, including a tie for ninth at the RBC Canadian Open and a tie for 21st at the U.S. Open. Cantlay also shot a round of 60 at the Travelers Championship, the lowest round ever by an amateur in a PGA Tour event. Cantlay turned professional after playing three PGA tournaments as an amateur in the 2012 season. Cantlay played in ten tournaments on the PGA Tour in that season and made the cut in eight. He also played in four tournaments on the Web.com Tour. Cantlay had conditional exempt status on the Web.com Tour heading into 2013.

Cantlay's 2013 season consisted of splitting time between PGA Tour and Web.com Tour events. By the end of the first week in May, Cantlay played in six PGA Tour events, but he made the cut in only two. One of those was a tie for ninth at the AT&T Pebble Beach Pro-Am. Cantlay also made six appearances in Web.com Tour events. He had his first professional tournament win in February 2013, when he was victorious at the Web.com Tour's Colombia Championship.

In May 2013, Cantlay felt a sharp pain in his back while warming up for his second round at the PGA Tour's event at Colonial. He played seven holes before deciding to withdraw. Cantlay was later diagnosed with a stress fracture in his lower back. The injury would linger for several seasons. Colonial would be Cantlay's last event on the PGA Tour that season. Cantlay did return that season to play in three events on the Web.com Tour. He missed the cut in two tournaments, but the other effort resulted in a second-place finish. Injuries would plague his 2013–2014 and the 2014–2015 seasons as Cantlay made it to the tee box on only six occasions. The OHL Classic at Mayakoba in November of 2014 was his last tournament for the next 27 months.

The 23-year-old Cantlay endured a far greater tragedy in 2016 when he and his friend and caddie, Chris Roth, were crossing a street together when Roth was killed by a hit-and-run driver. As quoted by Ryan Lavner in an article on golfchannel.com, Cantlay said, "you don't know how you're going to react in that situation. I'm standing there talking to the police officer and he says, 'do you want a towel or something to wipe yourself off?' I was completely covered in blood. I didn't realize it." Cantlay delivered the eulogy at the funeral for the friend whom he played golf with on their high school team. It was an incomprehensible low point. Cantlay told Lavner, "for a while, it just made me feel like nothing was important. Nothing made me sad. Nothing made me happy. I'm sure I was just in depression and grieving mode. I was just dull." Still not able to play golf due to his injury, the one activity that might provide some solace, Cantlay could only do one hour of physical therapy per day for months.

Cantlay was granted a Web.com Tour medical extension entering the 2015–2016 season. After he didn't play at all during that season, it carried over to 2016–2017. Cantlay would have ten tournaments on the PGA Tour to earn 389 FedEx Cup points or $624,746 to get out of the medical extension group. He finally returned to competitive play on the PGA Tour at the 2017 AT&T Pebble Beach Pro-Am. Cantlay finished that tournament in a tie for 48th place, three under par, to earn $17,897.

Cantlay obtained the prize money needed to regain status one month later in his next start when he finished in second place at the Valspar Championship. Cantlay posted rounds of 71–66–66–68. He had a stretch of 41 holes where he made 12 birdies and only one bogey. Cantlay finished one stroke behind Adam Hadwin. He trailed Hadwin by two strokes when Hadwin hit into the water on the 16th hole in the final round. However, when Cantlay bogeyed the 18th hole, it was Hadwin who won his first PGA Tour championship. Cantlay earned $680,400 and 300 FedEx Cup points for his tournament performance.

Cantlay went on to make the cut in all nine regular season tournaments that he played. He finished the RBC Heritage in a tie for third place to earn $338,000. In the PGA Championship, he tied for 33rd. It was his first major tournament appearance since the 2012 U.S. Open. The regular season concluded with Cantlay in 78th place in the FedEx Cup standings. He earned exempt status for the 2017–2018 season in the top 125 in the FedEx Cup points standings group.

Cantlay started the playoffs with a tie for tenth at the Northern Trust. That outcome moved him up to 50th. Cantlay had 29 holes without a bogey, making seven birdies in that stretch, to finish in a tie for 13th at the Dell Technologies Championship. He advanced to 41st place in the FedEx Cup standings. At the BMW Championship, Cantlay was at nine under par through the first 26 holes. He finished the tournament at 12 under par. He could not have afforded one more additional stroke. It was Cantlay's ten-foot, nine-inch birdie putt on the 18th hole in the final round that earned him a tie for ninth and put him into the Tour Championship by being number 29 in the FedEx Cup standings.

Cantlay finished the Tour Championship in a tie for 20th. Cantlay earned more than $2 million for the 2016–2017 season, with $747,500 of that total coming in the FedEx Cup Playoff tournaments. He was also awarded a bonus of $180,000 for finishing 29th in the final FedEx Cup standings. The accomplishment of getting to the Tour Championship meant an invitation to all four major tournaments in the following season.

11

Web.com Tour

In 2013, the PGA altered its system for how golfers are awarded their Tour cards. Previously, the PGA Tour Qualifying School, Q School, was the method of advancement onto the PGA Tour (a topic covered in detail by David Gould in his 1999 book, *Q School Confidential: Inside Golf's Cruelest Tournament*, and by John Feinstein in his 2007 book, *Tales from Q School: Inside Golf's 5th Major*). Q School used to be a single tournament that consisted of six rounds. The top 25 golfers in that event received a PGA Tour card. Another 25 PGA Tour cards were given to the golfers on the top 25 of the developmental tour's season prize money list, then named the Nationwide Tour until Web.com became the title sponsor with a ten-year agreement starting in 2012. The Q School process of reaching the PGA Tour was replaced by the Web.com Tour qualification system. Q School tournaments are still held, with the golfers emerging from those events awarded membership on the Web.com Tour.

The Q School process is four stages. Each stage has an entry fee, with the total cost of $14,700 to play in all stages and paying the fee by the earliest deadline. The beginning stage is pre-qualifying. In 2017, there were six pre-qualifying tournaments held in early September. Each field is approximately 78 golfers in a no-cut, 54-hole tournament. Approximately 40 golfers from each tournament advance to the first stage. The final position needed to advance is announced prior to play, with the golfers who tie for that spot advancing out of that stage. This tie-breaker system is used for the pre-qualifying stage and the first two stages.

The first stage had 12 tournaments in 2017 held in early to mid–October. These are no-cut, 72-hole tournaments. The field for each tournament is approximately 78 golfers. There are several performance-based measures that allow golfers to skip a pre-qualifying tournament and go directly into the first stage. For example, the golfers who are members of the PGA Tour or made a tournament cut on the PGA Tour, Web.com Tour, or any international tours are exempt into the first stage. Golfers who reached the second stage of qualifying in the previous three years, were in the top 50 in the first qualifying stage in the past two years, played in a PGA major tournament in the past two years, have a high position in the Official World Golf rankings, or have a high position in the amateur rankings are also exempt into the first stage.

The 2017 second stage included five tournaments in early November. Each field had approximately 75 golfers in the no-cut, 72-hole tournaments. Among the exemptions into the second stage are those who finished 86 through 100 on the Web.com Tour regular season money list, any golfer with more than 100 made cuts combined on the PGA Tour and Web.com Tour, golfers who won a Web.com Tour tournament in the past three seasons, those who made the cut in a PGA major tournament or The Players Championship, or have a high position on an international tour money list.

In 2017, the field for the final qualifying stage was 144 golfers. The final qualifying stage tournament, held in early December 2017, is a 72-hole, no-cut event. A series of exemptions allow some golfers directly into this one tournament. They include the golfers who finished 76 through 85 on the Web.com Tour regular season money list, finished in the top 100 on the Web.com Tour Finals money list, or have a high position on any one of several international tour money lists.

The winner of the final stage of Q School is fully exempt on the Web.com Tour for the entire season. Lee McCoy captured a two-stroke victory at the final stage tournament in 2017. The golfers who finish the final stage tournament in second through tenth place, including ties, are fully exempt on the Web.com Tour for the first 12 tournaments. The golfers who finish the final stage tournament in 11th through 45th place, including ties, are exempt for the first eight tournaments. The other golfers who reached the final qualifying stage receive conditional status on the Web.com Tour for the following season.

In 2017, the Web.com Tour consisted of 22 regular season tournaments, starting with the Bahamas Great Exuma Classic tournament, completed on January 11, and ending with the WinCo Foods Portland Open, completed on August 27. The top 25 golfers on the Web.com Tour regular season prize money list earn their PGA Tour card.

The Web.com Tour season also consists of four Finals tournaments. In 2017, the first was held the weekend of September 3. After one week off, the other three tournaments of the Finals were played on consecutive weeks. The Web.com Tour Championship concluded on Monday, October 2, after Sunday's final round was postponed due to heavy rain. The Web.com Tour Championship concluded one week after the PGA Tour Championship and one week before the 2017–2018 PGA Tour regular season began.

The fields for the Web.com Tour Finals tournaments consist of the top 75 golfers on the regular season Web.com Tour money list, the PGA Tour golfers ranked 126 through 200 in the FedEx Cup points standings, and the non–PGA Tour members who, had they been members of the Tour, would have accumulated enough FedEx Cup points to be 126th through 200th. The top 25 golfers in prize money earned through only the four Web.com Tour Finals tournaments receive their PGA Tour cards. In the priority ranking group order, the 50 top finishers of the Web.com Tour group is placed after the PGA Tour golfers who receive a major medical extension and before the golfers who receive a Web.com Tour medical extension.

There is a ranking of the 50 top finishers of the Web.com Tour group. Although the top 25 golfers on the Web.com Tour regular season money list are already guaranteed their PGA Tour cards for the following season as they enter the Finals tournaments, it is their combined earnings from both the regular season and the Finals that creates the ordering of these 25 golfers. They are essentially competing against each other to be placed higher on the priority list within the top finishers of the Web.com group. The golfers who earned more prize money in the regular season do begin the Finals tournaments with an advantage, but with all four Finals tournaments having prize money totaling $1 million, the winner of each Finals tournament receives $180,000, the ordering can easily change. The overall positioning of top finishers of the Web.com Tour group is then done on an alternating basis, with a golfer from the combined regular season and Finals money list followed by a golfer from the Finals money list. Again, the final golfer of the 50 within the Web.com ranking group is the 25th finisher on the Finals money list.

For the 50 golfers who graduate onto the PGA Tour, the system is designed for two to be placed in their own higher group for the following season. One is the combined money leader from both the Web.com Tour's regular season and Finals tournaments. The other is the leading money winner from only the four Web.com Finals tournaments. There will be only one golfer in this group if he is the leader on both money lists. Other golfers can potentially join this higher priority group by winning three Web.com tournaments during the season. The golfers in this higher priority group receive some important benefits in the following PGA Tour season. They are not part of the reordering of the golfers within the top finishers of the Web.com Tour group that occurs at various points during the PGA Tour regular season. These golfers are also exempt into The Players Championship.

In the 2014 season, Adam Hadwin was the combined regular season and

Finals money leader, Derek Fathauer was the Finals tournaments money leader, and Carlos Ortiz was a three-time Web.com tournament winner. Ortiz won two of the first six tournaments that he played and then won the regular season-ending WinCo Foods Portland Open. By winning three tournaments, that golfer will obviously be among the top 25 on the regular season money list. Ortiz ended the regular season atop the money list with $515,403.

When Ortiz missed the cut in all of the Finals tournaments that he competed in and did not add any prize money to his regular season total, he was overtaken by Hadwin as the combined regular season and Finals money leader. Hadwin finished the Web.com Tour regular season in fourth place on the prize money list with $293,667. He won the regular season's Chile Classic, then in the Finals won the Chiquita Classic to earn $180,000. He had two other top-ten finishes in Finals tournaments to earn an additional $56,125. His total of $529,792 gave him the combined regular season and Finals prize money championship over Ortiz by $14,389.

Derek Fathauer finished in a tie for ninth, tied for 16th, and tied for eighth at the first three Finals tournaments in 2014 to win $70,133. He then won the Web.com Tour Championship to collect another $180,000 and finish atop the Finals prize money list.

In 2015, Patrick Kizzire was the combined regular season and Finals money leader, while Chez Reavie was the Finals money leader. In 2016, Wesley Bryan emerged as the combined regular season and Finals money leader. Bryan was also the winner of three Web.com tournaments. The moment that Bryan was victorious at the Digital Ally Open on the weekend of August 7, 2016, with a win on the second playoff hole over Grayson Murray and J. T. Poston, he knew that the following season, he would be a member of the PGA Tour with the advanced placement above the top finishers of the Web.com Tour group.

Grayson Murray was the Finals tournaments money leader in 2016. Murray ended the regular season 18th on the Web.com Tour money list, winning $159,963, so he did have his PGA Tour card secure entering the Finals. After withdrawing from the DAP Championship, a third-place finish in the Albertsons Boise Open netted him $68,000. The following week at the Nationwide Children's Hospital Championship, Murray won the tournament and its $180,000 top prize. It should be noted that in 2016 the Web.com Tour Finals consisted of only three tournaments, as the Web.com Tour Championship was canceled when Hurricane Matthew hit Florida. Officials ruled that the results of the first three Finals tournaments would determine the 25 golfers who received their PGA Tour cards.

Chesson Hadley made it onto the PGA Tour for the first time after graduating from the Web.com Tour in 2013. Hadley ended up third on the Web.com

Tour regular season money list in a season that included his first professional tournament victory, the Rex Hospital Open in his hometown of Raleigh, North Carolina. Rex Hospital was where Hadley was born. Hadley also won the Web.com Tour Championship in 2013. He was only $567 short of John Peterson for the top spot on the Finals money list.

Hadley won the Puerto Rico Open on the PGA Tour in 2014 when he defeated Danny Lee by two strokes. He entered the final round with a one-stroke lead over Lee. Hadley birdied the 17th and 18th holes to prevail as Lee made four birdies over the final six holes. Hadley earned $630,000 for the win. He appeared in 29 tournaments and made the cut in 13 in the 2013–2014 season. He had eight top-25 finishes and four top-ten performances. Hadley overcame stretches where he missed the cut in five consecutive tournaments and six consecutive tournaments to complete the regular season 72nd in the standings.

In the FedEx Cup Playoffs, Hadley finished 70th in the Barclays, and his position dropped to number 84 in the points standings. He finished in a tie for ninth at the Deutsche Bank Championship to jump up to 57th place. Hadley became the only PGA Tour rookie in 2014 to play his way into the third playoff tournament. He finished in a tie for 12th at the BMW Championship. Hadley earned $363,143 in the playoffs and by ending the season 49th in the FedEx Cup standings, he earned a bonus of $126,000. Hadley was named the PGA Tour "Rookie of the Year."

Hadley followed his rookie season with another strong performance in 2014–2015. He made the cut in 20 of his 30 tournament appearances, with eight top-25 and three top-ten finishes. He entered the playoffs in the 83rd position, but his season ended after missing the cut at the Barclays and coming in 74th at the Deutsche Bank Championship. Overall, Hadley earned more than $1.1 million in prize money, and he received a $75,000 bonus by ending the season 98th in the FedEx Cup standings. Hadley had one more season remaining with a tournament winners exempt status.

Hadley, however, did not play as well in 2015–2016. He made the cut in 13 of his 27 PGA tournaments. He had four top-25 finishes, but no performances in the top ten. The regular season ended with him in 159th place in the FedEx Cup standings, 26 points behind Greg Owen in the 150th position, which would have provided higher status. Hadley did earn $503,993 and spent the post-season in the Web.com Tour Finals to try to reclaim his PGA Tour card. Hadley finished in a tie for 22nd at the first Finals tournament, but he missed the cut in the other two events. He earned only $9,372 in the Finals.

At the age of 29, Hadley entered the 2016–2017 season with the status as the top golfer in the past champions group. Hadley says that an exempt status is "what you make of it." He points out that there will be some opportunities to play in PGA Tour events, but "you have to be realistic." In 2016–2017, Hadley participated in eight PGA Tour events, of which four were the opposite tournaments. He also received sponsor exemptions into two tournaments in his home state of North Carolina. Hadley, however, missed the cut at both the Wells Fargo Championship and the Wyndham Championship. Overall, he made the cut in four PGA tournaments, with his season highlighted by a tie for 25th at the John Deere Classic. Hadley earned $82,208, and his FedEx Cup points total put him 211th in the standings.

Hadley, however, flourished on the Web.com Tour. He made the cut in nine of his 15 starts. Hadley won the Lecom Health Challenge tournament by one stroke over Beau Hossler in July. He also had a second- and a third-place finish during the Web.com Tour regular season. In July, when Hadley essentially knew that he made it back to the PGA Tour, he describes his feeling: "there was jubilation, but relief. Pure relief." Hadley earned his PGA Tour card for being in ninth place on the regular season money list with $264,350 in prize money.

Hadley points out that with an improved short-game, he continued his strong play in the Web.com Tour Finals. He finished tenth in the Nationwide Children's Hospital Championship to claim $27,000. He then won the Albertson's Boise Open by one stroke over Ted Potter, Jr., and Jonathan Randolph. Hadley shot a final round 65 that included consecutive birdies on the 15th through 17th holes. Hadley collected $180,000 for that victory. Hadley was then part of the playoff, along with Rob Oppenheim, at the DAP Championship before losing out to Nicholas Lindheim.

Hadley entered the Web.com Tour Championship knowing that he would be either the top money winner from the combined regular season and the Finals or the top prize money winner from only the Finals. Although he finished the Web.com Tour Championship in a tie for 46th and added only $3,125, it was good enough to finish atop both Web.com Tour prize money leaderboards. Hadley's Finals total of $298,125 bested the $185,864 won by Peter Uihlein. His combined total of $562,475 was better than runner-up Brice Garnett, who won $395,212. Garnett, the regular season money leader, added only $26,452 in the Finals. Hadley would be the only Web.com Tour graduate with the advanced group status entering the 2017–2018 PGA Tour season.

As the method of advancement onto the PGA Tour, the Web.com Tour regular season offers a system of many critical dividing lines. The first is obviously getting into the top 25 on the regular season money list to earn a PGA Tour card. The second objective is to make the top 75 on the regular season money list, which qualifies a golfer for the Web.com Tour Finals and provides fully exempt status on the Web.com Tour for the following season, which simply allows him to participate in any Web.com Tour regular season tournament. These golfers do not have to go back to Q School. The other regular season dividing lines are those that provide advancement to the further stages of the Q School process.

Some golfers split time during a season between PGA tournaments and Web.com Tour events. In some instances, it is out of necessity as a golfer plays in whatever tournament provides the opportunity. The golfers who split time are obviously first simply trying to earn prize money. Professional golfers also need to play competitive rounds to keep their games sharp. In other instances, the golfers are being strategic in trying to maximize the number of paths possible to play somewhere in the post-season, obtain a PGA Tour card, and have the highest possible priority exempt status for the following season.

Chesson Hadley explains the difficulty of some scheduling decisions. In 2016–2017, playing out of the past champions group, he was "making strategic decisions about what is the best way to get back to the PGA Tour." For example, Hadley passed on playing the PGA Tour's FedEx St. Jude Classic in Memphis on the weekend that ended on June 11 so that he could play in the Rust-Oleum Championship on the Web.com Tour. Hadley ended up not making the cut in that tournament.

In playing in PGA Tour events, a golfer obviously hopes to qualify for the FedEx Cup Playoffs. However, if he finishes in position 126 through 200 in the FedEx Cup points standings, there is still the opportunity to compete in the Web.com Tour Finals. These golfers would improve their exempt status for the following PGA Tour season with a top-25 finish on the Web.com Tour Finals money list.

By playing in Web.com Tour events as well, a second path is available to obtain a PGA Tour card and be among the top finishers of the Web.com Tour group for the following season. A golfer could finish in the top 25 in regular season prize money, albeit he must play well in what might be limited Web.com Tour starts if he is also competing in tournaments on the PGA Tour. A golfer could also finish in the top 75 to qualify for the Web.com Tour Finals. He would then have to finish in the top 25 in prize money in those four Finals tournaments to obtain his PGA Tour card.

The golfers who finish in the 126 through 150 positions in the FedEx Cup points standings may have a little less pressure in the Web.com Finals tournaments. They do receive a bonus of $32,000 for their PGA Tour season's performance despite not qualifying for the playoffs. These golfers also retain some status on the PGA Tour in their own separate priority ranking group for the following season, placed after the Web.com Tour medical extension golfers and before the past champions group. These golfers are also fully exempt on the Web.com Tour for the following season. For these reasons, there is certainly value to finishing at least within the top 150 in the FedEx Cup standings.

Still, the opportunity to improve an exempt status group and leap over many golfers in the tournament priority selection process is significant. For example, if a golfer ranked number 126 in the FedEx Cup points standings became the top prize money winner in the Web.com Finals tournaments, he would automatically jump over 49 golfers and probably more as he also leaps ahead of the golfers on the Web.com Tour who will receive a medical extension for the following season. In 2016–2017, 11 golfers began the season with a Web.com Tour medical extension.

For the PGA Tour golfers who finished 151 through 200 in the FedEx Cup points standings, but not in the top 25 in prize money in the Finals, their placement for the following season will vary based on other career accomplishments. The golfers who won a PGA Tour event are placed in the past champions group. The golfers who made the cut in 150 tournaments in their career are placed in the veteran members group. Golfers who have neither of these achievements have conditional status on the Web.com Tour for the following season. They do have the opportunity to improve to a fully exempt status on the Web.com Tour through the Q School process. The PGA Tour golfers who finish the four Web.com Tour Finals tournaments in the top 75 on the money list are given entrance into the Q School final stage.

For the golfers who entered the Web.com Tour Finals through their play in the Web.com Tour regular season, their status for the following season will also vary. A golfer is fully exempt on the Web.com Tour for the following season if he won a Web.com Tour regular season tournament, finished 26 through 75 on the Web.com Tour regular season money list, or is one of the top 25 from only the Web.com Tour golfers on the Finals money list. Other golfers without those achievements receive conditional status for the following Web.com Tour season. They too have the chance to upgrade that status through the Q School process.

There are many different moments of increased pressure for a professional golfer attempting to cross a critical dividing line. Certainly, the quest to graduate from the Web.com Tour to the PGA Tour is among the most intense. As the last tournament of the Web.com Tour regular season, the WinCo Foods Portland Open is an extra pressure-filled event.

Joel Dahmen arrived at the WinCo Foods Portland Open in 2016 with his next season's Tour status very much on the line. Dahmen was 22nd on the regular season Web.com Tour prize money list. Getting to that point of his professional golf career had been a series of obstacles for Dahmen. In high school, he suffered through the tragedy of his mother Jolyn passing away from pancreatic cancer. Still trying to recover from the loss of his mother, Dahmen, on a scholarship to play golf at the University of Washington, dropped out of school. In 2009, his brother Zach was diagnosed with testicular cancer. Two years later, Joel himself was also diagnosed with testicular cancer. His treatment consisted of eight-hour-a-day chemotherapy sessions for many weeks.

In overcoming these hardships, Dahmen was able to play his way onto the Mackenzie Tour—PGA Tour Canada. In 2014, he won two of the season's first three tournaments. He went on to win the Order of Merit for being the money leader on the PGA Canadian Tour. He earned just under $81,000, more than $20,000 ahead of the second-place finisher. For that achievement, Dahmen got to play in his first PGA Tour event, the RBC Canadian Open, where he finished in a tie for 53rd to win $13,034. Dahmen also qualified for the Web.com Tour.

Dahmen played in 21 regular season tournaments and made the cut in 13 in his first season on the Web.com Tour. He had six top-25 finishes, with three top-ten outcomes. He finished in 62nd place on the regular season Web.com Tour money list. Dahmen did qualify to compete in the Web.com Tour Finals, but he made the cut in only one of the four tournaments. Dahmen earned $86,344 for the entire season. He returned to the Web.com Tour for the 2016 season by being in the top 75 on the regular season prize money list in 2015.

Dahmen's 2016 season started well. His results included a tie for 11th and a tie for third in two of his first three tournaments. Dahmen played in eight tournaments from the beginning of June through the middle of July, and he made the cut in all of them. That stretch of play was highlighted by a tie for third and a tie for fifth. Dahmen felt he was well positioned to finish in the top 25 of the Web.com Tour money list and earn his PGA Tour card, with only four tournaments remaining in the regular season. Dahmen seemed to continue his steady play at the first tournament in August as he shot an opening round 68, three under par. However, he shot a 71 in the second round and missed the cut by two strokes. He missed the cut the following week as well.

Dahmen decided to take a week off before the season-ending tournament in Portland. He believed that if he made the cut in Portland, he would be in position to earn his PGA Tour card, but he assessed his game at the time as "trending in the wrong direction." In what he described as the most pressure that he ever felt in a golf tournament, Dahmen did not play well in Portland, missing the cut after rounds of 73 and 74. He spent part of Friday in tears about what could easily result in a lost opportunity. Dahmen would now have to wait out the performance of other golfers to see if his total season's accomplishments were enough to get him to the PGA Tour. He says, "I was so disappointed to let it slip through my fingers. As golfers, we want to take care of it on our own."

Dahmen did not pay much attention to the golf results on Saturday other than receiving some text messages. He did watch the leaderboard closely on Sunday. It would come down to the final two holes. Xander Schauffele needed to par the 17th and 18th holes to surpass Dahmen. Schauffele made a bogey on the par-4 17th and could only manage a par on the par-5 18th hole. Dahmen finished the Web.com Tour regular season with $150,267, holding off Schauffele by $975. What were tears of disappointment only 48 hours earlier were now tears of joy. Dahmen was going to the PGA Tour.

Dahmen was not the only player to celebrate earning his PGA Tour card after the final round in Portland in 2016. Ryan Brehm entered the 2016 WinCo Foods Portland Open 30th on the Web.com Tour money list. Brehm posted a first-round eight under par 63. After 54 holes, he was in a tie for the lead. A final-round, three under par 68 would give him a total score of 15 under par to win the tournament by one stroke. The victory vaulted Brehm all the way to fourth on the regular season Web.com Tour money list and onto the PGA Tour for the first time in his career. Brehm earned $281,808 for the Web.com Tour regular season.

Two other golfers earned their PGA Tour cards in Portland in 2016. Mark Anderson finished the tournament in second place. He earned $86,400 to jump from 51st place to 16th on the money list. Anderson birdied the 18th hole in the final round to finish off a five-birdie, four under par, back nine score of 31. The prize money for third place in Portland, one stroke higher, was $54,400. Anderson, whose total money was $169,499, would have been out of the top 25 had he finished in third and earned $32,000 less. Anderson graduated from the Web.com Tour in 2011 and 2013. He entered the 2016–2017 season having played in 45 PGA Tour events, making the cut in 21 with one top-ten finish.

Rick Lamb arrived in Portland 27th on the regular season Web.com Tour money list. Lamb's season included a victory in a playoff at the Lecom Health Challenge tournament. He gained entrance into that tournament by shooting a 63 in the Monday qualifier. Lamb was tied for 14th, six strokes off the lead, after 54 holes at the Lecom Health Challenge. In the final round after he birdied the 7th and 8th holes, Lamb played the first four holes of the back nine in five under par. He added a birdie on the 15th to complete a nine-hole stretch at eight under par. Lamb's final-round 63 got him into a four-man playoff. After waiting an hour for the other golfers to complete their rounds, Lamb won the tournament on the second extra hole. He earned $108,000 for the tournament instead of the $44,800 awarded to the three golfers that he defeated at the Lecom Health Challenge tournament.

In the final round of the WinCo Foods Portland Open, Lamb used a back nine 32 to put him at ten under par and into a tie for 19th. Lamb moved into 24th on the money list for the 2016 season. When he placed his tee in the ground at the Safeway Open in October 2016, it was for the first time in a PGA Tour event. After missing six cuts to start his PGA Tour career, Lamb made his first cut at the AT&T Pebble Beach Pro-Am in February 2017. He finished tied for 62nd at that tournament.

With the top 75 on the Web.com Tour regular season money list gaining entrance into the Finals tournaments and a fully exempt status on the Web.com Tour for the following season, one other golfer made a critical advancement at the WinCo Foods Portland Open. Eric Barnes moved from 82nd on the money list to 72nd when he tied for 11th in Portland. Barnes earned $18,075 through the first two tournaments of the Finals, but he did not make the cut in the third. Barnes ended up in 37th place on the Finals money list and had to return to the Web.com Tour for the 2017 season.

In 2017, Barnes earned only $29,973 in the Web.com regular season when he made nine cuts in 20 tournament starts and had only two finishes in the top 25. Instead of qualifying for the Finals, Barnes returned to Q School. He finished the final stage in a tie for 42nd place. That result provided Barnes with fully exempt status on the Web.com Tour for the first eight tournaments in 2018.

Joel Dahmen was truly fortuitous to make it to the PGA Tour through the regular season, as one week after achieving his PGA Tour card he suffered an injury when he slipped on a cart path. Dahmen broke the base of his thumb and was not able to compete in the Web.com Tour Finals. Dahmen lost out on a critical opportunity to try to improve his positioning within the top finishers of the Web.com Tour group heading into the following PGA Tour season. Dahmen entered the 2016–2017 season 48th in the top finishers of the Web.com Tour group.

For some golfers who just missed out on earning their PGA Tour card through the Web.com Tour regular season, redemption did come in the Web.com Tour Finals. Xander Schauffele, who was 26th on the money list, started the Finals with a tie for 50th at the DAP Championship followed by a tie for 18th at the Albertsons Boise Open. He was once again right on the cusp of earning his PGA Tour card as he was 25th on the Finals money list.

Schauffele finished in a tie for ninth to take home $27,000 at the Nationwide Children's Hospital Championship. Schauffele's total earnings of $42,395 for the three tournaments put him 15th on the Finals money list and onto the PGA Tour after only one season on the Web.com Tour. Once the alternate selection process was completed, Schauffele entered the 2016–2017 season 31st in the top finishers of the Web.com Tour group. Despite finishing behind Dahmen on the regular season prize money list, Schauffele was now 17 spots higher than Dahmen within the Web.com Tour group heading to the PGA Tour.

Kevin Tway missed the cut in Portland and finished 27th on the money list. His season total of $148,746 left him $1,521 short of Dahmen. Tway would play his way onto the PGA Tour through the Web.com Tour Finals. Tway missed the cut in the opening tournament of the Finals, then tied for 31st at the Albertsons Boise Open to pocket $5,975. Tway was 52nd on the Finals money list after two tournaments. He tied for third and earned $58,000 at the Nationwide Children's Hospital Championship. Tway's total of $63,975 earned him a ninth-place finish on the Finals money list. Tway entered the 2016–2017 season 19th in the top finishers of the Web.com Tour group. It marked the second time that Tway graduated from the Web.com Tour onto the PGA Tour, previously doing so in 2013.

With the potential to move up within the top finishers of the Web.com Tour group for next season, the Finals tournaments represent a significant opportunity for the golfers who already secured their PGA Tour card through the Web.com Tour regular season. Roberto Diaz earned his PGA Tour card for the first time through the 2017 Web.com Tour regular season. He, however, explains that the excitement needs to be tempered as a golfer heads into the Finals. He points out, "positioning is so important. You still have to focus."

In addition to Grayson Murray, who jumped from 18th during the regular season to become the Finals money leader, Julian Etulain and Nicholas Lindheim greatly improved their position through their performance in the 2016 Web.com Tour Finals. Etulain entered the Finals 20th on the money list, which would equate to 38th after the alternate process for placing the golfers within the top finishers of the Web.com Tour group. He earned $158,860. In the Finals, Etulain was one of three golfers, along with Nicholas Lindheim and Andres Gonzalez, who lost in a playoff at the DAP Championship to Bryson DeChambeau. Etulain earned $74,667 for that tournament. He added another $2,950 for finishing in a tie for 48th at the Albertsons Boise Open before missing the cut in the last tournament of the Finals. After the alternating selection process, Etulain moved up to the 16th position within the top finishers of the Web.com Tour group.

Lindheim finished the Web.com Tour regular season 21st, having earned $158,654. After losing in the playoff to DeChambeau, winning $74,667, he missed the cut at the Albertsons Boise Open and finished tied for 24th at the Nationwide Children's Hospital Championship to earn $8,426. After the alternating selection process, Lindhelm moved up to 14th within the top finishers of the Web.com Tour group.

Brandon Hagy finished in 19th place on the Web.com Tour regular season money list. He missed the cut in two of the three Finals tournaments, with a tie for 12th for which he earned $19,000. After the alternating system, Hagy found himself 41st within the Web.com Tour group. Despite earning more prize money in the regular season than Etulain or Lindheim, Hagy now found himself below them in the PGA tournament priority selection process by 25 and 27 positions, respectively.

Of the 25 golfers who made it to the PGA Tour through the Web.com Tour regular season in 2016, 18 were rookies and seven already had stints on the PGA Tour. Eight of those 18 rookies would qualify for the FedEx Cup Play-offs in 2017. Six of the Web.com golfers who graduated onto the PGA Tour through the path of the Web.com Tour Finals were rookies, three of whom qualified for the FedEx Cup Playoffs in 2017.

Neither Mark Anderson, Ryan Brehm, Joel Dahmen, Julian Etulain, Rick Lamb, nor Nicholas Lindheim made it to the FedEx Cup Playoffs in 2017. For Anderson, Brehm, and Etulain, their 2016–2017 season would end without PGA Tour status. Anderson played in 20 PGA Tour events in 2016–2017 but made the cut in only six. The highlight of his season was a tie for tenth at the Puerto Rico Open. His one other top-25 finish was a tie for 24th at the Wells Fargo Championship. Anderson earned $188,806 for the season and finished 194th in the FedEx Cup standings. In the Web.com Tour Finals, Anderson missed the cut in three of the four tournaments.

Etulain made the cut in 13 of his 22 PGA Tour appearances. He had three top-25 finishes, highlighted when he and his playing partner, Angel Cabrera, tied for fifth at the Zurich Classic of New Orleans. Etulain finished 161st in the FedEx Cup standings; his 220 points were 49 behind the 150th-position total of 269 held by Rick Lamb. Etulain earned $448,214 in prize money on the season. In the Web.com Tour Finals, he won $20,696 in prize money, but that amount was not enough to get him into the top 25. Anderson and Etulain entered the 2017–2018 season with conditional status on the Web.com Tour for finishing in the top 200 in the FedEx Cup points standings.

Brehm had 25 tournament starts and made the cut in 17 in the 2016–2017 season. A tie for 18th at the Sanderson Farms Championship was his best performance of the season. He earned $396,258 and finished 164th in the FedEx Cup standings with 188 points. In the Web.com Tour Finals, he missed the cut in two tournaments and could accumulate only $19,200 in the other two. With only conditional status on the Web.com for the 2018 season, Brehm tried to upgrade that position to a fully exempt status. However, in the Q School final stage, he tied for 85th. Brehm would remain with conditional status on the Web.com Tour for 2018.

12

Getting Back to the PGA Tour

Like the golfers who play on the Web.com Tour and miss out on earning their PGA Tour card through the regular season, the golfers who play on the PGA Tour and did not qualify for the FedEx Cup Playoffs must quickly respond and perform well in the Finals to reclaim their Tour card. The Web.com Tour Finals tournaments present an opportunity for all of these golfers to improve their priority ranking group status for the following season, as well as another opportunity to earn prize money. For the golfers who finished 126 through 200 in the FedEx Cup points standings, where they were positioned at the conclusion of the regular season no longer has relevance in terms of the opportunity to improve their priority ranking group. That advancement into the top finishers of the Web.com group is solely based on a golfer's total prize money accumulated in the four Web.com Tour Finals tournaments.

In terms of the opportunity to earn prize money, there are even some scenarios where golfers can benefit financially through playing in the Web.com Tour Finals rather than the FedEx Cup Playoffs. The golfers who finish 101 through 125 in the FedEx Cup points standings at the end of the season receive a bonus of $70,000. Again, despite not qualifying for the playoffs, the golfers who finish 126 through 150 in the FedEx Cup standings receive a $32,000 bonus. So the golfers who qualified for the playoffs are already earning $38,000 more than the finishers in the 126 through 150 positions.

The rest of the financial evaluation will depend on how a golfer performs in the post-season. The golfers in the 101 through 125 positions in the standings at the end of the regular season who miss the cut in the first FedEx Cup Playoff tournament will not earn any additional prize money and will not advance to the second playoff tournament. These golfers receive only the playoff bonus. Those playing in the Web.com Tour Finals know that they are competing in four tournaments, and they may earn a greater amount than the $38,000 bonus difference.

For example, in 2016, Michael Thompson finished 145th in the regular season FedEx Cup points standings to earn the $32,000 playoff bonus. Thompson tied for 39th and earned $4,000 in the first tournament of the Web.com Tour Finals. The following week, Thompson won the Albertsons Boise Open by three strokes to claim $180,000 in prize money. Thompson did not make the cut in the last Web.com Tour Finals tournament. His total of $184,000 for the three Web.com Tour Finals tournaments overcame the $38,000 difference in playoff bonus money received by the FedEx Cup Playoff participants who did not advance to the second tournament. It is important to note that the cancelation of the fourth tournament of the Web.com Tour Finals in 2016 due to Hurricane Matthew curtailed all of the Finals golfers' earning potential.

Of course, no golfer would prefer to miss the FedEx Cup Playoffs and compete in the Web.com Tour Finals. A golfer can get hot in the FedEx Cup Playoffs and earn far greater prize money. For example, the $180,000 that Michael Thompson earned for his win in a Web.com Tour Finals tournament is less than the prize money for finishing in the top ten of the first three FedEx Cup Playoff tournaments and in the top 15 of the Tour Championship. Good performances in FedEx Cup Playoff tournaments will also allow a golfer to move up in the final standings to earn a higher playoff bonus.

Perhaps with greater significance, heading into the following season the golfers who qualify for the FedEx Cup Playoffs are in a much higher exempt status group than those in the top finishers of the Web.com Tour group, let alone the golfers who remain 126th through 150th in the FedEx Cup points standings group. The important point, however, is that opportunities exist in the Web.com Tour Finals, and those tournament outcomes have a significant impact on all of the golfers' current season and future prospects.

Quickly refocusing after what was certainly a disappointing season that resulted in missing the FedEx Cup Playoffs, to play well in the Web.com Tour Finals can be especially difficult for those golfers who were only a couple of points away from a qualifying position. At the conclusion of the 2015–2016 regular season, David Toms earned 455 points to place him 124th, and Seung-Yul Noh amassed 454 points to place him at number 125 in the FedEx Cup standings. Four golfers were within 13 points of Noh: Matt Jones, 445 points, Whee Kim 444, Scott Stallings 443, and Nick Taylor 441. The four golfers who were left out of the playoffs could have erased that margin with the slightest alteration of regular season tournament outcomes.

If a golfer does not play well in the season following his tournament win, the two-season exemption is incredibly meaningful. Nick Taylor had his exempt status for the 2016–2017 season in the tournament winners group secure for his victory at the Sanderson Farms Championship in 2014. After not qualifying for the FedEx Cup Playoffs, Taylor did not have to participate in the Web.com Tour Finals. Kim and Stallings improved their priority ranking group through their performance in the Web.com Tour Finals, but Jones was not able to do so.

Kim ended the 2015–2016 regular season 127th in the FedEx Cup points standings. Kim was in the 125th and final qualifying position for the FedEx Cup Playoffs heading into the regular season's final tournament, the Wyndham Championship. He dropped to number 127 after missing the cut. Kim made the cut in the first two Web.com Tour Finals tournaments, but he was still 35th on the Finals money list.

At the third Finals tournament, the Nationwide Children's Hospital Championship, Kim shot an opening-round 65 that featured a 31 on the back nine. Kim's entire tournament play on the back nine proved to be pivotal as he shot 11 under par over that stretch of holes on the week. Kim posted a two under par 33 on the back nine in the final round. He finished the tournament in a tie for ninth place.

Kim earned $27,000 of his Finals total of $36,975 at the Nationwide Children's Hospital Championship. He finished 18th on the Finals prize money list. If Kim shot even par on the back nine in the final round, with the two additional strokes, he would have earned only $12,600. The difference of $14,400 would have dropped his prize money to $22,575, below the 25th position. Kim would have entered the 2016–2017 season in the lower-ranked 126 through 150 finishers in the FedEx Cup points standings priority group.

Stallings played in 27 PGA Tour events, but he made the cut in only ten, with one top-ten finish. Stallings actually just missed the top 125 cut-off list for FedEx Cup points and prize money. He finished 128th in the regular season FedEx Cup points standings. Stallings earned $697,434 in prize money to place him 129th position on the PGA Tour money list. Stallings trailed Morgan Hoffmann for the 125th position by $20,456.

Stallings shot an opening-round four over par 74 in the first tournament of the Web.com Tour Finals. He was in jeopardy of missing the cut before he birdied the 17th and 18th holes to finish the second round with a four under par 66. Stallings made the tournament cut by one stroke. He took full advantage of his opportunity and shot an even par 70 in round three. In the fourth round, Stallings produced a seven hole stretch, from the 9th through the 15th, in which he shot four under par. He completed the round with a 65 and vaulted into a tie for sixth. He earned $32,375.

Stallings continued his strong play at the Albertsons Boise Open when he finished in a tie for fifth place. Stallings added $36,500 to his Finals total and earned an additional $6,630 after finishing in a tie for 29th at the Nationwide Children's Hospital Championship. Stallings amassed $75,505 in the Web.com Tour Finals, which made him the sixth-highest earner. Instead of being in the 126 through 150 group, Stallings now found himself in the 13th position in the top finishers of the Web.com Tour group. Due to his performance in the Finals, Stallings jumped over 49 golfers in the PGA tournament priority selection process.

Tim Wilkinson also just missed both top 125 cut-off lists on the PGA Tour in 2015–2016. His $708,623 in prize money placed him 127th on the PGA Tour money list. Wilkinson was less than $10,000 behind Morgan Hoffmann's $717,890 total in 125th. Wilkinson suffered from an end-of-season slump where he missed the cut in four consecutive tournaments. At the season-ending Wyndham Championship, where Hoffmann did not make the cut, Wilkinson posted rounds of 69–67–64 heading into the final day. By carding a 70 on the final day, Wilkinson finished in a tie for 22nd to earn $45,665. The golfers who finished in a tie for 20th, one stroke better than Wilkinson, earned $70,000. Wilkinson earned 44 FedEx Cup points for his finish at the Wyndham Championship. His season total of 426 FedEx Cup points put him 132nd, only 28 points behind Seung-Yul Noh's 454 points.

Wilkinson was 41st on the Web.com Tour Finals money list after finishing 33rd and 48th in the first two tournaments. At the Nationwide Children's Hospital Championship, Wilkinson shot an opening-round, one over par 72 and a second-round, two under par 69. A third-round bogey on the 6th hole would be the last blemish on his scorecard for the tournament. Wilkinson shot two under par on the back nine in round three and four under par 67 in the final round. Wilkinson earned $19,000 after tying for 12th.

Wilkinson needed every one of those stokes not only in the Nationwide Children's Hospital Championship, but throughout all of the Web.com Tour Finals tournaments. One additional stroke, and the resulting difference in lower earnings, would have caused him to lose the 25th and final position on the Web.com Tour Finals money list. Wilkinson's $27,425 bested Rob Oppenheim's $27,033 by a mere $392. Ironically, it was Oppenheim who the year before earned the final spot for his PGA Tour card through the Web.com Tour Finals path by a margin of only $101. After the alternate player selection process, Wilkinson claimed the 50th and final spot in the top finishers of the Web.com Tour priority group for the 2016–2017 season.

Wilkinson had 22 tournament starts in the 2016–2017 season, making the cut in 11. His five top-25 finishes featured a tie for 14th along with playing partner Michael Thompson at the Zurich Classic of New Orleans and a tie for 14th at the Wyndham Championship. He completed the season earning $411,459 and finished 156th in the FedEx Cup standings, 36 points behind Rick Lamb in position 150. Wilkinson missed the cut in three of the four Web.com Tour Finals tournaments and won only $3,000 in the other. He entered the 2017–2018 season with conditional status on the Web.com Tour for finishing in the top 200 in the points standings.

Securing a bonus payment and having some exempt status on the PGA Tour for the following season do create another critical dividing line at the 150/151 position in the FedEx Cup points standings. Greg Owen ended his 2015–2016 regular season 150th with 319 points. In the Web.com Tour Finals, he finished 39th in the first tournament, earning $4,000, and 12th in the second tournament, to add $19,000 to his Finals earnings total. He was 18th on the overall Finals money list. Owen, however, missed the cut in the last Finals tournament and was passed on the money list. His $23,000 Finals total put him 32nd and left him heading into the 2016–2017 season as the last of ten golfers in the FedEx Cup finishers 126 through 150 priority ranking group.

Will MacKenzie, two-time PGA tournament champion with wins at the 2006 Reno-Tahoe Open and the 2008 Viking Classic, ended the 2015–2016 season with 317 FedEx Cup points, 151st in the standings. MacKenzie missed out on the $32,000 bonus by only two points, as he trailed Greg Owen's 319. MacKenzie played in 26 PGA Tour events. He made the cut on 15 occasions, with four top-25 finishes and one top-ten performance. MacKenzie did not make the cut in three of the last four tournaments of the PGA Tour regular season. He completed the John Deere Classic in a tie for 56th to earn 13 FedEx Cup points. Owen missed the cut in three consecutive tournaments, but by finishing in a tie for 42nd at the season-ending Wyndham Championship, he earned 28 points to overtake MacKenzie.

MacKenzie, however, took full advantage of the Web.com Tour Finals. He finished in a tie for sixth place at the opening Finals tournament, the DAP Championship, to collect $32,375. MacKenzie missed the cut in the second Finals tournament but rebounded with a tie for fifth in the Nationwide Children's Hospital Championship to earn $35,125. MacKenzie concluded the Finals eighth on the money list. After the alternate selection process, he was 17th in the top finishers of the Web.com Tour priority group. MacKenzie entered the 2016–2017 season 54 positions higher than Greg Owen in the PGA tournament priority selection process.

In 2016–2017, MacKenzie appeared in only 16 tournaments, with his last being the Travelers Championship in June. He made the cut in eight events, with a tie for 14th at the AT&T Pebble Beach Pro-Am his best performance of the season. His other top-25 finish was a tie for 17th at the Travelers. MacKenzie earned $272,288. He ended up number 183 in the FedEx Cup standings after not playing in the final two months of the season. MacKenzie did try to return in the Web.com Tour Finals, but he missed one cut and withdrew in his two tournament starts. MacKenzie began the 2017–2018 season on a Web.com Tour medical extension. He had six tournaments to earn 238 points, which when added to his 2016–2017 points total of 127 would equal the 125th position in the 2016–2017 standings, the 365 points J. J. Henry.

For the PGA Tour golfers who do not take advantage of the opportunity to improve their exempt status through the Web.com Finals tournaments, redemption will have to wait until the following season. Brian Stuard had an exempt status for being in the top 125 in the previous season's FedEx Cup points standings entering the 2014–2015 season. He played in 31 tournaments that season. Only four golfers played in more: Danny Lee 36, Zac Blair 34, and Steven Bowditch and Carl Pettersson 32 each. Lee and Bowditch played in all four FedEx Cup Playoff tournaments, while Blair played in three and Pettersson competed in two.

Stuard made 17 cuts in his 31 tournament starts. He had seven top-25 finishes with one top ten, a tie for tenth at the Waste Management Phoenix Open. He missed the cut in two of his last three regular season tournaments, including the season-ending Wyndham Championship, when a first-round score of 68 was paired with a second-round 74. He ended the regular season in 128th place in the FedEx Cup standings, 11 points behind the total needed to qualify for the FedEx Cup Playoffs. Stuard was also number 133 on the PGA Tour money list. He earned $687,109, but that total was $60,790 short of the 125th position.

Stuard was not successful in the Web.com Tour Finals. He made only one cut in the four Finals tournaments. By not improving his exempt status, Stuard began the 2015–2016 season in the 126 through 150 in the FedEx Cup points standings priority group. Stuard explains that "to play out of that category is tough. You are not getting many starts. You have no expectations and you are happy when you do get into a tournament."

Stuard was part of the field for the Zurich Classic of New Orleans that concluded on the first weekend of May 2016. Stuard played in six PGA Tournaments at that point in the season. He made the cut in three tournaments, highlighted by a tie for 25th in the RSM Classic. Stuard also participated in two Web.com Tour events. In February, Stuard played in the Web.com Tour event while the PGA Tour's Waste Management Phoenix Open was being played, and in April he played in the Web.com tournament on the same weekend as the Masters. Stuard missed the cut in both Web.com Tour events.

Stuard also missed the cut in three of four PGA Tour tournaments in the weeks leading up to the Zurich Classic. At the Valero Texas Open, the week before, Stuard tied for 55th. His fourth round of that tournament featured five bogeys and four birdies in shooting one over par.

At the Zurich Classic, the thunderstorm-riddled tournament was reduced to 54 holes. Stuard shot an eight under par 64, with eight birdies in the first roun to tie for the lead with Jhonattan Vegas. After a second-round score of four under par, Stuard emerged with a one-stroke lead over Vegas and Jamie Lovemark, and a four stroke lead over six golfers.

Lovemark played the final round at four under par 68, shooting three under on the final nine holes. Vegas opened the final round with a birdie on the 1st and 2nd holes, but he could only par the other 16 holes for a two under par 70. Byeong Hun An was one of the golfers who trailed Stuard by four strokes. An posted a 65 with five birdies on the back nine, including a birdie on the 18th hole. Stuard shot a final-round 69 and, after he converted a putt from seven feet, four inches for a birdie on the par-5 18th to tie for the lead, he joined An and Lovemark in a playoff.

An was eliminated on the first playoff hole. On the second extra hole, back at 18, Lovemark missed the green on his approach shot. Sensing an opportunity to put some pressure on Lovemark, Stuard said he "wasn't too nervous and that the shot was from a perfect yardage." Stuard stuck his approach shot from 177 yards to only a couple of feet from the cup. Stuard made the birdie putt, and the 33-year-old claimed his first career PGA tournament championship in his 120th Tour start.

Stuard ended up making 46 of 46 putts from inside ten feet. Stuard attests "how much fun it is to play golf when you are feeling really good putting." He was the only golfer to play the entire tournament without a bogey on his scorecard. While Stuard recalls the exceptional shots that he made during the tournament, he also points out that "executing the difficult par save, going up-and-down from a tough spot" is incredibly meaningful during a tournament and it can really "boost momentum and confidence." In the final round on the front nine, Stuard hit only two greens in regulation, with holes 3 through 8 all being one-putt pars. Stuard felt the victory was "validation for all of the hard work that I put into my golfing career." He reflected, as many other golfers also contend, that sometimes in golf "when it's your week, it's your week."

Stuard earned $1.26 million for the victory. His previous high for a single tournament was $648,000, when he finished second at the OHL Classic at Mayakoba in 2014. Stuard also accumulated 500 FedEx Cup points and jumped from 184th in the standings to number 38. He ended the regular season in 76th position with 680 points. The difference in winning the Zurich Classic and finishing second was 255 points. Had a victory not been the result for Stuard, his FedEx Cup points total would have been 425 and not within the top 125 in the standings to qualify for the playoffs.

Stuard claims that the win "took the pressure off a bit" for the rest of the season. The Zurich Classic of New Orleans was one of only 17 PGA tournaments that Stuard competed in during the 2015–2016 regular season. He made the cut in ten, and aside from his tournament victory he had two finishes in the top 25 in regular season tournaments, including a tie for 16th at the World Golf Championships—Bridgestone Invitational.

Participating in the FedEx Cup Playoffs for the third time in his career, Stuard finished in a tie for 41st at the Barclays and a tie for 21st at the Deutsche Bank Championship. These performances moved Stuard into the top 70 in the standings and advanced him into the BMW Championship. Stuard tied for 56th in the no-cut, guaranteed prize money BMW Championship. Although he did not qualify for the Tour Championship, Stuard earned $144,160 through his performances in the FedEx Cup Playoff tournaments. He completed the FedEx Cup Playoffs 60th in the standings to earn a bonus of $110,000. The 2015–2016 season became the third in which Stuard surpassed the $1 million mark in prize money. He won more than $1.66 million.

With the victory in New Orleans, Stuard competed in the 2017 Tournament of Champions. He finished in a tie for 22nd to earn $78,500 and 40 FedEx Cup points. Stuard also competed in his first Masters tournament in 2017. Stuard calls playing in the Masters "the highlight of my career." He finished the Masters in a tie for 36th to earn almost $53,000 and 20 FedEx Cup points.

Stuard appeared in 31 tournaments and made the cut in 16 in the 2016–2017 season. He had four top-25 finishes, but none in the top ten. Stuard missed the cut in his final seven tournaments of the season. He finished the season in 145th place in the FedEx Cup standings, which provided a bonus of $32,000. Stuard played 2017–2018 as his final season in the tournament winners priority ranking group.

13

Graduation 2017

The system of the PGA Tour, as well as the Web.com Tour, is such that golfer storylines along the critical dividing lines are guaranteed. There are certain tournaments where the dividing line outcomes are ultimately decided. The WinCo Foods Portland Open in 2017 once again produced considerable drama as the last tournament of the Web.com Tour regular season. Brice Garnett entered the tournament 11th on the money list. Garnett birdied the 13th hole in the final round to take sole possession of the lead. He added birdies on the 15th, 17th, and 18th holes to complete a back nine 30 in his final round of 65 for the four-stroke win. Garnett won $144,000 for his second title of the season. He completed the Web.com Tour regular season as the leader in prize money, earning $368,761.

A spot in the top 75 on the money list is needed to gain entrance into the Finals and obtain fully exempt status on the Web.com Tour for the following season. If not advancing to the PGA Tour through the Finals, these golfers at least can essentially set their own playing schedule on the Web.com Tour. Again, it should be noted that the golfers who finish in positions 76 through 85 on the Web.com Tour regular season money list advance to the final stage of Q School, while those golfers in positions 86 through 100 on the list advance to the second stage of Q School in their quest to get fully exempt on the Web.com Tour.

Two golfers moved into the top 75 on the regular season money list through their performance in Portland. David Skinns came into the tournament at number 115. The only way that he could secure his PGA Tour card in Portland was to win the tournament. In the final round he posted a two under par 34 on the front nine. Skinns shot a five under par 30 on the back nine. He made birdies on the 11th, 12th, and 13th holes. After a bogey on the 14th, Skinns had another three-hole stretch of consecutive birdies on the 16th through 18th holes. Skinns' nine-birdie, seven under par 64 gave him the clubhouse lead. Skinns would not win the tournament with many golfers having several holes left to play. What Skinns did achieve with his performance was to move into 58th on the money list. Skinns earned $85,449 for the Web.com Tour regular season. He did not earn any money in the Finals as he missed the cut in two tournaments and had to withdraw from another.

Ben Kohles also moved into the top 75 through his performance in Portland. Kohles entered the tournament 85th after earning $52,032 in 19 Web.com Tour starts. Kohles could only get his PGA Tour card in Portland by winning the tournament. Kohles says that he had a "great week of preparation" leading up to Portland. He opened the tournament with a two under par 70 and a three under par 69. After shooting a 66 in the third round, Kohles was well-positioned to finish in the top 75 of the regular season money list. Kohles explains that in the final round he "did not look at the leaderboard" as he tried to "stay in the present." He claims that he "did not want any outside thoughts that had no impact" on his performance. His strategy prevailed. In the final round, Kohles bogeyed the 1st hole, but he responded with a birdie on the 2nd, 4th, and 7th holes. He gave a stroke back with a bogey on the ninth hole. Kohles then rallied on the back with a birdie on the 11th, 13th, 14th, and 17th holes to finish the round with a 67 and play his way into a tie for eighth, 12 under par. Kohles claimed $20,800. That amount helped get him into 68th on the money list. Kohles earned $72,832 in the Web.com Tour regular season.

Kohles' spot in the Finals was obtained by playing nine consecutive weeks, from July 9 until a week off between the first and second tournaments of the Finals. Kohles explains that on the Web.com Tour, it is "hard to take a week off." It is a challenge to have to play every week as it is often "necessary to get a physical and mental break." Kohles points out that good finishes early in the season can set you up so that the stretch run is not as daunting.

Kohles did not make it to the PGA Tour through the path of the Finals. He missed the cut at the first two Finals tournaments. Kohles then finished in a tie for 11th at the DAP Championship to earn $20,500. He was now in contention for a PGA Tour card, but he came up short as he finished in a tie for 32nd at the Web.com Tour Championship and added only $5,975. However, simply by getting into the top 75 on the regular season money list, Kohles would not have to go to Q School as he had fully exempt status when the 2018 Web.com Tour season began.

The two golfers Skinns and Kohles replaced in the top 75 were Samuel Del Val, who began the tournament in 74th place, and Brady Schnell, who had the 75th position entering Portland. Alex Kang started the week at number 81 on the prize money list. He projected into the 74th position when he birdied the 14th and 15th holes in the final round. Kang added another birdie on the 18th hole, but it was not enough to stay in the top 75. That final spot went to Jacques Blaauw. After entering Portland 72nd, despite missing the cut in that tournament, Blaauw's season total of $64,005 eclipsed Kang's total of $63,243.

Kang played in the final stage of Q School, where he finished tied for seventh, 19 under par, after rounds of 70–67–66–66. This top-ten result made Kang fully exempt on the Web.com Tour for the first 12 tournaments in 2018. Brady Schnell shot a 65 in the final round of Q School to be one of 15 golfers tied for 42nd place at 14 under par (the finishers at 13 under par tied for 57th). With the golfers who finish the final stage tournament in 11th through 45th place, including ties, fully exempt on the Web.com Tour for the first eight tournaments, had Schnell's score been one stroke higher, he would not have that status going into 2018. Instead, for the golfers who reach the final stage of Q School, but do not finish in the top 45, only conditional status on the Web.com Tour is given. That was the status of Samuel Del Val entering 2018 after he finished the final stage of Q School in 141st place, shooting two under par for the tournament.

The most dramatic dividing line of the 2017 WinCo Foods Portland Open was, as always, which golfers would make the top 25 on the prize money list to earn their PGA Tour cards. In 2017, for the first time since going to the Web.com Tour qualifying format for the PGA Tour, the final regular season tournament did not produce a change in the golfers who comprised the top 25 on the regular season money list. That result, however, was not without excruciating moments for the golfers positioned near that dividing line.

Roberto Diaz and Beau Hossler were in the precarious 24th and 25th positions on the money list heading into Portland. Diaz earned $155,023 in 19 tournaments, and Hossler collected $154,966 in only ten events. Hossler finished tied for 19th in Portland, adding $9,360 to his season total. Hossler was able to elevate two positions and end the regular season in 23rd on the money list. Ethan Tracy dropped down one spot after not making the tournament cut in Portland to end the season 24th.

Diaz explains that during the week of the WinCo Foods Portland Open, he was "very nervous and it was tough to play." He adds, "there are so many possibilities. You are just running through the numbers. It is a tough situation." Diaz still felt that he was in control of the outcome and that he would be fine if he made the cut. Diaz did make the cut with a tie for 43rd, but it did not yet secure his PGA Tour card as he hoped. After completing his round earlier in the day, Diaz had to wait several hours before his status was determined. All control that Diaz believed he had was gone. Diaz could now only watch the tournament's conclusion from his hotel room, along with his coach and his agent. At times during the remainder of the final round, Diaz was projected to be out of the top 25.

Keith Mitchell was the golfer in pursuit of Diaz. Mitchell earned $123,644 in the 17 tournaments that he played on the Web.com Tour prior to Portland, putting him 36th on the money list. He trailed Diaz by $31,379. Facing pressure in trying to reach the next level of professional golf was not a new experience for Mitchell. The crossing of each dividing line was often by one stroke. It took the seventh hole of a playoff for Mitchell to gain status on the PGA Latinoamerica Tour. He then missed out on advancing to a further stage in the Q School process by one stroke, before playing his way out of Q School and onto the Web.com Tour by one stroke.

Mitchell says of the 2016 season, his first on the Web.com Tour, that "I was just happy to be on the Web." Mitchell played in 17 regular season events and made the cut in 11 in that season. He had five top-25 finishes, with two performances in the top ten. He ended the regular season 70th on the money list. In the Finals, Mitchell missed the cut in the first tournament before a tie for 37th and a tie for 34th. He earned $9,493 in the Finals of his season total of $69,275 in prize money. Staying on the Web.com Tour would not be a satisfying result for the 2017 season. That season for Mitchell was about getting a PGA Tour card.

After rounds of 70, 69, and a 62 in round three, Mitchell started the final round of the WinCo Foods Portland Open in a four-way tie for the lead. He was projected to be in the number seven position on the money list if he remained atop the leaderboard. Mitchell was in the last pairing for the final round, playing alongside Brice Garnett. Mitchell bogeyed the 6th, 7th, and 9th holes to find himself in the projected 29th position. After stabilizing his round with a par on the 10th and 11th holes, Mitchell's regular season quest to join the PGA Tour was still not decided with seven holes to play

At the par-3, 160-yard 12th hole, Mitchell dropped his nine-iron tee-shot within a few feet of the hole. He moved to 12 under par for the tournament upon draining the birdie putt, which elevated his projection to number 28. He was two strokes off the lead. Based on the projections, Mitchell needed to finish the tournament in fourth place. After the 12th hole, he was tied for fifth.

At the par-4, 440-yard 13th hole, Mitchell's drive was perfectly placed in the fairway. His second shot from 84 yards hit the green, but bounced into the rough behind the hole. With little green to work with, he wedged the ball within a couple of feet of the hole, seemingly in a good position to save par. Mitchell's putt, however, hit the right edge of the cup and lipped out for a bogey five.

Mitchell says that after missing the putt on 13, "nerves were present." Mitchell talked it over with his caddie, Pete Persolja, and they both understood that playing afraid was not going to help. Mitchell responded with a birdie on 14. When Mitchell made a birdie at the par-3, 184-yard 15th hole, he was in sole possession of fifth place in the tournament, right on the cusp of his PGA Tour card in the projected 26th position. Mitchell hit another outstanding tee-shot on the par-4, 432-yard 16th hole that put him in the fairway, only 98 yards from the flagstick. His lob wedge placed him on the green. The putt for birdie hit the left edge of the cup, but did not drop. Mitchell needed to play the final two holes at one under par to earn his PGA Tour card.

The 17th hole is a par-4, 422 yards. Mitchell hit a four-iron off the tee, once again in the fairway. His second shot, a nine-iron from 157 yards, put him on the green. If Mitchell made the birdie putt, his projected position on the money list would jump to 21. Mitchell's putt was on a direct line toward the center of the hole but incredibly stopped on the edge of the hole. An extra quarter-revolution of the golf ball appeared to be all that was needed for it to drop. Mitchell bent over in disbelief.

Mitchell still had the opportunity to earn his PGA Tour card with a birdie on the par-5, 545-yard 18th hole. Mitchell, however, approached the final hole believing that he needed an eagle, not birdie, to obtain his PGA Tour card. In the first two rounds, Mitchell birdied the 18th. Mitchell eagled that hole in the third round. In the final round on 18, Mitchell obliterated his tee-shot, 355 yards in the fairway. His second shot was from 206 yards away from the hole. With a six-iron, Mitchell's ball headed slightly left. It landed on a hill just off of the green and rolled down to the bottom of the hill that left a difficult up-and-down for birdie. The ball would have rolled onto the green had it landed a few feet to the right. Mitchell says that "it started to cross my mind that it [getting his PGA Tour card] might not happen."

Mitchell, again, believing that he needed an eagle for his PGA Tour card, thought he had to hole out from the bottom of the hill. Mitchell was aggressive as he tried to bump-and-run his chip shot, but it rolled approximately 15 feet past the hole. The reality was that Mitchell could still get to the PGA Tour by making the birdie putt, even if he now thought that achievement was no longer possible. Mitchell's putt traveled to the right of the hole.

Mitchell finished the tournament in a tie for sixth place. A birdie on either 17 or 18 would have allowed him to tie for second place. Mitchell hit 4,430 shots in 18 starts during the Web.com Tour regular season, but he needed to have one fewer at the WinCo Foods Portland Open to earn his PGA Tour card. With $157,823 in winnings, Roberto Diaz obtained the 25th position as his regular season money total was $6,379 better than Mitchell's total of $151,444, in the 26th position.

Upon arriving at the scorer's tent, Mitchell learned that he needed only a birdie, not an eagle, on the 18th hole. Mitchell says that "finding out that I needed birdie was the hardest part of the golf tournament." Mitchell explains that in the week leading up to the tournament, all he hoped for was "a putt to win the tournament or a putt to go the PGA Tour. I had it and I didn't even know it."

Every golfer arrives at the Web.com Tour Finals from a different path. Some golfers probably knew for months that barring a miraculous result at one of the late-season tournaments, either at a PGA Tour or the Web.com Tour event, they would be playing in the Finals. Others begin the Finals disappointed that they just missed either reaching the FedEx Cup Playoffs or had not already secured their PGA Tour card through the Web.com Tour regular season. For Keith Mitchell, arriving at the Finals came with the emotion of just missing out on his Tour card in Portland and the frustration over the circumstances in which that tournament ended.

With golf, as in any other sport, the way a player responds to a setback is critical to future success. Over the next three tournaments in the Finals, Mitchell would display his resolve and his ability to rebound from a difficult outcome on a golf course.

Mitchell says that it was beneficial that the first tournament of the Web.com Tour Finals began only four days after the last round in Portland. There was not time to dwell on any past failure. After staying up until 5:00 a.m., Mitchell left for the Nationwide Children's Hospital Championship in Columbus, Ohio, on Monday. He arrived at that tournament very motivated.

In the first round, Mitchell was paired with Roberto Diaz. Mitchell opened the tournament with a par and a bogey. Mitchell recalls that despite this start, "I was not mad, was not frustrated," and that "my game felt great." Mitchell would prove himself correct by making seven birdies in the remainder of his opening round to shoot a six under par 65. Mitchell was "shaking and on the verge of tears" as he signed his scorecard in front of some of the same officials who just a few days earlier informed him that he needed only a birdie, not an eagle, on the final hole and witnessed the profound disappointment that could only come with being one stroke short of earning a PGA Tour card in that manner.

Mitchell would go on to finish in a tie for sixth at the Nationwide Children's Hospital Championship. Although he was proud of his determination and his overcoming what occurred in Portland, Mitchell points out that he was in no way satisfied with the outcome in the first Finals tournament. He explains that "it is good to be disappointed when you tie for sixth." With earnings of $34,750, Mitchell was now well-positioned on the Finals money list with three tournaments remaining.

There was one week off before the start of the second Finals tournament, the Albertsons Boise Open. Mitchell missed the cut in that tournament. Mitchell's excellent position after the first Finals tournament was a bit more precarious after that result.

The following week was the DAP Championship. Mitchell opened with a three under par 67 and a second-round 71. Mitchell played the first seven holes of round three at even par and completed the round with three birdies and no bogeys for another 67. Mitchell played the final round of the DAP Championship knowing that a good 18 holes would indeed complete his journey to the PGA Tour. A bogey on the 13th hole left Mitchell at two over par for the round. Again, Mitchell's resolve would come through as he birdied the 14th and 15th holes. His current position on the tournament leaderboard would put his Finals total earnings in the top 25, and a PGA Tour card would be his.

When Mitchell hit the green at 18, he felt a tremendous sense of relief. He still wanted to close out the tournament and his PGA Tour card with a defining moment that he created. On the birdie putt, Mitchell was aggressive and hit the ball past the hole to about six feet. Putting for par, Mitchell delivered what he calls "by far the best putt I hit all season, best read, best speed." He says making that putt "made it all feel real." Mitchell finished the DAP Championship in a tie for sixth place to earn $31,300. Only a few weeks after the ultimate disappointment in Portland, Mitchell now had the ultimate redemption, his PGA Tour card.

Mitchell was not the only golfer to secure his PGA Tour card at the DAP Championship. Nicholas Lindheim finished the 2016 season 21st on the Web.com Tour regular season money list to earn a PGA Tour card for the 2016–2017 season. Lindheim played in 21 tournaments on the PGA Tour in 2016–2017 and made the cut in nine, with his best finish a tie for 23rd at the Sanderson Farms Championship. Lindheim ended the regular season 197th in the FedEx Cup standings, dangerously close to the top 200 dividing line for even qualifying for the Web.com Tour Finals. Lindheim's 93 FedEx Cup points were only 11 better than Padraig Harrington in position number 200, and 12 points better than Miguel Angel Carballo and Will Wilcox in positions 201 and 202.

Lindheim's struggles continued as he missed the cut in the first Finals tournament. A tie for 46th at the Albertsons Boise Open yielded only $3,020. Lindheim was looking at having nothing more than conditional status on the Web.com Tour with only two Finals tournaments remaining. The 32-year-old then had the four days that he needed. He opened the DAP Championship with a 64, including a six under par 29 on the back nine. Lindheim carded a one under par 69 in round two and a two under par 68 in round three. In the final round, Lindheim withstood a bogey on the 17th and 18th holes to remain tied for the tournament lead, along with Chesson Hadley and Rob Oppenheim. Lindheim prevailed on the first hole of the playoff. He pocketed the $180,000 winner's share, and he was heading back to the PGA Tour.

Troy Merritt started 2016–2017 in his final season in the tournament winners group for his victory at the 2015 Quicken Loans National tournament. Merritt was part of the field at 28 PGA tournaments with this high exempt status. He made the cut in 12, with five top-25 finishes. Merritt's season was highlighted by his only top-ten finish, a tie for eighth at the Travelers Championship. Merritt finished number 151 in the FedEx Cup points standings, one spot outside of a position that would have awarded him a $32,000 bonus as well as placed him in the 126 though 150 FedEx Cup standings group heading into the following PGA Tour season. Merritt's total of 265 was only four points behind Rick Lamb in the 150th position and 11 points shy of Alex Cejka in 149th place. Merritt was now faced with improving his status through the Web.com Tour Finals or being relegated to the past champions group.

Merritt, facing for his second time the challenge of competing in the Finals, says, "the pressure is there, but I have an idea what to expect." He also contends that this system is fairer than the previous one-tournament Q School system. Merritt began the Finals by missing the cut at the Nationwide Children's Hospital Championship. Merritt, who grew up in Iowa but now residing in Idaho, would have a bit of a home advantage in the Albertsons Boise Open. Merritt responded with a stretch of 25 holes, from the 16th hole of round one to the 4th hole in round three, that produced eight birdies and only one bogey. He added consecutive birdies on the 15th through 17th holes in round three. Merritt finished the tournament at 11 under par to tie for ninth place. He earned $22,375.

Still needing to play well to earn his PGA Tour card, Merritt left no doubt at the following week's DAP Championship. After an opening-round three over par 73, Merritt posted scores of 65–67–70. He ended the tournament in a tie for sixth to add $31,300 to his Finals total. Merritt played his way back onto the PGA Tour in those two Finals tournaments.

Joel Dahmen was another golfer who ended the DAP Championship in a tie for sixth place, along with Mitchell, Merritt, Chad Collins, and Matt Atkins. By entering the 2016–2017 season in the 48th spot in the top finishers of the Web.com Tour, Dahmen played in only 16 PGA Tour events. He made the cut in seven, with two top-25 finishes and a season-best tie for ninth at the AT&T Byron Nelson. Dahmen ended the regular season 176th in the FedEx Cup standings.

Dahmen began the Finals with a tie for 63rd at the Nationwide Children's Hospital Championship that gave him $2,510. He added $8,132 to his Finals total with a tie for 25th at the Albertsons Boise Open. Dahmen reclaimed his PGA Tour status with his performance at the DAP Championship. His rounds of 69,66 (which included a five under par stretch over eight holes) and 68 helped him withstand a final-round 72 that included a double-bogey on the 18th hole. The $31,300 in prize money from the DAP Championship put his total at $41,942, $1,317 more than the eventual 25th-place prize money total.

While Dahmen had suspenseful finishes to the 2016 and 2017 seasons with his qualifying for the PGA Tour closely decided, no golfer straddled the PGA Tour/Web.com Tour dividing line as often and dramatically as Rob Oppenheim. Oppenheim began competing regularly on the Web.com Tour in 2010. In some events, even making the cut did not cover the expenses of his participating in the tournament. Oppenheim recalls that at times he was "fighting to keep the dream alive, to pay bills."

Oppenheim did not have fully exempt status on the Web.com Tour for some seasons. He played in only 14 Web.com Tour events in 2014, making the cut in five. It was a Web.com Tour Q School win by one stroke that made him fully exempt on the Web.com Tour for the 2015 season. All it took for Oppenheim to achieve that status was to make a hole-in-one in the tournament's final round.

The dramatics for Oppenheim in relation to qualifying for the PGA Tour began in the 2015 season. Oppenheim played in all 25 tournaments on the Web.com Tour that season. In June, he scored his first Web.com tournament victory at the Air Capital Classic in Wichita, Kansas. The final round began with Oppenheim trailing Andy Winings by six strokes. Oppenheim shot a final-round 64 to finish at 13 under par. He had to wait in the clubhouse for the rest of the golfers to finish their rounds. Winings was 13 under par at the 17th hole, but he could not convert a ten-foot birdie putt. Winings bogeyed the 18th to give Oppenheim the victory. With the $108,000 winner's purse, Oppenheim rocketed up the prize money leaderboard from position number 70 to 13.

Oppenheim made only three cuts in his next seven tournaments. He arrived at the WinCo Foods Portland Open having dropped to number 24 on the money list. When Oppenheim did not make the cut in Portland, posting rounds of 71 and 70, he could only watch as his following season's status was determined. Oppenheim ended up on the wrong side of the PGA Tour card dividing line by $943 as he dropped to number 26 on the Web.com Tour regular season money list.

He would have another opportunity to earn his PGA Tour card at the Web.com Tour Finals. Although he made the cut in the first three tournaments of the Finals, Oppenheim was 50th as he entered the Web.com Tour Championship. Oppenheim essentially staved off elimination when he made the cut by two strokes. When he needed it most, Oppenheim turned in back-to-back rounds of 67. He still did not believe that his performance got him high enough on the Finals money list to get his PGA Tour card. He left the scorer's trailer thinking that he was 28th based on the computer projections.

Disappointed, Oppenheim and his family began the two-hour drive home to Orlando as some golfers remained on the course finishing their final rounds. Thirty minutes into his drive, while at a gas station filling up and getting snacks for his wife, Lacey, who was pregnant, and his three-year-old daughter, Zoey, Oppenheim received a phone call from a Tour official. Due to a Lucas Glover bogey on the 18th hole, he moved up into a six-way tie for 12th place at the Web.com Tour Championship. The Finals money list calculations were now altered. Oppenheim was 25th just $101 ahead of Eric Axley. Ironically, it was Axley who secured the final PGA Tour card spot one year earlier.

Oppenheim returned to the golf course to take the group photo of the PGA Tour card winners, where he was greeted with an ovation by his fellow recipients. After playing regularly on the Web.com Tour for six seasons, Oppenheim was finally a member of the PGA Tour. As quoted by Steve DiMeglio in *USA Today*, Oppenheim stated, "it's amazing how it all turned out. You've been grinding for so long, it just shows you how fine a line there is between playing the PGA Tour and the Web.com Tour. If Lucas makes par, I'd be playing the Web.com Tour. But, you keep working hard, keep hoping one day something will turn your way."

Although having a PGA Tour card, getting PGA tournament starts from the 50th position in the top finishers of the Web.com Tour group is precarious. Oppenheim appeared in 21 PGA tournaments in the 2015–2016 season. He made the cut in 11 events, with two top-25 finishes and his season-best tie for tenth at the Quicken Loans National tournament. For that result, Oppenheim earned $179,400 of his season total prize money of $462,427. Oppenheim found himself within the top 150 of the FedEx Cup standings in early July, reaching as high as 140. Had he remained in that position, he would have status in the 126 through 150 finishers group for the following season and collected a bonus of $32,000. Oppenheim, however, missed the cut in four of his final five tournaments and dropped to 158th in the FedEx Cup standings. He was headed back to the Web.com Tour Finals.

Oppenheim missed the cut in the first Finals tournament. A tie for 24th awarded him $8,033. That was followed by a tie for 12th that added $19,000 to his Finals total. Oppenheim was 26th with $27,033 heading into the Web.com Tour Championship, $392 behind Tim Wilkinson in the 25th spot. Oppenheim would not get the chance to play his way back to the PGA Tour as Hurricane Matthew canceled the Web.com Tour Championship. Again, it was determined that the results of the first three Finals tournaments would decide the 25 golfers who received their PGA Tour card.

The 2016–2017 regular season ended with Oppenheim right back on the bubble between the PGA Tour and the Web.com Tour. He appeared in four PGA Tour events in that season. He finished in a tie for 22nd at the Sanderson Farms Championship, earning $8,190. Oppenheim received a sponsor exemption into the AT&T Pebble Beach Pro-Am, where he finished in a tie for eighth. Oppenheim earned $216,000 at Pebble Beach, more prize money than he earned in any one complete season on the Web.com Tour. By finishing in the top ten at Pebble Beach, Oppenheim got to play in the next PGA tournament, missing the cut at the Genesis Open at Riviera Country Club. Oppenheim also missed the cut at the Arnold Palmer Invitational, his other PGA Tour start.

In 2017, Oppenheim made 15 cuts in 20 starts in the Web.com Tour regular season. He had seven top-25 finishes, with four in the top ten. Oppenheim also almost broke through to the winner's circle at the Utah Championship in July. Oppenheim, along with two other golfers, finished the tournament one stroke back of Brice Garnett.

Oppenheim entered the WinCo Foods Portland Open 26th in prize money. His $148,709 trailed Beau Hossler, in the 25th position, by $6,257. In Portland, Oppenheim finished in a tie for 65th place, one over par. He would add only $1,984 to his season total. It was not enough, and Oppenheim, at position number 27, was denied entrance back on the PGA Tour through that path. Oppenheim's total of $150,693 was $7,130 behind Robert Diaz's 25th-place total of $157,823.

The Finals would once again determine Oppenheim's status for the following season. He played with great consistency in the 2017 Web.com Tour Finals. He finished all four tournaments in the top 17. His rally back to the PGA Tour began with a tie for 11th at the first playoff tournament, for which he earned $24,000. Oppenheim then tied for 17th at the Albertsons Boise Open to earn an additional $12,650. On the cusp of his PGA Tour card, but with it still not a certainty, Oppenheim removed any doubt when he made it into a three-man playoff at the DAP Championship. Although he came up short to Nicholas Lindheim, Oppenheim earned $88,000. Oppenheim says, "the great thing is if you work hard, you keep giving yourself chances. Each week can change your life. Each week is the Super Bowl." With his PGA Tour card secure, Oppenheim arrived at the Web.com Tour Championship with a new feeling, "knowing I'm not going to be stressing out." He won another $36,500 in prize money with a tie for fifth at the Web.com Tour Championship.

Of his 16 rounds in the Finals, Oppenheim played 13 under par and another round at even par. He played eight straight rounds of golf under 70. He collected $161,150 in the Finals to finish fourth on that money list. After the alternate selection process, Oppenheim entered the 2017–2018 PGA Tour season in the ninth position in the top finishers of the Web.com Tour group. It is the best exempt status to begin a season on the PGA Tour of his career.

14

Past Champions

Winning one tournament leads to many opportunities on the PGA Tour, but they can be short-lived in terms of an entire career. While it may seem like ample time, a golfer has only two seasons to win another tournament to maintain that high priority ranking group status. Graeme McDowell and Hideki Matsuyama both entered 2015–2016 in their final season in that group. McDowell, the 2010 U.S. Open champion, achieved his status for his victory at the 2013 RBC Heritage, Matsuyama for his win at the 2014 Memorial (it was not until 2015 that the winners of the Memorial and the Arnold Palmer Invitational received a three-season exemption).

Both McDowell and Matsuyama obtained victories during the 2015–2016 season to extend their high exempt status for multiple seasons. McDowell won at the season's sixth tournament, the OHL Classic at Mayakoba in the autumn of 2015. He entered 2017–2018 once again in his final season in the tournament winners group.

Matsuyama was victorious in the season's 12th tournament, the 2016 Waste Management Phoenix Open that provided his exempt status as a tournament winner through 2017–2018. Matsuyama extended his exempt status even longer when he won the World Golf Championships—HSBC Champions tournament in the autumn of 2016. He would go on to win three tournaments in the 2016–2017 season. He repeated as the champion of the Waste Management Phoenix Open and won the World Golf Championships—Bridgestone Invitational. Matsuyama has an exempt status as a tournament winner through 2021–2022.

In the final season of that tournament winners exempt status, if a golfer is not victorious, he must play well enough to at least maintain a status where he can set his tournament schedule for the following season by finishing in the top 125 FedEx Cup points standings and reaching the playoffs. Anything short of that, and the opportunities to play in PGA Tour events will be less frequent, although there are certainly some opportunities for playing out of the top finishers of the Web.com priority group or settling into the 126 through 150 in the FedEx Cup standings group.

If that former tournament winner does not qualify for the playoffs, improve his status in the Web.com Tour Finals, or reach the top 150 of the FedEx Cup standings, he drops even further in the priority rankings to a group of past champions. Ken Duke, winner of the Travelers Championship in 2013, points out that with a tournament win, you forever have some status on the PGA Tour by being part of the past champions group. At the very least, it means never having to go back to Q School to get fully exempt on the Web.com Tour.

D. A. Points, who played the 2015–2016 season out of the past champions group, explains that when you are in that group, it is a struggle to get tournament starts. A golfer ends up participating in many Monday qualifiers or hoping for a sponsor exemption into tournaments. Points explains that he would write and call tournament directors, hoping for an opportunity to play. He even offered on one occasion to play in a tournament's Monday pro-am event rather than playing in a qualifying tournament in his attempt to get into the U.S. Open. Points says, "I needed opportunities."

Rod Pampling, who played out of the past champions group for multiple seasons, adds that one challenge of being in that group is waiting just to get into tournaments. He points out that it is difficult to prepare correctly when you may get to play one week, but then you are off for two or three weeks. Pampling explains that "you are forced to go and play when you have to, instead of playing the tournaments that you want to."

Pampling first competed in a PGA tournament in 1999. By 2002, he was playing regularly on the PGA Tour, with 29 tournament starts in that season. Entering the 2016–2017 season, Pampling earned more than $14.1 million in PGA Tour events with a resume that includes winning the International in 2004 and the Bay Hill Invitational in 2006, as well as tying for fifth at the 2005 Masters. Pampling last qualified for the FedEx Cup Playoffs in 2012, when he competed in only the first playoff tournament.

Pampling was part of the past champions group in the 2013–2014 and 2014–2015 seasons. In 2014–2015, he split time between the PGA Tour and the Web.com Tour. He played in ten PGA tournaments and nine regular season Web.com tournaments. Pampling won the Web.com Tour's BMW Charity Pro-Am and ended the regular season among the top 25 in prize money on the Web.com Tour. Pampling rejoined the PGA Tour out of the top finishers of the Web.com Tour group for the 2015–2016 season.

Pampling played in 18 PGA Tour events in 2015–2016. He made the cut in nine tournaments, but he did not have a top-25 finish. Pampling found himself 195th in the FedEx Cup points standings. For the fourth consecutive season, Pampling did not qualify for the FedEx Cup Playoffs, and he had to spend his post-season competing in the Web.com Tour Finals.

Pampling found success at the first tournament of the Web.com Tour Finals, the DAP Championship. After an opening-round 74 at the par-70 course, he carded rounds of 66 and 68. In the fourth round, two bogeys on the front nine put Pampling at even par for the tournament. He shot four under par on the back nine to finish with another round of 68, finishing in a tie for tenth place to earn $25,000. He finished tied for 24th in the second Finals tournament on the strength of a final-round 65 that featured seven birdies and only one bogey. Pampling added $8,033 to his Finals total.

At the Nationwide Children's Hospital Championship, the third tournament of the Web.com Tour Finals, Pampling tied for 12th. Again, it was his excellence on the back nine of the final round that propelled his movement up the leaderboard. Pampling posted a four under par 31 on the back nine to finish six under. He earned $19,000 for the tournament. Pampling finished 11th on the Web.com Tour Finals money list with a total of $52,033 in the three events. Had it not been for his Web.com Tour Finals success, Pampling would have again been relegated to the past champions group.

The 2016–2017 season for Pampling began with missing the cut at the season-opening Safeway Open. After a tie for 42nd at the Sanderson Farms Championship, his next start came at the Shriners Hospitals for Children Open at TPC Summerlin in Las Vegas. This was the fifth tournament of the regular season. Pampling opened the Shriners with a blistering 60 in the first round at the par-71 course. His round included two eagles and seven birdies. In round two, he made three more birdies in the first seven holes to bring his tournament total to 14 under par through 25 holes. Pampling, however, played the rest of round two and round three, the next 29 holes, at even par. He had a one-stroke lead after round two, but after round three found himself tied with Brooks Koepka for second place, trailing Lucas Glover by one stroke.

Pampling very much remained in contention for the tournament championship when he shot four under par on the front nine in the final round, including a birdie on the 8th hole when he chipped in from 50 feet. Pampling bogeyed the 10th and 12th holes, but he rebounded on the last six holes. A 13-foot birdie putt on the 13th was followed by an 18-foot birdie putt on the par-3 14th to tie him for the lead with Glover at 18 under.

Both players matched birdies on the 15th hole, with Pampling making a putt of 11 feet. Pampling parred both the 16th and 17th holes. After a Glover bogey on 17, the door was open for Pampling to win the tournament. Glover made another bogey on the 18th, and Pampling countered by continuing his superb back nine putting when he made a 32-footer on 18. It was his eighth birdie of the day and his fourth on the final six holes of the tournament.

For the 47-year-old Pampling, his decade-long victory drought ended. His 20 under par was his lowest score to par in a tournament since he shot 16 under at the Bob Hope Classic in 2010. Pampling earned $1.18 million for his win at the Shriners. It was the highest tournament earning for his career, eclipsing the $990,000 he was awarded for winning the Bay Hill Invitational in 2006.

With the win early in the season, Pampling could then set his schedule. He played in 22 tournaments in 2016–2017 and made the cut in 13. His other top finish was a tie for 17th at the Tournament of Champions, where he earned over $98,000. Of course, Pampling only gained entrance into that tournament because of his win two months earlier. He also got to play in his fourth Masters, his first since 2007, though he was not able to make the cut at Augusta.

Of his points total of 630, 500 were earned at the Shriners. On the strength of that victory alone, Pampling amassed a FedEx Cup points total that qualified him for the playoffs. Pampling was one of eight golfers who were previously on the PGA Tour, returned to the Tour via the Web.com Finals in 2016, and qualified for the FedEx Cup Playoffs in the 2016–2017 season.

Pampling entered the FedEx Cup Playoffs in the 70th position. He made the cut in the first two playoff tournaments, a tie for 54th at the Northern Trust and 79th at the Dell Technologies. His placement at 74th in the FedEx Cup standings did not allow him to advance further. Pampling earned $35,613 in the two FedEx Cup Playoff tournaments and received a bonus of $80,000. He earned more than $1.53 million for the season.

Finally, in the scope of his career, with the victory, Pampling reclaimed an exempt status in the tournament winners priority ranking group for the following two seasons. Pampling states that to win at that point in his career was "more special" and that the timing "could not get any better." For the 48-year-old entering the 2017–2018 season, Pampling specifically receives an extra benefit from having the tournament winners status for the next two seasons: he will be able to play consistently on the PGA Tour leading into his transition to the Champions Tour. Pampling explains that not many golfers are able to obtain that status late in their career.

The golfers within the past champions group are ranked based on their combined earnings on both the PGA Tour and the Web.com Tour from the previous season. Aaron Baddeley, Vaughn Taylor, and Jhonnattan Vegas all won tournaments in the 2015–2016 season after starting that season in the past champions group. They were three of the top four players ranked within the past champions group at the beginning of the season.

Vaughn Taylor entered the 2015–2016 season as the top-ranked golfer in the past champions group. He last won a tournament in 2005, a three-stroke victory over Jonathan Kaye in the Reno-Tahoe Open. Taylor had four tournament starts prior to the AT&T Pebble Beach Pro-Am in 2015–2016, two on the PGA Tour and two on the Web.com Tour. In his PGA Tour starts, Taylor missed a cut and tied for 20th at the Sanderson Farms Championship, for which he earned $41,359. In his two Web.com Tour starts, Taylor missed a cut and, the week before the tournament at Pebble Beach, withdrew from the Club Colombia Championship in Bogota, Colombia.

Taylor entered the final round of the AT&T Pebble Beach Pro-Am at ten under par after posting rounds of 70–68–67. He was six strokes behind tournament leader Phil Mickelson. Taylor shot two under par on the front nine of the final round with four birdies and two bogeys. A birdie on the 10th, 13th, and 14th holes rallied Taylor to within one stroke of the lead. His second shot from the rough on the par-4 15th bounced on the green and caromed off the ball of Roberto Castro to roll within inches of the cup for an easy birdie. Another birdie on 16 gave Taylor the lead. He finished the round with nine birdies to shoot seven under par 65. Taylor's score of 17 under par sent him to the clubhouse with the lead.

Mickelson was at one over in the final round after he bogeyed the 14th hole. He needed to rally to catch Taylor. A birdie from the fringe on 17 got Mickelson to within one stroke. He then stood over a birdie putt from five feet away on 18 to force a playoff. The putt hit the left edge of the cup and rolled around the lip, but did not drop. After rounds of 68–65–66, and a final-round 72, Mickelson ended the tournament at 16 under par. Taylor had his third PGA Tour championship.

Taylor competed in 21 tournaments during the PGA Tour regular season in 2015–2016. He made the cut in ten, with two finishes in the top 25. His win accounted for 500 of his season total of 726 FedEx Cup points. Taylor ended the regular season 64th in the standings. After missing the cut at the Barclays, Taylor rebounded with a tie for 24th at the Deutsche Bank Championship and a tie for 42nd at the BMW Championship. Although he did not qualify for the Tour Championship, Taylor earned $94,067 for his playoff performances. His total season earnings were more than $1.64 million. He completed the season 62nd in the FedEx Cup points standings to earn a playoff bonus of $110,000. Moving forward, Taylor obtained an exempt status in the tournament winners group through the 2017–2018 season.

For the 2016–2017 season, 53 golfers comprised the past champions group including major tournament winners such as Angel Cabrera, Ben Curtis, Trevor Immelman, Bernhard Langer, and Justin Leonard, as well as players with three or more PGA tournament wins, such as Cameron Beckman, Jonathan Byrd, and Camilo Villegas. Some golfers in this group are long-time veterans who may play a very limited schedule while predominantly playing on the Champions Tour. Others, however, are younger players who could not sustain their early career success and are trying to reclaim a position in a higher group.

Camilo Villegas has four PGA tournament victories, including two in FedEx Cup Playoff tournaments. He entered the 2016–2017 season in the second position within the past champions group. For 2015–2016, Villegas was in the final season of the tournament winners group for his victory at the 2014 Wyndham Championship.

In 2015–2016, Villegas made the cut in 15 of his 27 starts on the PGA Tour. He had two-top 25 finishes, highlighted by a tie for 14th at the Honda Classic. Villegas ended the season 152nd in the FedEx Cup standings with 313 points, only six behind Greg Owen in position number 150. Villegas earned $450,056 and finished 158th on the PGA Tour money list in the 2015–2016 season, the first time since 2012 that Villegas did not participate in the FedEx Cup Playoffs. He participated in the playoffs in eight of the previous nine seasons. His career playoff record includes three appearances in the Tour Championship, a tournament that he won in 2008 by defeating Sergio Garcia on the first playoff hole.

Villegas participated in the Web.com Tour Finals to try to improve his status. He missed the cut in the first two events, and his 34th-place finish at the third tournament earned him only $5,475. That was not nearly enough to advance into the top finishers of the Web.com Tour priority group. For the 2016–2017 season, the difference between Villegas's position in the past champions group and the final position in the top finishers of the Web.com Tour was 25 players. In a starker contrast, the difference compared to the position of Graeme McDowell and Hideki Matsuyama, who both extended their status by winning in 2015–2016 was more than 160 players.

Jonathan Byrd is the winner of five PGA tournaments. His first win was at the 2002 Buick Challenge, when his final-round 63 produced a one-stroke victory over David Toms. His most recent victory was in the 2011 Tournament of Champions, when his par on the second playoff hole defeated Robert Garrigus. Byrd qualified for the Tournament of Champions with a win in the autumn of 2010 at the Shriners Hospitals for Children Open. He also won that tournament in a playoff when he defeated Cameron Percy and Martin Laird, the tournament's defending champion.

In the 2010 Shriners at the second playoff hole, the 17th, Byrd came close to ending the tournament when his 25-foot putt went around the rim of the cup, but did not drop. At the third playoff hole, the 18th, Byrd's approach shot was only a couple of feet from going into the water. He saved par by getting up-and-down from that tricky location, chipping to approximately seven feet and draining the putt. Byrd withstood the four opportunities that Laird had to win the championship with his putter in hand, four failed attempts.

The golfers debated whether to play a fourth extra hole in the growing darkness. They agreed to play one more hole, the 17th. Byrd had the honors. Using a six iron at the 204-yard par-3, Byrd's tee-shot landed on the green, ten feet short of the hole, and miraculously rolled its way to the bottom of the cup. It was the only time on the PGA Tour that a playoff was decided by a hole-in-one. Byrd stated on the broadcast, "I hit it perfect, but for it to go in, that's just luck."

Byrd was ranked third within the past champions group entering the 2015–2016 season. He played in only six PGA Tour events and made the cut in four tournaments, highlighted by a tie for 39th at both the Sanderson Farms Championship and the Puerto Rico Open. He earned $58,655 on the PGA Tour. Byrd did play in 17 regular season tournaments on the Web.com Tour, making the cut in nine, earning $102,899. That amount was well below what was needed to be in the top 25 on the regular season money list to earn his PGA Tour card.

Byrd participated in the three Web.com Finals tournaments, but after missing the cut in the first two events and finishing 18th at the third tournament, earning $12,600, he did not qualify for a PGA Tour card through that path. For the 2016–2017 season, Byrd once again had status as a past champion, 14th within that group.

Starting the 2016–2017 season in the last positions in the past champions group, the 52nd and 53rd spots, were Richard S. Johnson and Brett Wetterich. Neither earned any money in PGA Tour events in the 2015–2016 season. Richard S. Johnson won the 2008 U.S. Bank Championship in Milwaukee by one stroke on the strength of a first-round 63 and a final-round 64. Johnson played in five Web.com Tour events in the 2015–2016 season, missing the cut in four. He earned $3,038 for finishing tied for 36th at the Panama Claro Championship.

Wetterich was the winner of the 2006 Byron Nelson. He played in only one PGA Tour event in the 2015–2016 season, missing the cut in the Valero Texas Open. He played in two tournaments on the Web.com Tour, making the cut in the Chitimacha Louisiana Open, where his tie for 58th earned him $1,446.

Matt Bettencourt, 51st within the past champions group, did earn prize money on the PGA Tour. Bettencourt was the champion of the 2010 Reno-Tahoe Open. He made the cut in one of the five PGA Tour events that he played in 2015–2016. He tied for 81st in the Barbasol Championship to earn $6,195. Bettencourt missed the cut in his only appearance on the Web.com Tour.

15

Veteran Members

If the golfers in the past champions group offer the ultimate stories of redemption on the PGA Tour, it is the veteran members who provide the ultimate stories of perseverance. The veteran members exempt status is the final group in the PGA's priority system. This group consists of golfers who made a minimum of 150 tournament cuts in their career. The golfers are ranked within this group based on their position on the PGA Tour career money list.

The veteran members group is where Greg Chalmers found himself at the beginning of the 2015–2016 season. Chalmers, who turned professional in 1995 and first played in a PGA Tour event in 1998, had two second-place finishes that served as the best PGA tournament performances of his career, one in 2000 and the other in 2009. It must be noted that Chalmers does have five international tournament victories, twice winning the Australian PGA Championship, in 2011 and 2014. For his career, entering the 2015–2016 season, Chalmers earned more than $9.2 million in PGA Tour events.

Chalmers career featured seasons when he had to play exclusively on the Web.com Tour. After finishing 156th on the PGA Tour's money list in 2004, Chalmers played 26 tournaments on the Web.com Tour in 2005. His victory at the 2005 Albertsons Boise Open on the Web.com Tour helped get him back to the PGA Tour. After a 2006 season in which he made the cut in only eight of 28 PGA tournaments, with no top-25 finishes, Chalmers was back playing on the Web.com Tour. He played all of 2007 and 2008 on the Web.com Tour with no appearances in PGA Tour events during those seasons. Again, he showed his resolve as a victory at the Web.com Tour 2008 Henrico County Open, along with 16 top-25 finishes and ten top-ten finishes in 24 tournaments, propelled him back to the PGA Tour.

Chalmers played exclusively on the PGA Tour from 2009 through 2013 and qualified for the FedEx Cup Playoffs each season. Chalmers' PGA Tour career was highlighted by the 2012 season, in which he earned more than $1.16 million. In 2012, Chalmers made the cut in 20 of 25 tournaments, with seven top-25 finishes. He ended the regular season 78th in the FedEx Cup points standings. Chalmers then had his most successful playoff performances. He finished ninth in the Barclays and in a tie for 39th at the Deutsche Bank Championship to advance to the third playoff tournament. He tied for 16th in the BMW Championship and earned $375,000 in the three playoff tournaments, vaulting to 35th in the final FedEx Cup standings, which awarded him a playoff bonus of $142,000.

In 2013, Chalmers advanced to the FedEx Cup Playoffs by finishing number 122 in the regular season points standings. He tied for 37th in the Barclays, earning $36,800, to qualify for the Deutsche Bank Championship. Although he missed the cut in that tournament, Chalmers did end the season in 97th place in the FedEx Cup points standings to earn a playoff bonus of $75,000.

In the 2013–2014 season, however, Chalmers finished just short of qualifying for the FedEx Cup Playoffs, 132nd. Chalmers played in the Web.com Tour Finals, but he did not earn the needed prize money to improve his exempt status group for the following season. He entered the 2014–2015 season in the 126 through 150 finishers in the FedEx Cup points standings group.

Chalmers played in 17 tournaments on the PGA Tour in the 2014–2015 season and made the cut in 12, but he did not have any top 25 finishes. Chalmers also played in two Web.com Tour tournaments, earning less than $3,400. After finishing 177th in the regular season FedEx Cup points standings, Chalmers again played in the Web.com Tour Finals. He had the same result as the previous season, not improving his status and began the 2015–2016 season in the veteran members group.

Chalmers claims that one of the key attributes of a golfer is "how you deal with adversity." He describes golf as a sport with "many fork in the road moments." He says that professional golfers "constantly think that something good is right around the corner." Chalmers, however, approached the 2016 Barracuda Championship in Reno, Nevada, telling his wife Nicole that it might very well be his last PGA Tour event of the year. That season, Chalmers played in six PGA Tour events, but he missed the cut in five. His only made cut was a tie for 58th at the World Golf Championships—HSBC Champions tournament. He earned $44,792 for that effort. He also played in nine Web.com Tour events and made the cut in three, highlighted by a tie for seventh. Chalmers' combined PGA Tour and Web.com Tour prize money was $78,701.

The Barracuda Championship in 2016 was played opposite the World Golf Championships—Bridgestone Invitational in Akron, Ohio, on the weekend of June 30–July 3. The Barracuda Championship is the only tournament on the PGA Tour that uses the modified Stableford scoring system rather than stroke play or match play. In the Stableford system, the objective is to have the highest score. The system rewards excellence on a given hole, while not punishing a golfer too severely if he struggles. The modified Stableford scoring system assigns points based on the outcome of each hole. A par equals zero, a birdie +2, an eagle +5, and a double-eagle +8. A bogey means -1, and a double-bogey or worse is -3. With this scoring system, aggressive play in encouraged and rewarded.

Chalmers' score was +14 after the first round of the 2016 Barracuda Championship, one point behind tournament leader Martin Laird. Chalmers made five birdies over the last eight holes in the second round and finished the day with 10 points. He took the overall lead in the tournament by two points over Laird and Gary Woodland, the 2013 champion of the same tournament (then named the Reno-Tahoe Open). Chalmers posted his best score of the tournament in round three when, after making birdies on five of the last six holes, he finished the day at +15. His total score was +39 for the tournament.

Chalmers took a six-point lead over Woodland and Ben Martin into the final round. Chalmers opened with a bogey on the 1st and 3rd holes. He rebounded with a birdie at the 4th. A bogey on 12 was offset by a birdie on 13. Woodland, meanwhile, birdied the 9th, 13th, and 14th holes. When Chalmers bogeyed the 15th and 17th, he was tied with Woodland, or so he thought.

After finishing the 17th hole, Chalmers saw the large scoreboard behind the green indicating that he and Woodland were tied. The scoreboard, however, had not yet posted Woodland's bogey on the 18th hole to give Chalmers a one-point lead. As Chalmers was about to hit his tee-shot at 18, Robert Dickerson, his caddie, learned that his golfer did indeed have the lead and needed only to par the par-5 18th hole for the victory.

Chalmers birdied the 18th hole in each of the first three rounds of the tournament. Knowing that Chalmers was driving the ball well, Dickerson chose not to tell Chalmers that he was still the tournament leader. It was not until after Chalmers perfectly placed his drive on 18 that Dickerson finally told him the correct tournament score. On his second shot from 210 yards in the altitude of Reno that Chalmers explains was "playing like 180," he delivered another perfect shot as his 7-iron placed him only five feet from the hole. An eagle putt on the 18th hole in his 386th career PGA Tour start gave Chalmers a six-point win and a newfound title for all to call him—PGA tournament champion.

At their home in Texas, Chalmers' wife, Nicole, watched the first nine holes of the final round, but she became so nervous that she went outside and sat on the curb for the remainder of the tournament. She would receive updates from family and friends. After Chalmers' drive put him in the fairway on 18, Nicole finally received a message that she should go inside and watch the conclusion.

Chalmers explains that while the 7-iron to the green appeared to be the more significant shot, considering the pressure he believes the tee-shot was one of the best shots of his career. He states, "the tee shot sets up that hole." After the approach shot sealed his win, Chalmers describes the 200-yard walk to the green as one of the greatest feelings. He adds that it was difficult for him to control his emotions as he thought about his journey from the start of his career and having his dream as a child finally fulfilled.

The victory gave Chalmers the highest tournament earning for his two-decade career as he claimed the $576,000 winner's share. His previous high was second place at the 2009 Buick Open, when he took home $380,800.

The win came with one additional unexpected opportunity. When the Greenbrier Classic, scheduled to conclude on Sunday, July 10, was canceled due to heavy rain and flooding that damaged the West Virginia golf course, the final spot in The Open Championship which was to be awarded to the top finisher at the Greenbrier was instead awarded to the top finisher at the Barracuda. For the fourth time in his career, Chalmers would play in The Open Championship. Despite finishing 81st, Chalmers earned $18,331 in a major tournament that he was not expected to compete in.

For the rest of the 2015–2016 regular season after the Barracuda Championship, instead of playing in Web.com Tour events, Chalmers played in five PGA tournaments. He made the cut in four, only missing the cut at the PGA Championship. Chalmers earned $74,396 in PGA Tour events that he might not have even qualified for. The 300 FedEx Cup points accumulated for his win helped Chalmers achieve a final placement of 142 in the standings to earn a $32,000 bonus.

As for the 2016–2017 season, with the tournament winners exempt status, Chalmers would get to play in tournaments that he would not have if he remained in the veteran members exempt status group. Although it would appear that there would be less pressure entering the season, Chalmers contends that his day-to-day approach as a competitor is the same and that it is still bothersome when he misses a cut, knowing that "you failed in what you were trying to do. You didn't play well enough to get in the mix and win the tournament." Chalmers also says that there is something about a golfer which insures that he "can't be happy. Nothing is ever quite good enough. You could always be one shot better." He explains that in a tournament, "one guy is genuinely happy. The others are all wishing they had one shot different." He then adds that you can extrapolate that sentiment to an entire season and an entire career.

Chalmers made the cut in nine of his 29 starts in the 2016–2017 season. His season was highlighted by a tie for 17th at the Arnold Palmer Invitation. For the season, Chalmers earned $344,631 and was 173rd in the FedEx Cup standings. With the victory at the Barracuda Championship in 2016, Chalmers entered 2017–2018 in his final season in the tournament winners group.

Brendon de Jonge is another golfer who began the 2016–2017 season with a veteran member status. de Jonge competed in at least 30 PGA tournaments in the seven seasons between 2010 and 2016. From 2010 through 2015, he qualified for the FedEx Cup Playoffs, reaching the Tour Championship in 2013. That result provided de Jonge entry into his only Masters, in 2014, where he finished in a tie for 37th. de Jonge won more than $9.98 million in prize money from 2010 through 2015.

In 2010, de Jonge earned more than $2.18 million on the strength of three third-place finishes. He made 24 cuts in 30 tournament starts in that season. He also earned more than $2 million in 2012, when he made the cut in 27 of his 31 tournament appearances. The 2012 season included a second-place finish at the Shriners Hospitals for Children Open. He opened that tournament with a 62, but he was one stroke behind Ryan Moore. The two would be in contention throughout the tournament. It was a Moore birdie on the 16th hole in the final round that provided the one-stroke victory over de Jonge.

de Jonge also had a second-place finish at the McGladrey Classic in October 2014, losing in a playoff to Robert Streb. The 2014–2015 season was the last time that de Jonge qualified for the FedEx Cup Playoffs. He had 31 starts, with 22 made cuts and nine top-25 finishes. In addition to the second-place effort at the McGladrey, de Jonge tied for fifth at the Shell Houston Open and for tenth at the Puerto Rico Open. He completed the season 48th in the FedEx Cup standings. After missing the cut in the first playoff tournament, he finished tied for 22nd and tied for 32nd. He earned over $1.59 million in prize money as well as a bonus of $128,000.

In 2015–2016, de Jonge once again made 30 tournament starts, but this season was not as successful. He made the cut in 11 tournaments, with only two finishes in the top 25. He ended up 156th in the FedEx Cup standings. His 304 points were 15 behind Greg Owen in the 150th position, a threshold that would have provided a bonus and status for the following season. de Jonge did earn $415,583. He competed in the Web.com Tour Finals, but he missed one cut and he withdrew from two others. His status for the 2016–2017 now became as a veteran member.

The 2016–2017 season produced 14 PGA Tour starts but de Jonge made the cut in only two. He tied for 26th at the Sanderson Farms Championship and for 71st, MDF, at the Shell Houston Open. He played in four regular season Web.com Tour events, but he missed the cut in all. de Jonge earned $54,773 in prize money. He once again started the 2017–2018 season as a veteran member with a career of 284 tournament starts and 185 made cuts. He won more than $11.4 million in career prize money.

16

The Autumn Tournaments

For the golfers who do not have an exempt status that allows them entrance into all PGA Tour regular season tournaments, navigating the schedule is very much about recognizing the prime opportunities to compete. Three types of tournaments provide the prime opportunities to play when higher-ranked golfers might not be competing. The autumn tournaments, when many golfers take time off after a grueling regular season and the FedEx Cup Playoffs, begin only a couple of weeks after the Tour Championship. Next, four PGA tournaments are played opposite the three World Golf Championships events and The Open Championship. Finally, tournaments played in the weeks leading up to and the week after a major represent another opportunity when higher-ranked golfers might not play. For any golfer in a lower group, gaining entrance into a PGA tournament presents the opportunity to alter his career. However, with fewer opportunities to play, those limited tournament entrances amplify the pressure to perform well.

In the autumn that started the 2015–2016 regular season, there were seven tournaments played over six consecutive weekends. The season began with the Frys.com Open from Napa, California, on the weekend of October 18. The Frys.com tournament was followed by the Shriners Hospitals for Children Open from Las Vegas and the CIMB Classic in Malaysia. In week four, there were two tournaments, the World Golf Championships—HSBC Champions in Shanghai, China, and the Sanderson Farms Championship in Jackson, Mississippi. The following week was the OHL Classic at Mayakoba from Playa del Carmen, Mexico. The autumn portion of the PGA Tour regular season concluded with the RSM Classic at St. Simons Island, Georgia, on the weekend of November 22.

In the 2015–2016 regular season, of the 30 golfers who comprised the field in the Tour Championship, only seven competed in the Frys.com tournament and only eight in the Shriners tournament. The CIMB Classic in Asia had 11 golfers from the Tour Championship field, and the World Golf Champions—HSBC Champions tournament had 17. This tournament might be the best opportunity to win a World Golf Championships event, as some of the top golfers inevitably do not travel to Asia. This autumn event is also an especially important opportunity considering that the winner gets an exempt status as a World Golf Championships tournament winner, which is for the current season and the following three seasons.

The same weekend as the World Golf Championships tournament, no golfers from the Tour Championship field participated in the Sanderson Farms Championship. The OHL Classic in Mexico, one week after the World Golf Championships in China, had only three golfers from the Tour Championship field competing. The final tournament of the autumn season, the RSM Classic, had seven golfers from the Tour Championship. Some of the top golfers did not participate in any of the 2015 autumn tournaments, including Phil Mickelson and Jason Day. Others participated in only one tournament, such as Dustin Johnson, Jordan Spieth, and Jimmy Walker.

Some golfers who had successful seasons in 2014–2015 used the autumn schedule to propel their 2015–2016 seasons. Justin Thomas earned more than $2.2 million in 2014–2015 and finished the season 32nd in the final FedEx Cup points standings. He was 36th entering the playoffs, but he was not able to crack the top 30 and, thus, did not compete in the Tour Championship. Thomas was awarded a playoff bonus of $155,000.

To begin the 2015–2016 regular season, Thomas participated in four autumn tournaments. He tied for third place in the season-opening Frys.com tournament. After taking a week off, Thomas got his first career PGA tournament win with a one-shot victory over Adam Scott in the CIMB Classic in Malaysia. Thomas birdied the 15th through 17th holes in the final round to secure the victory. His 61 in the second round set a new course record, and his 26 under par set the tournament record in relation to par.

Thomas earned more than $1.2 million, 500 FedEx Cup points, an exempt status in the tournament winners priority group through 2017–2018, and entrance into January's Tournament of Champions for the win. Thomas concluded his autumn season with a tie for 27th in the World Golf Championships—HSBC Champions and, after a week off, a tie for 58th in the RSM Classic.

Including his autumn performances, Thomas made the cut in 22 of 28 tournaments. He had ten top-25 finishes, with seven in the top ten and four in the top three. He ended the 2015–2016 regular season tenth in the FedEx Cup points standings. Thomas earned just over $4.1 million—almost $2 million more than he won in the previous season. Thomas got to compete in the Tour Championship for the first time in his career and tied for sixth place to earn $297,500. He earned a bonus of $290,000 for his 12th-place finish in the final FedEx Cup points standings.

Kevin Kisner also used the autumn tournaments to start his successful 2015–2016 regular season. Unlike Justin Thomas, Kisner did participate in the Tour Championship in 2015. He did not win a tournament in 2014–2015, but in 30 starts, including the playoffs, he had three second-place finishes. He lost each time in a playoff. Overall, he had ten top-25 and six top-ten finishes. Kisner earned more than $3.56 million as well as a playoff bonus of $220,000.

Kisner did not participate in the Frys.com tournament before playing in four autumn events in the 2015–2016 season. He tied for 25th at the Shriners Hospitals for Children Open before traveling to Asia for the CIMB Classic and the World Golf Championships—HSBC Champions. At the CIMB Classic, he finished 37th. At the World Golf Championships—HSBC, he came in second for the fourth time in his PGA Tour career, losing to Russell Knox by two strokes.

After skipping the OHL Classic in Mexico, Kisner broke through as a PGA tournament champion. He won the RSM Classic by shooting 22 under par in a commanding six-stroke victory. Kisner posted rounds of 65–67–64–64 at the par-72 course to set the tournament record by four strokes. Kisner had only two bogeys over 72 holes. In his 109th tournament start, Kisner's first PGA tournament victory earned him just over $1 million, the highest tournament earning for his career. He was awarded 500 FedEx Cup points and an exempt status as a tournament winner through the 2017–2018 season. In the last event of the autumn portion of the season, Kisner secured the final slot in January's Tournament of Champions, where he finished ninth to earn $178,000 and 80 FedEx Cup points.

Overall, in the 2015–2016 season, Kisner participated in 27 tournaments and made the cut in 22. Including his victory and his second-place finish, Kisner had ten top-25 finishes and six top-ten finishes. He ended the season 20th on the PGA Tour money list for the second consecutive season, earning more than $3.4 million. Kisner finished the FedEx Cup playoffs in the 23rd position and was awarded a $210,000 bonus.

Several golfers used the autumn portion of the regular season essentially to launch their PGA Tour careers. Nick Taylor entered the WinCo Foods Portland Open in 2014 in the precarious 74th position on the Web.com Tour prize money list. A tie for 26th allowed Taylor to move up to 69th to qualify for the Finals, where he went on to earn his PGA Tour card. Taylor began the 2014–2015 season 37th in the top finishers of the Web.com Tour group.

Taylor had not played in any PGA Tour events in the 2013–2014 season. One of the benefits of an autumn victory is the dramatic shift in the type of tournaments a golfer gets to play. After he won the Sanderson Farms Championship in the autumn of 2014, Taylor played in 28 PGA Tour events in 2014–2015. Taylor has not played in any Web.com Tour events since the Sanderson Farms victory.

In the autumn of the 2015–2016 season, there were six first-time winners on the PGA Tour. Emiliano Grillo, Smylie Kaufman, and Peter Malnati participated in only five, two, and one PGA tournament respectively in the 2014–2015 season. The autumn tournament winners shifted their exempt status from the top finishers of the Web.com Tour group to the tournament winners group. That jump moved them ahead of 90 to 100 golfers in the priority selection process. Grillo, Kaufman, and Malnati now had that tournament winners exempt status through the 2017–2018 season.

Grillo won the season-opening Frys.com tournament in a playoff over Kevin Na when he birdied the second extra hole. At age 23, it was Grillo's first victory in his seventh PGA Tour event, but it was his first tournament as an official member of the Tour. The last golfer to win his first tournament was Russell Henley, who won the 2013 Sony Open. Grillo earned more than $1 million and 500 FedEx Cup points for the win.

Grillo participated in 25 PGA Tour events in 2015–2016. Beside his victory, the high point was a tie for second place, along with Sean O'Hair, in a one-stroke loss to Patrick Reed in the Barclays. Grillo earned $748,000 for that tournament. He entered the playoffs 32nd in the FedEx Cup standings, but on the strength of his performance in the Barclays, along with a tie for 33rd at the Deutsche Bank Championship and a tie for 32nd at the BMW Championship, he advanced to the Tour Championship. A tie for tenth in the Tour Championship earned Grillo $218,620 of his season total of more than $3.37 million. He ended the season 11th in the final FedEx Cup points standings and was awarded a bonus of $300,000. Grillo won the 2016 PGA Tour "Rookie of the Year" Award.

Peter Malnati scored a one-stroke victory over William McGirt and David Toms in the 2015 Sanderson Farms Championship when he posted a final-round, five under par 67. He earned $738,000 and 300 FedEx Cup points. After a 2015 season in which he played in 24 tournaments on the Web.com Tour, Malnati played 31 regular season tournaments on the PGA Tour in 2015–2016. He made ten cuts, with four top-25 finishes and three top-tens.

The Sanderson Farms Championship was one of five autumn tournaments Malnati played. He made the cut in four. Malnati earned $900,193 and 377 FedEx Cup points during that portion of the season. At the Tournament of

Champions, he tied for sixth to take home an additional $202,333 and 92 FedEx Cup points. These performances helped Malnati endure a stretch from the middle of February through early August in which he missed the cut in 18 of 19 tournaments. His only made cut during that stretch was a tie for 13th at the Valero Texas Open that earned him $103,075 and 55 FedEx Cup points. Malnati completed the season with earnings of more than $1.29 million.

Largely on the strength of his victory at the Sanderson Farms Championship, Malnati finished the season at number 93 in the FedEx Cup regular season points standings. He accumulated 596 points. Had Malnati added two more strokes and finished behind McGirt and Toms in the Sanderson Farms Championship, instead of obtaining 300 FedEx Cup points, he would have received only 105 points for that tournament. The difference of 195 points would have dropped his points total to 401, which would have put him 137th in the standings and out of the FedEx Cup Playoffs. Malnati only qualified to participate in the first playoff tournament, a tie for 78th. He finished 104th in the final FedEx Cup points standings to earn a $70,000 bonus.

The autumn season again featured seven tournaments played over six consecutive weekends in the 2016–2017 PGA Tour regular season. Of the 30 golfers who comprised the field in the Tour Championship from the 2015–2016 season, only eight played in the season's first tournament, the Safeway Open (renamed as Safeway replaced the previous year's sponsor, Frys.com). Aside from the World Golf Championships tournament, the other autumn tournaments had even fewer top golfers. Only five golfers from the Tour Championship played in the Shriners Hospitals for Children Open and the OHL Classic at Mayakoba, with seven playing in the RSM Classic. There were 23 golfers in the World Golf Championships—HSBC Championship, once again held the same weekend as the Sanderson Farms Championship. Similar to the previous season, several top golfers opted not to participate in autumn tournaments. Jason Day and Jordan Spieth did not compete in any autumn tournaments. Rory Mcllroy and Dustin Johnson competed only in the World Golf Championships tournament. Brandt Snedeker and Phil Mickelson each played in only one autumn tournament.

Obviously, playing in the autumn does not guarantee season or career-altering results. After all, only one player can be the tournament winner. However, not winning a tournament during this portion of the season does not lessen the opportunity to contribute to a season's success. For example, both Charles Howell III and Luke List entered the 2016–2017 season with an exempt status in the top 125 of the FedEx Cup standings group. Both Howell and List competed in five tournaments in the 2016 autumn schedule.

Howell made the cut in four tournaments, with three finishes in the top

15, including a tie for seventh at the OHL Classic at Mayakoba. Howell accumulated 199 points of his regular season total of 1,102 in the autumn. He also earned $438,757 in these autumn tournaments. Howell went on to make the cut in 20 of 23 tournaments, with ten top-25 and five top-ten finishes. He made it to the BMW Championship in the playoffs and completed the season earning more than $2.6 million. He received a bonus of $135,000 for finishing 40th in the final FedEx Cup standings.

List made the cut in all five of his autumn appearances. He had four of his season's nine top-25 finishes and two of his three top-ten finishes in the autumn tournaments. List tied for second at the Sanderson Farms Championship, winning $313,600 and 117 points, and tied for seventh at the OHL Classic at Mayakoba, winning $218,167 and 85 points. List earned $765,190 and accumulated 329 of his regular season total of 741 points in the autumn. These results helped List overcome a stretch of the season where he made the cut in only two of nine tournaments, from the RBC Heritage that ended on April 16 through the Greenbrier Classic that ended on July 9. Overall, List made the cut in 20 of his 31 appearances. He made it to the BMW Championship in the playoffs. List completed the season earning more than $1.81 million and received a bonus of $125,000 for finishing 50th in the FedEx Cup standings.

As in the previous season, a pattern of career-changing results occurred during the autumn portion of the 2016–2017 PGA Tour. The winners would all make it to at least the second round of the playoffs in the 2016–2017 season. Justin Thomas again used the autumn to begin a season that culminated with him lifting the FedEx Cup Championship trophy. After finishing eighth in the season-opening Safeway Open, Thomas returned to the CIMB Classic in the autumn of 2016 and successfully defended his championship with a three-stroke victory over Hideki Matsuyama. Thomas then competed in the World Golf Championships—HSBC Championship, where he finished 23rd.

It was his win at the CIMB Classic that qualified Thomas for the 2017 Tournament of Champions. Thomas tied for 21st in the 2016 Tournament of Champions, but in 2017 Thomas claimed victory when he defeated Matsuyama by three strokes. He earned more than $1.2 million for his Tournament of Champions win.

Thomas continued his torrid play the following week with a record-setting performance at the Sony Open in Honolulu, Hawaii, a first-round 59. After three birdies on the first four holes, his three under par round quickly became seven under when he eagled both the 9th and 10th holes. After a bogey at the par-3 11th hole, Thomas responded with five birdies on the back nine. Thomas followed his first-round 59 with rounds of 64–65–65 to shoot 27 under par and earn a seven-stroke victory over Justin Rose. His four-round stroke total of 253 eclipsed Tommy Armour III's 254 at the Texas Open in 2003 for the lowest 72-hole score in PGA Tour history. Thomas also became the first player since Ernie Els in 2003 to win both of the Hawaii tournaments.

By the time the Sony Open concluded on January 15, 2017, Thomas made the cut in all five tournaments in which he participated. He won three and had another finish in the top ten. Thomas amassed $3.8 million in earnings and 1,614 FedEx Cup points, and already secured his return trip to the following year's Tournament of Champions.

Hideki Matsuyama would play in only two autumn tournaments in 2016. The week after his second-place loss to Thomas at the CIMB Classic, Matsuyama had a dominating seven-stroke victory over Henrik Stenson and Daniel Berger at the World Golf Championships—HSBC Champions tournament. Matsuyama shot rounds of 66–65–68–66. In only two tournaments, with his outstanding performances, Matsuyama earned just under $2.4 million.

While Thomas and Matsuyama were coming off seasons in which they finished in the top 11 of the PGA Tour money list (Matsuyama, 9; Thomas, 11) and the top 13 of the final FedEx Cup points standings (Thomas, 12; Matsuyama, 13), other players used the autumn tournaments to improve their exempt status priority ranking group. Three golfers returned to being tournament champions after years without a victory, Rod Pampling, Pat Perez, and Brendan Steele. The autumn tournaments also produced two first-time PGA Tour champions, Mackenzie Hughes and Cody Gribble.

Brendan Steele's jump in the priority list was not as significant as the other golfers in altering the prospects of their season and their career. Steele entered the season with an exempt status after he finished 63rd in the FedEx Cup points standings. Steele had a one-stroke win over Patrick Kizzire at the season-opening Safeway Open, his first PGA Tour victory since the 2011 Valero Texas Open. With the victory, the greater significance for Steele than the jump in the priority order in that current season was the security of being in the tournament winners group for the remainder of the season and the following two seasons.

Mackenzie Hughes played on the Web.com Tour in the 2016 season. In the third-to-last regular season tournament, Hughes poured in a birdie putt on the 72nd hole to win the Web.com Tour's Price Cutter Charity Championship by one stroke. He held off Richy Werenski, who eagled the same hole. The win earned Hughes $121,000, and his earnings of $167,369 put him 17th on the Web.com Tour regular season prize money list. Hughes earned another $42,070 in the Web.com Tour Finals, with $36,500 coming from his tie for fifth at the Albertsons Boise Open. Hughes started the 2016–2017 season ranked 28th in the top finishers of the Web.com Tour priority group.

Hughes played in four PGA Tour events, but he had yet to make a cut.

His rookie season on the PGA Tour started well. Hughes shot under 70 in all four rounds at the first tournament of the regular season, the Safeway Open, tying for 13th to earn $120,000 and 58 FedEx Cup points. He made the cut in his next two tournaments before missing the cut at the OHL Classic. With the top finishers of the Web.com Tour group reordered after the autumn schedule, making three cuts, including a tie for 13th significantly improve the prospects of playing in PGA Tour events during that season.

The week after the OHL Classic was the RSM Classic from St. Simons Island, Georgia, the final tournament of the autumn, where Hughes made any concerns about a reordering moot. Playing the par-70 Seaside Course in the opening round, Hughes put nine birdies on his scorecard in shooting a 61 for a one-stroke lead over Jonathan Byrd and Stewart Cink. A second-round 67 at the par-72 Plantation Course grew his lead by an additional stroke, two shots better than C. T. Pan.

The third and fourth rounds were played back at the Seaside Course. It was not until the 11th hole in round three, a streak of 46 holes, that Hughes put the first blemish on his scorecard. The result at that hole, however, was a triple-bogey seven. It was the same hole that Hughes birdied only two days earlier. Hughes' third-round 68 kept him in the lead, but it was trimmed to one stroke. There were three golfers just off the lead, Pan, Billy Horschel, and Camilo Villegas.

In competing for the tournament championship, Hughes points out that the victory on the Web.com Tour was a big help in that he knew to remain calm and just continue doing the same things that put him in contention for the win. Hughes explains that the rookie year on the PGA Tour is about getting a sense of Tour life and what the golf courses are like. He describes that playing on the PGA Tour is "different golf." Hughes' final score in his victory on the Web.com Tour was 24 under par. He points out that that type of score does not happen often on the PGA Tour. Hughes explains that when playing on the PGA Tour, a golfer has to learn to be patient and understand that on occasion "par is a great score." He adds that a golfer has to learn to "manage the course, to hang in there, and that a golfer can have an over par round and still be in it."

Hughes shot even par through the first 13 holes in the fourth round of the RSM Classic, including a bogey at the same 11th hole that derailed his round the previous day. Hughes birdied the 14th hole on his way to a final-round, one under par, 69. He was being caught by four other golfers. Horschel and Villegas made up the one stroke that they needed to tie. Horschel shot three under on the back nine, while Villegas birdied the 16th and 17th holes. Blayne Barber and Henrik Norlander came from further back to complete the five-player group that went to the playoff. Barber was three shots behind Hughes starting the day. He birdied the 14th and 15th holes to tie for the lead. Norlander was four strokes behind Hughes and birdied 18 to join the quintet in the playoff.

All of the golfers survived the first extra hole, with Horschel eliminated on the second playoff hole. Play was then suspended due to darkness. The four remaining golfers returned to the course on Monday morning to determine the tournament champion. Only one hole was needed. At the par-3, 192-yard 17th, a hole Hughes parred three times, he made another three when he converted a putt from just off the edge of the green. The others missed their tying putts, the last being Villegas, who was hoping to make the huge jump from the past champions group to the tournament winners group.

In only his ninth PGA Tour start, and two days before his 26th birthday, Hughes was a tournament champion. He earned $1.08 million and 500 FedEx Cup points. In the last tournament of the autumn, Hughes became the final golfer to qualify for the Tournament of Champions, where he tied for 25th to earn $70,000 and 34 FedEx Cup points.

Hughes competed in 31 tournaments and made the cut in 22 in the 2016–2017 season. He had nine top-25 finishes and one top ten, a tie for tenth at the AT&T Pebble Beach Pro-Am. He entered the FedEx Cup Playoffs 34th in the standings. After a tie for 62nd at the Northern Trust, Hughes finished the Dell Technologies Championship in a tie for 13th. He earned $159,250 in that tournament. A tie for 44th at the BMW Championship left Hughes 36th in the standings and out of the Tour Championship. Hughes earned $206,763 in the playoff tournaments and collected a bonus of $140,000. For the season, Hughes earned more than $2.35 million, a substantial increase from the $209,439 that he earned on the Web.com Tour in the previous season.

Mackenzie Hughes was not the only rookie golfer whose career quickly changed in the autumn of the 2016–2017 regular season. Cody Gribble's young career had already seen some close calls. In the 2015 season, Gribble made 16 of 24 cuts in Web.com Tour events and two cuts in four PGA Tour events. He finished 27th on the regular season Web.com Tour money list, just missing out on obtaining his PGA Tour card by $1,067. He would return to the Web.com Tour for the 2016 season.

At the Web.com Tour's United Leasing Championship in 2016, a bogey by Gribble on the 17th hole and a birdie by Seamus Power on 17 created a tie for the tournament lead. After Power parred the par-4 18th hole, the opening was there for Gribble to birdie and win his first Web.com tournament. Gribble was in the middle of the fairway on 18 for his second shot. His ball hit approximately five feet from the flagstick. Seeing Gribble's ball land, announcer Craig

Perks exclaimed, "what a shot!" However, the seemingly perfect shot bounced and began spinning away from the cup. Perks pleaded, "stay right there. Be careful." The ball rolled off the green, down a steep bank, and into the water. Victory could now only be obtained by chipping in on his next shot and defeating Power in a playoff.

That was not the result, but in showing the tremendous resolve needed for a professional golfer, after taking his drop, Gribble got up-and-down to secure a bogey and preserve his spot in a three-way tie for second place. Gribble earned $44,800. The next place prize money was $24,000. Seamus Power took home the top prize of $108,000. For the regular season, Gribble made the cut in only nine of 24 tournaments on the Web.com Tour. His $89,000 in prize money put him once again outside of the top 25 on the money list.

The Web.com Tour Finals in 2016 offered Gribble the final opportunity of the season to earn his PGA Tour Card. Gribble missed the cut in the first two tournaments. In the third, Gribble found redemption to his season. He shot rounds of 70–70–69 leading into the final 18 holes. A seven-hole stretch from the 6th through the 12th in which Gribble played seven under par, five birdies and one eagle, changed the entire outcome of his season. Gribble posted a final-round 67 and tied for fifth place. He earned $35,125 and moved from being tied for the 84th position to 19th on the Web.com Tour Finals money list.

When the fourth tournament of the Web.com Tour Finals was canceled due to Hurricane Matthew, the three Finals tournaments determined which golfers would receive their tour card. Gribble earned his PGA Tour card for the 2016–2017 season, finishing $7,700 ahead Tim Wilkinson in 25th and $8,092 ahead of the 26th-place finisher, Rob Oppenheim. By finishing 19th, after the alternate ordering of the Tour card recipients, Gribble entered the 2016–2017 season 40th within the top finishers of the Web.com Tour priority group.

Gribble's 2016–2017 autumn season began with a trip to Napa, California, hoping to gain entrance into the Safeway Open. When he arrived, Gribble believed that he would have to play in the Monday qualifying round to gain entrance into the main tournament starting on Thursday. While having break-fast on Monday morning, he received a call from the PGA Tour office telling him that he made the main tournament field and would not have to play in that day's qualifier. Gribble capitalized on the opportunity by posting rounds of 67–69–70–68 to finish that tournament at 14 under par, tying for eighth place along with Phil Mickelson, Justin Thomas, and Chris Kirk, four shots back of tournament champion Brendan Steele.

The finish was significant for Gribble for many reasons, starting with the prize money of $162,000. Gribble felt secure that his improved positioning after the autumn reordering would get him into many PGA tournaments. The Dallas native was especially excited about the opportunity to play in his hometown tournament, the AT&T Byron Nelson, as well as the other tournaments played in Texas. Gribble says of his start to the regular season, "the pressure was off immediately."

Two weeks later at the Sanderson Farms Championship, held opposite the World Golf Championships—HSBC Champions tournament, Gribble "played stress free." Even after an opening round of 73, Gribble felt confident. He texted his swing coach, Randy Smith, that he felt he was just a little fast with his swing, and if he could slow it down and control it a little more, he could score very well. Gribble responded with rounds of 63–67–65. He recorded 22 birdies and only one bogey in rounds two through four. His play was highlighted by six birdies in a nine-hole stretch in round two, finishing round three with birdies on three of the last five holes, and playing the fourth round at seven under par with five birdies on the back nine. His final tournament score of 20 under par was four strokes better than Greg Owen, Luke List, and Chris Kirk. Gribble's win at the Sanderson Farms Championship marked the third straight year that the winner of that event was a first-time PGA tournament winner.

The win was Gribble's first individual tournament victory since high school. He never won on the Web.com Tour, and despite a career at the University of Texas highlighted by being on the 2012 national championship team that included Jordan Spieth, never won an individual tournament as a Longhorn. Gribble earned $756,000 and 300 FedEx Cup points for the Sanderson Farms win.

With the victory occurring in the third week of the season, Gribble's win essentially gave him a three-season exempt status in the tournament winners group. Practically speaking, Gribble simply points out that the tournament win gives him a "steady job for the next couple of years."

Gribble now qualified for all other regular season events, including the Tournament of Champions, where he tied for 14th to earn $122,000 and 55 FedEx Cup points. By the end of the Tournament of Champions, played on the seventh tournament weekend of the 2016–2017 season, Gribble already amassed 481 FedEx Cup points, easily enough for entrance in the FedEx Cup Playoffs, as the 125th place points total that season was 365.

Gribble appeared in 28 tournaments with 17 made cuts in the 2016–2017 season. He had four top-25 finishes and two in the top ten. Gribble completed the regular season 89th in the FedEx Cup points standings. In the playoffs, Gribble missed the cut at the Northern Trust but remained within the top 100 threshold to advance into the second playoff tournament. He tied for 30th at the Dell Technologies Championship to earn $54,338. Gribble's season concluded with a $75,000 bonus for finishing 87th in the FedEx Cup standings. For the season, he earned more than $1.3 million in prize money. The 2017–2018 season was Gribble's first full season in the tournament winners group.

17

The Opposite-Field
Tournaments

A victory at the Sanderson Farms Championship in the autumn portion of the regular season is noteworthy for one other reason—the win occurs in one of the opposite tournaments on the PGA Tour. While certainly not viewed with the same prestige as other tournaments by the casual sports fan, for many golfers they provide the most significant opportunities to change the trajectory of their career.

These opposite tournaments do have lesser value in terms of prize money, FedEx Cup points (only 300 points are awarded to the winner as opposed to 500 points), and the winner does not get immediate admission into majors and World Golf Championship events. However, winning any PGA Tour event carries significant meaning and opportunities. Most notably, a golfer who wins an opposite tournament acquires the same multi-year exempt status as any other regular season tournament winner. The fact that the fields for these opposite tournaments might not feature many highly-ranked players is completely immaterial. In actuality, it only makes the opportunity more significant. Greg Chalmers, winner of the 2016 Barracuda Championship, describes the opposite tournaments as "the weeks where guys can change their situation, change their career." Ian Poulter, who entering the 2016–2017 season earned more than $18 million on the PGA Tour and is the winner of two World Golf Championships tournaments, explained, "I think these events are important. Obviously, it's very difficult to schedule so many tournaments in a calendar year, and when you've got an event opposite WGC's or other events, it gives a playing opportunity to other players and enables the Tour to continue to expand and grow."

Several of the PGA Tour's top golfers had their first tournament victory at an opposite event. For example, Chris Kirk won his first tournament in July 2011, during his first full regular season on the PGA Tour. He won the Viking Classic, the tournament that is now the Sanderson Farms Championship, when it was played opposite The Open Championship. Kirk has now won four PGA tournaments, including a FedEx Cup Playoff tournament in 2014. Kirk qualified for the FedEx Cup Playoffs in every season since 2011. In 2014, he finished second in the final FedEx Cup standings to Billy Horschel and collected a playoff bonus of $3 million.

The winners of the opposite tournaments are obviously going to alter their careers significantly because of the dramatic improvement of their priority ranking group. After all, the reason that these golfers are playing in an opposite tournament rather than the more elite PGA Tour event is that they were in a lower-ranked group. In 2015–2016, Tony Finau, winner of the Puerto Rico Open, moved up from the top 125 of the FedEx Cup standings priority ranking group. Peter Malnati, winner of the Sanderson Farms Championship, moved up from the top finishers of the Web.com Tour group. Aaron Baddeley, winner of the Barbasol Championship, made a significant jump when he advanced past as many as 165 to 170 golfers from the past champions group to the tournament winners group. Greg Chalmers, winner of the Barracuda Championship, moved from the last group in the priority ranking system, the veteran members group, to the tournament winners group. For Finau, Malnati, and Chalmers, the victory also provided them with their highest tournament earning for their career. Baddeley earned more than $1.1 million for his victory at Riviera in 2011.

No player took advantage of participating in the opposite tournaments in the 2015–2016 season as much as Baddeley. He was awarded $630,000 for his win at the Barbasol Championship. After the second round at the Barbasol, Baddeley found himself 11 shots off the lead. He closed to within three strokes after round three when he shot a 64, with nine birdies and two bogeys. In the final round, Baddeley shot a five under par 66 to force a playoff with Si Woo Kim. The tournament was not decided until the fourth extra hole, when Baddeley made a 28-foot birdie putt for the win. His combined earnings through his participation in all four opposite tournaments was $919,570. His total prize money for all 28 PGA Tour events in the 2015–2016 regular season was more than $1.64 million.

Baddeley earned 436 FedEx Cup points through the four opposite tournaments. His FedEx Cup points total for all PGA tournaments was 874, in 45th place in the regular season standings. Baddeley missed the cut in the Barclays, tied for 67th in the Deutsche Bank Championship, and tied for 61st in the BMW Championship. Though he did not qualify for the Tour Championship,

Baddeley ended the FedEx Cup Playoffs in 69th place to receive a bonus of $110,000.

With four opportunities in these opposite events, even having one good performance can catapult a season. Steve Marino does not have a PGA Tour win in his career, with his career-best finishes being a loss in a playoff in 2009 and 2016. Marino played in all four opposite tournaments in 2015–2016. He did not make the cut in the Sanderson Farms Championship. He lost on the third playoff hole to Tony Finau in the Puerto Rico Open. Marino earned $324,000 at that tournament. He won just over $15,000 for his performance in the Barracuda Championship and the Barbasol Championship, when he tied for 35th in both events. Marino earned $354,758 at the four opposite tournaments of his season total of $768,200 that was compiled in all 24 PGA tournaments that he played.

Marino tied for eighth in the John Deere Classic, earning $124,000, and a 12th-place finish in the AT&T Byron Nelson earned $138,000. His prize money total placed him 120th on the official PGA Tour money list, the performance measure that provided Marino with his exempt status for the 2016–2017 season. Marino acquired 276 of his season total 429 FedEx Cup points in the opposite tournaments. He ended the regular season 130th in the FedEx Cup points standings, 35 points behind Seung-Yul Noh, who qualified for the final playoff position. Marino did take home a $32,000 bonus.

In 2016–2017, Marino was able to make only 15 tournament starts due to injury. He made the cut in five and earned $98,573. He began the 2017–2018 season on a major medical extension. He had ten tournaments to accumulate 320 points, which when added to his 2016–2017 points total of 45 would equal the 125th position, the 365 points total of J.J. Henry.

Even veteran players with stellar careers continue to exploit the opportunities of the opposite tournaments. David Toms' career features 13 PGA tournament victories, including the 2001 PGA Championship with a one-stroke victory over Phil Mickelson. Toms finished the season in the top ten on the PGA Tour prize money list on five occasions. Toms was seventh on the career money list with more than $41 million in prize money entering the 2015–2016 season.

In 2015–2016, Toms, along with William McGirt, finished one stroke behind Peter Malnati at the Sanderson Farms Championship. Toms earned $360,800 for that performance. Toms also participated in the Puerto Rico Open, earning $11,400 for his tie for 39th, and the Barbasol Championship, where he took home $65,333 after a tie for 11th. He did not play in the Barracuda Championship. Toms' combined earnings in the four opposite tournaments totaled $437,533. His regular season total in all 19 PGA starts was $774,592.

Toms earned 135 FedEx Cup points for his second-place finish in the Sanderson Farms Championship. He added 49 points in the other opposite tournaments. His season total of 454 points was good for 124th place in the standings. Toms did play in the first playoff tournament, but he did not make the cut. He earned a $70,000 bonus for qualifying for the FedEx Cup Playoffs.

Toms appeared in only three PGA Tour events in 2016–2017. He missed two cuts and finished in a tie for 50th at the Sanderson Farms Championship, earning $9,984. He did compete in 22 tournaments on the Champions Tour. He made the cut in 21 events, with 15 top-25 finishes, seven top-tens, and one third-place performance. Toms won $925,818 in prize money.

The 2015–2016 regular season schedule did offer one additional unique opportunity to play in an "opposite" PGA event when some of the top golfers were not competing, as the John Deere Classic was played during the Olympics golf tournament. Only four of the golfers who competed in the Tour Championship in the previous season were part of the John Deere Classic field. Ryan Moore won the tournament with a two-shot victory over Ben Martin. Moore's fifth PGA Tour victory earned him $840,000.

On the weekend concluding on Sunday, March 26, 2017, the PGA held the World Golf Championships—Dell Match Play, with a total purse of $9.75 million, and the Puerto Rico Open, with a purse of $3 million. One of the interesting scheduling dilemmas during the week of the opposite tournaments involves the golfer who is the first alternate to play in the more elite event. While 64 of the top 69 golfers in the Official World Golf rankings were playing in the World Golf Championships—Dell Match Play in Austin, Texas, another 132 golfers were playing at the Puerto Rico Open. In 2017, Tony Finau opted to attend the World Golf Championships—Dell Match Play as the first alternate rather than choosing the guaranteed option to play in the Puerto Rico Open, where he was the defending champion. Finau, as quoted by the *Associated Press*, stated, "that was the only scenario that would pull me from Puerto Rico." He added, "it was a tough decision because I loved being in Puerto Rico and I told the fans last year in my winning speech I'd be back if I wasn't playing the Match Play." None of the 64 golfers in the World Golf Championships—Dell Match Play field dropped out, and Finau did not swing a club in PGA Tour competition that weekend.

The final round of the 2017 Puerto Rico Open featured a crowded leaderboard when Chris Stroud took his 18 under par, one-stroke advantage over five players to the back nine. Among those chasing Stroud was Retief Goosen, the 48-year-old, two-time winner of the U.S. Open. Goosen birdied six of the first ten holes in the final round. He added another birdie on 14. When Goosen's eighth birdie of the day dropped at the 18th hole, he completed a final round of 64, tied for the lead at 18 under. With other contenders having several holes left to play, a victory for Goosen was unlikely.

Another golfer chasing Stroud was D. A. Points. From 2011 through 2013, Points found great success on the PGA Tour. He earned more than $2 million in 2011 and 2013, and more than $1.5 million in 2012. In 2011, he won the AT&T Pebble Beach Pro-Am. Points and his playing partner, Bill Murray, also won the Pro-Am portion of the event that season.

Points, with the help of a putter from his mother's golf bag that he used as a child, shot an opening-round 64 at the Shell Houston Open in 2013. In that tournament, he had a 32-hole stretch of bogey-free golf. Points shot six under par in the final round. When he made a 13-foot par putt on the 72nd hole, he won the Shell Houston Open by one stroke over Billy Horschel and Henrik Stenson. It was Points' second title on the PGA Tour.

Two weeks later, Points tied for 38th at the Masters. It was the only time that Points made the cut in his three starts at Augusta National. Points also finished second at the Zurich Classic of New Orleans in 2013 on his way to the highest season earning for his career of more than $2.6 million. Points ended the regular season 25th in the FedEx Cup standings.

That season was also the one occasion in his career when Points advanced in the FedEx Cup Playoffs to the Tour Championship. At the Barclays, after shooting even par through the first two rounds, Points shot nine under par over the last two rounds to tie for sixth place. He was two strokes behind tournament winner Adam Scott. Although Points missed the cut in the Deutsche Bank Championship and finished in a tie for 57th at the BMW Championship, his season performances qualified him for the Tour Championship and the Masters. Upon tying for 26th at the Tour Championship, Points ended up 30th in the FedEx Cup standings. Points won $419,600 in prize money in the FedEx Cup Playoff tournaments, and he earned a playoff bonus of $175,000.

Points then had three consecutive seasons in which he did not qualify for the FedEx Cup Playoffs. He played in 27 PGA tournaments in the 2013–2014 season and made 12 cuts, but with only one top-25 finish. He ranked 173rd in the FedEx Cup standings. His exempt status for the 2014–2015 season, however, remained secure in the tournament winners group thanks to his victory in the previous season's Shell Houston Open.

In the 2014–2015 season, Points again did not have the success that he enjoyed only a few seasons prior. Points participated in 26 tournaments, but he made the cut in only 11. His three top-25 finishes were not enough to reach the FedEx Cup Playoffs, as he ended the season 171st. Without the security of an exempt status in the tournament winners group for the following season, Points competed in the Web.com Tour Finals. His struggles continued. Points missed the cut in the first two Finals tournaments. A 52nd-place and a 35th-place finish in the remaining two Finals tournaments could not salvage the season, and Points was not able to improve his priority status group. He entered the 2015–2016 season in the past champions group.

Points played in 18 PGA tournaments and made the cut in 11 that season. He had three finishes in the top 25, with his best performance a tie for 14th at the season-ending Wyndham Championship. Points completed the regular season 184th in the FedEx Cup standings. This result led Points back to the Web.com Tour Finals tournaments.

Two and a half weeks after the Wyndham, Points began the Web.com Tour Finals. He shot a five under par 65, with five birdies and no bogeys on his scorecard, in the first round of the DAP Championship. He finished that tournament in a tie for sixth to earn $32,375. He made the cut in the next two Web.com Finals tournaments, a tie for 53rd and a tie for 56th, for a Finals total of $37,950. His performances were good enough for the 17th position on the Web.com Tour Finals money list. After the alternate selection process, Points ended up 35th in the top finishers of the Web.com Tour priority group heading into the 2016–2017 PGA Tour season. Without those performances in the Web.com Tour Finals, Points would have again dropped to the past champions group.

Points played in six PGA tournaments with three made cuts in the 2016–2017 season prior to the Puerto Rico Open. He earned $54,783 at that point in the season. His best tournament finish was a tie for 39th at the AT&T Pebble Beach Pro-Am. It was five weeks in between Points competing at Pebble Beach and playing in Puerto Rico.

Points posted scores of 64–69–69 in the first three rounds of the Puerto Rico Open. His first-round, eight under par 64 was achieved with six birdies plus an eagle at the par-4 9th hole when his nine-iron from 149 yards found the bottom of the cup. Consistency in rounds two and three, with only one bogey in each round, put Points at 14 under par, only one stroke behind Chris Stroud with 18 holes to play.

Points had a spectacular start in the final round of the Puerto Rico Open with birdies on the first five holes. He bogeyed the 6th and 8th holes to put him at 17 under par for the tournament. Another bogey on the 10th hole left him two strokes off the lead of Stroud. Despite the number of golfers in contention for the championship, Points says that he has "never been much of a leaderboard watcher," but he knew he needed "a momentum switch to head in the right direction."

After Points parred the 11th and 12th holes, the 13th and 14th holes would significantly alter the top of the leaderboard. Stroud parred 13, but a birdie by Points moved him to within one stroke of the lead. Stroud went par-birdie-par on the par-4 14th hole in the previous three rounds. Playing at 459 yards in the final round, Stroud pulled his tee-shot left. The ball landed just short of the water, but it plugged in the soft ground only a few feet beyond the red hazard line. He was forced to take a one-stroke penalty and drop for his third shot of the hole.

Stroud's choice of where to drop represented one of the critical decisions that a golfer has to make during the management of a round. When a tournament championship is at stake, these strategic decisions are magnified. Rather than dropping in an area that would have left his ball in an uphill lie in the rough, Stroud chose to take his drop on the gravelly cart path. His shot from the cart path landed in the front-side bunker on the right of the green, with the added misfortune of the ball burying into the sand up against the lip. Stroud was able to pop the ball out of the trap and onto the green on his fourth shot, but he was not able to make his bogey putt. The double-bogey on 14 dropped his score to 16 under par. Points, who parred the 14th in each of the first three rounds, countered with another birdie to move to 18 under and complete the two-hole, four-stroke turnaround between himself and Stroud.

Stroud did respond to his difficulties on the 14th hole with a birdie on 15 to go to 17 under par. He, however, eliminated himself from contention with a bogey on 17. His final round of 71 left him in a tie for eighth place, along with J. J. Henry, at 16 under. Stroud earned $90,000 and 48 FedEx Cup points.

Points was now tied with Goosen for the lead. They were later joined by Bryson DeChambeau, who birdied 14, 16, and 18 to complete his final round of 67 to put him at 18 under par. With holes left to play, the advantage remained with Points. At the par-3, 198-yard 16th hole with a downwind and water coming into play, Points recounts that tee-shot as the moment during the tournament when he was the most nervous. Hitting a six-iron, Points put his tee-shot 15 feet from the cup. By making the putt, Points for the third time in the tournament birdied 16 to take the outright lead at 19 under par. Points calls the tee-shot on 16 "one of the best shots I ever hit under the pressure."

On the par-4, 411-yard 17th hole, Points put his nine-iron approach shot from 143 yards safely on the green. Although he missed the birdie putt, the par helped Points maintain the lead. Bill Lunde emerged to put some pressure on Points when he chipped in at the 17th to pull within one stroke of the lead.

In the previous three rounds at the 630-yard, par-5 18th hole, Points went birdie-birdie-par. His strategy for the 18th hole was determined earlier in the week. With trouble on the left and a reachable bunker if using his driver on the right, Points hit three-wood off the tee all week. His strategy and execution in the final round at the 18th never endangered his one-stroke lead over Goosen, DeChambeau, and Lunde.

After placing his tee-shot in the fairway and hitting his second shot with a two-iron hybrid, Points was 136 yards from the green. A pitching wedge left Points well-positioned on the green. When Lunde missed his birdie putt, Points now had two putts for the championship. Only one was needed as Points nailed his birdie putt to finish the round at six under and win the tournament with a score of 20 under par. It was Points' ninth birdie of the day and his fourth in the final six holes, when he took charge of the tournament.

For Points, who says he "hit some of the worst parts of golf, mentally and physically," the win ended a drought of 95 starts since his last PGA title in 2013 and was Points' third career title. Points earned $540,000 for the win, more than the $305,000 that he won in the 2015–2016 season in 18 PGA Tour events, the $390,000 total that he collected over 26 PGA events in 2014–2015, and the $364,000 he earned over 27 events in the 2013–2014 season. The 300 FedEx Cup points earned for the championship in Puerto Rico were more than the 167 total points that he accumulated in the previous season. Points also secured his entrance into The Players Championship, the PGA Championship, and the 2018 Tournament of Champions.

Moments after the tournament concluded, an emotional Points told Golf Channel reporter Billy Ray Brown, "I can't even begin to explain. A couple of really awful years. I pretty much hit rock-bottom and I put my family through a lot. To be able to find the strength and the courage to stay calm and win was something I didn't know I had in me."

For the season, Points played in 22 tournaments and made the cut in 12. He had three top-25 finishes, but no other top-ten performance aside from his win. Points earned 300 of his 435 FedEx Cup points in Puerto Rico. He ended the regular season 104th in the standings. He tied for 54th at the Northern Trust to conclude his season with a bonus of $70,000, and his season's earnings totaled $893,700.

After the Puerto Rico Open, Chris Stroud missed the cut in his next four tournaments. He made the cut in five of his next six tournaments, highlighted by consecutive top-20 finishes, a tie for 20th at the Greenbrier Classic and a tie for 19th at the John Deere Classic. Stroud missed the cut at the RBC Canadian Open the week before arriving at the Barracuda Championship, the last opposite tournament of the season, played on the same weekend as the World Golf Championships—Bridgestone Invitational.

Using the modified Stableford scoring system, Stroud ended the first day with +9 points to find himself tied for 26th. He regressed in the second round when he added only three points and dropped into a tie for 45th. Stroud was 14 points behind the tournament leader, Richy Werenski. Stroud doubled his points total to +24 in the third round, moving up into a tie for 22nd, but he remained 13 points behind tournament leader Greg Owen's total of +37. Owen brought himself back to the pack when a double-bogey on the 18th hole cost him three points.

Stroud quickly began to make up the gap in points as he birdied the first three holes in the final round. A bogey on the 4th hole was offset by a birdie on the 5th. A bogey on the 7th hole was responded to with a birdie on the 8th and 9th holes. Stroud added ten points on the front nine to get to +34.

After a bogey on the 12th hole, for the third time on the day, Stroud rebounded on the next hole with a birdie. He then birdied the 14th and 15th holes. On 15, Stroud made the birdie putt from off the green. He now stood at +39 points. Greg Owen, the tournament leader, completed the front nine with a four-point gain to reach +41.

At the par-3, 232-yard 16th hole, Stroud's tee-shot found the bunker. His shot from the sand hit the cup, went around and out, but by saving par Stroud did not lose any points. At the 17th, for the second consecutive hole, Stroud had a birdie chance roll around the cup and out.

The 18th is a par-5, 616-yard hole. Stroud's second shot hit a small hill just off the left side of the green and rolled perfectly to five feet from the cup. Stroud buried the eagle putt. The five points that he gained transformed a three-point deficit into a two-point lead over Owen. Stroud took his +44 point total to the clubhouse, where he waited for more than two hours to see if he would be caught.

Richy Werenski started the final round with +30 points and was at +33 after the 13th hole. He began his charge with a birdie on the 14th hole. At the par-4, 439-yard 15th, his approach hit the green and, on the ball's second bounce, its backspin allowed it to roll back to the left toward the hole, where it fell for an eagle. The five points immediately brought Werenski into the championship mix at +40 points.

Like Stroud, Werenski went into the bunker with his tee-shot on the par-3 16th. His sand-shot ran across the green and the fringe before settling in the edge of the rough. For the second consecutive hole, Werenski did not need a putter as he chipped in for the critical par save. He needed an eagle or two birdies on the final two holes to match or possibly surpass Stroud. Werenski made a birdie at the par-4, 464-yard 17th hole to pull to within two points of Stroud. He completed the comeback when he converted an eight-foot birdie putt on 18 to get to +44 points. Werenski added 11 points over the final five holes. He would now play the waiting game with Stroud.

The golfer most likely to topple Stroud and Werenski remained Greg Owen. On the back nine, however, Owen made three bogeys. His last came at the 17th hole after he drove his tee-shot left into a creek. Owen's total fell to

+42 points. The leader coming into the final round now needed a birdie on the 18th hole to get into the playoff. Owen responded with his third birdie on the back nine when he converted a seven-foot putt on 18 to equal Stroud's and Werenski's +44 total. All three golfers heading to the playoff never won a PGA tournament.

Owen was eliminated on the first playoff hole. On the second extra hole, back at 18, Stroud hit a five-iron for his second shot to within five feet of the flag. Werenski went long on his approach shot to the green. After chipping to 25 feet away, Werenski missed his birdie putt. When the 35-year-old Stroud converted a two-putt birdie, he had his first PGA Tour victory in his 290th tournament start. Stroud earned $594,000 for the win and 300 FedEx Cup points. He jumped from 144th to 76th in the FedEx Cup points standings.

Stroud obtained the long-term benefits of two seasons in the tournament winners exempt group and a spot in the 2018 Tournament of Champions. One immediate dividend was that Stroud would now be traveling from Reno, Nevada, to Quail Hollow Golf Club in Charlotte, North Carolina, to play in the following week's PGA Championship. For Stroud, it was his first appearance in a major since the 2014 PGA held at Valhalla Golf Club in Louisville, Kentucky. Stroud tied for 64th in that tournament. Stroud also played in The Open Championship in 2014, but he missed the cut.

It is one thing for a golfer to create an additional opportunity, but it is initially just that, an opportunity. There are certainly no guarantees of any great success, especially in this instance with the increased competition and pressure that comes with playing in a major. However, when a player capitalizes on that one opportunity, considerable additional rewards emerge.

At the 2017 PGA Championship, Stroud played the first round in three under par 68, with no bogeys on the day and three birdies on the back nine. He was one stroke behind Kevin Kisner and Thorbjorn Olesen. Stroud posted another 68 in round two, ending the day two strokes behind Kisner and Hideki Matsuyama. It was Stroud's third made cut in his nine major appearances. A third-round even par 71 that ended with a bogey on the 17th and 18th holes, left Stroud at six under par. He was tied with Matsuyama, one stroke behind tournament leader Kisner. Stroud shot a one-under 34 on the front nine of the final round. On the back nine, however, Stroud struggled and posted a six over par 42. Instead, Justin Thomas won his first major when a final round, three under par 68 allowed him to finish eight under and lift the Wanamaker Trophy for winning the PGA Championship.

Stroud tied for ninth place at the PGA, a tournament whose entrance seemed highly unlikely only eight days earlier after the third round of the Barracuda Championship. Stroud earned $250,000 and 80 FedEx Cup points and jumped from 76th to 69th in the FedEx Cup points standings.

Stroud went on to finish 71st in the regular season FedEx Cup points standings. He missed the cut at the first two tournaments in the playoffs and ended the season 84th in the standings to earn a $75,000 bonus. For the season, Stroud played in 22 PGA tournaments. He made the cut in 11, with seven top-25 and three top-ten finishes. Stroud earned more than $1.3 million. He entered 2017–2018 in his first season in the tournament winners group.

18

The Weeks Before
and After Tournaments

Aside from the major tournaments and the World Golf Championships, a certain number of golfers decide to skip a given regular season tournament. However, the weeks leading up to and the week after a major represent another opportunity when more of the higher-ranked golfers do not play. It must be pointed out, however, that these weeks are not nearly the opportunity for lower ranked players to gain entrance that they have in the autumn tournaments, and certainly not in the opposite tournaments.

In 2015, Jordan Spieth committed to playing in the RBC Heritage tournament in Hilton Head, South Carolina, the week after the Masters, where Spieth shot 18 under par to win his first major championship. The win tied Spieth with the 1997 performance of Tiger Woods for the best score in relation to par at the Masters. Spieth spent the Monday and Tuesday after the Masters in New York City doing media appearances. He kept his commitment to play in the RBC Heritage, a tournament that gave him a sponsor exemption in 2013. Spieth explained to the media at the press conference on the Wednesday before the RBC Heritage the difficulty of playing in another tournament only a few days after his Masters championship. He stated, "yesterday, my energy level was maybe at a two. Today, I'm back up to about a six and I should be at a nine tomorrow. Fortunately, I'm in the afternoon in the first round, otherwise that might have been tough."

Spieth posted a three over par 74 in the first round but responded with a nine under par 62 in the second round. Spieth finished the RBC Heritage in a tie for 11th with a final score of ten under. Spieth did not enter the RBC Heritage in 2016 or 2017. Jason Day was one of the top-ranked golfers who did compete in the RBC Heritage in 2016. He too acknowledged the difficulty of playing the week after the Masters. Day was quoted in *USA Today*, stating, "you just have to suck it up and get through the week."

The week after the 2017 Masters, only two golfers in the top ten and eight in the top 20 in the current FedEx Cup points standings played in the RBC Heritage. PGA Tour rookie Wesley Bryan was part of the field. Bryan won three tournaments on the Web.com Tour in the 2015–2016 season to obtain his PGA Tour card. Prior to that, Bryan was best known for the golf trick-shot videos that he and his brother George posted on the Internet.

Bryan's record for the 2016–2017 season entering the RBC Heritage was nine made cuts in 13 appearances. His began the season with three consecutive made cuts, with his best performance a tie for 41st at the Shriners Hospitals for Children Open. He then had a stretch of four consecutive missed cuts, but responded by making the cut in six straight tournaments leading into the RBC Heritage, including three consecutive top tens. Bryan tied for fourth at both the Genesis Open and the Honda Classic, and he tied for seventh at the Valspar Championship. Bryan was in 44th place in the FedEx Cup standings and earned more than $820,194.

Bryan shot 69–67–68 in the first three rounds of the RBC Heritage. He was at nine under par, four strokes behind former major champion Jason Dufner. Bryan's four birdies in a row on holes 4 through 7 in the final round offset a bogey on the 3rd and the 8th to put him at 11 under heading into the final nine holes. Dufner shot two over on the front nine.

At the par-4 13th, Bryan stuck a 54-degree wedge from 113 yards to nine feet, five inches, where he converted his birdie putt. He was now even with PGA Tour rookie Ollie Schniederjans at 12 under par, one stroke ahead of Dufner, Webb Simpson, another former major champion, and Luke Donald, a five-time PGA tournament winner.

Having birdied the 9th hole, Donald chipped in out of a sand trap from 75 feet at the 11th hole. He continued his charge up the leaderboard with a birdie on 13. On the par-3 14th, Donald's tee-shot took him to four feet from the cup. He made that birdie putt to join Schniederjans and Bryan in the lead. It was, however, Donald's last birdie of the day.

Dufner's struggles continued as he shot three over on the back nine for a final-round 76, 11 strokes more than the round of 65 that he posted one day earlier. Dufner completed the RBC Heritage in 11th place.

Bryan repeated his approach shot brilliance from two holes earlier on the par-5 15th when his 58-degree wedge from 88 yards left him four feet, 11 inches from the cup. When Bryan made the birdie putt, he gained the lead that he would hold for the rest of the day to win his first tournament on the PGA Tour. Bryan, who only ten days earlier attended the first round of the Masters as a member of the gallery, secured his entrance into next year's major tournament. Bryan told Jim Nantz and Nick Faldo on the CBS broadcast, "honestly, I wasn't nervous at all, all day. Then number 17, I got up and honestly, I just threw up a little in my mouth and I was like, shoot, I guess this is what nervous feels like." With Nantz and Faldo now laughing, Bryan continued, "that's how it went down. Then I was able to get it back together."

Golfers' decisions as to which tournaments they compete in often center around trying to prepare for and give an optimum performance at the major tournaments. In the 2016–2017 season, the four-week stretch leading up to the Masters offered a variety of strategies. The stretch began with the Arnold Palmer Invitational at Bay Hill that concluded on Sunday, March 19, 2017. That tournament is always a popular stop on the PGA Tour, with the significance of a three-season exempt status awarded to the champion, as well as the reverence that the golfers desire to show for Palmer. The 2017 tournament was particularly special, the first time that the event was being held since Palmer passed away on September 25, 2016, at the age of 87. Marc Leishman earned the victory at the 2017 Arnold Palmer Invitational with a one-stroke win over Kevin Kisner and Charley Hoffman.

The next week was the World Golf Championships—Dell Match Play, a format that has only 16 golfers advancing to the weekend. The *Associated Press* reported that after not advancing out of his group, Jordan Spieth spent the weekend at the Augusta National Golf Club playing practice rounds in preparation for the Masters, including one round with New England Patriots quarterback Tom Brady. Some of the golfers who qualified for the match play event, such as Justin Rose, Adam Scott, Henrik Stenson, and Rickie Fowler, all of whom played at the Arnold Palmer Invitational on the previous weekend, chose not to compete and used this weekend as their time off in preparation for the Masters.

There is, of course, no perfect strategy for how to prepare for a major. Examples can be found of major tournament champions choosing to play or not play the week before a major. Justin Rose, Adam Scott, Henrik Stenson, and Rickie Fowler all resumed their preparation for the 2017 Masters by playing in the Shell Houston Open, held the week before the Masters. Jordan Spieth and Phil Mickelson were among those who played in Austin and Houston. Jon Rahm, who lost in the World Golf Championships—Dell Match Play final to Dustin Johnson, also chose to compete in Houston. Stenson, who played in the Scottish Open the week before his victory at The Open Championship in 2016, was quoted by the *Associated Press* stating, "I like to play the week before a major if I can." He explained that it "sets me up better, puts me in game mode, and instead of coming straight from practice, I tend to analyze a little bit too much at times, I guess. I like to play." Adam Scott, whose only major championship is the 2013 Masters, said of his start in Houston, "part of my plan for the rest of the year is to play the week before the majors and doing something a little different than I have the past few years."

As the Masters gets closer, the field for the season's first major begins to solidify. If a golfer has not yet qualified to play at Augusta National, there is one last opportunity to do so—win the Shell Houston Open. Considering that a spot in the Masters is at stake, the Shell Houston Open offers an opportunity for high drama.

In 2014, Matt Jones began the final round of the Shell Houston Open six strokes behind leader Matt Kuchar. Jones' rally was capped off with his eighth birdie of the day on the 18th hole when he made an improbable 46-foot putt to shoot 66 and remain in contention for the championship. Of the lengthy birdie putt, Johnny Miller, NBC lead golf analyst, 25-time PGA tournament winner, and two-time major champion, stated on the broadcast, "that is a one-in-a-hundred putt right there. A double-breaker. Somehow he read it and put it right in the center." Miller added, "that's the best pressure putt we've seen in a long time on the Tour."

Jones still had to get some help. On the par-4, 472-yard 18th hole, Kuchar needed only par to win the tournament. From the middle of the fairway, Kuchar hit his second shot into the water to the left of the green. Kuchar, who only a few minutes earlier had a two-stroke lead over Jones, now had to get up-and-down after his drop to force a playoff. Kuchar was able to execute and make a bogey five on 18 to complete his round of 72 and keep his chances of victory alive.

Back at the 18th hole for the playoff, Kuchar again put his drive in the middle of the fairway. Jones hit his tee-shot into the fairway bunker, giving the advantage to Kuchar. Jones' second shot left him short of the green. For the second consecutive time on 18, Kuchar was not able to get his fairway approach shot onto the green. This time, rather than going left into the water, Kuchar hit the ball to the right into the bunker short of the green.

Jones' third shot produced another incredible highlight on the 18th hole. His chip shot from 42 yards went over the bunker and onto the green before rolling to the center of the cup. Kuchar, now having to hole out from the bunker to force a second playoff hole, did not match the heroics of Jones. For Jones, it remains his only PGA tournament victory and the only year that he qualified for the Masters.

After the tournament, as reported by the *Associated Press*, Jones said of his putt on 18 in regulation, "I was going to three-putt before I left it short. I didn't care about finishing second or third or fourth, it didn't matter. I was only trying to get the win." He commented about his qualifying for the Masters, stating, "going to Augusta is amazing. The win means everything to me right now because that's what we play for, is to win. To have Augusta as a reward for that win is amazing." Jones did not make the cut at the 2014 Masters.

Jim Herman never finished in the top three of a PGA tournament as he entered the 2016 Shell Houston Open. Herman did have three different seasons in which he had two top-ten finishes, with his best result a tie for fourth place at the 2015 Zurich Classic of New Orleans. For Herman, it was a long journey to the PGA Tour. He competed on mini-tours and missed Q School opportunities. He spent three seasons on the Web.com Tour before winning a tournament in 2010 and graduating onto the PGA Tour for the first time. Herman simply explains that "being able to call myself a PGA Tour member was a dream come true."

Herman describes his first season on the PGA Tour as a "tough year." He says that "just making the Tour is great, you are playing against the best players every week," but in reflection he concedes that at the time he needed to learn how to better prepare to compete on the Tour, and his short game, in particular, needed to improve. Herman had 22 starts on the PGA Tour in the 2010–2011 season. He made the cut in 13 tournaments, with two top-25s, finishing 178th in the points standings.

Herman appeared in only two PGA tournaments in 2011–2012. He instead played in 26 tournaments on the Web.com Tour. His performance earned him the 25th and final position on the Web.com Tour regular season money list to once again earn his PGA Tour card. Herman obtained the last spot by squeaking past Camilo Benedetti by $940.

In 2012–2013, Herman made the cut in ten of 19 PGA tournaments. He had four top-25 finishes in that season highlighted by the first two top-ten finishes of his career, a tie for tenth at the John Deere Classic and a tie for ninth the following week at the Sanderson Farms Championship. Herman won $490,000 on the Tour, at that time the best season of his career. Those performances, however, only got Herman to the 139th position in the FedEx Cup points standings. Herman did improve his exempt status for the following season through his performances in the Web.com Tour Finals. He entered the 2013–2014 PGA Tour season 28th in the top finishers of the Web.com Tour group.

Herman made the cut in 11 of 21 PGA tournaments in the 2013–2014 season, but without any top-25 performances. His earnings fell to $187,000, and FedEx Cup points ranking tumbled to 182. Once again, Herman performed well in the Web.com Tour Finals, where earning $101,725 in the four tournaments got him back to the PGA Tour. Herman qualified for the PGA Tour in the 15th position in the top finishers of the Web.com Tour group.

The 2014–2015 season represented a turning point in Herman's career. He posted two top-25 finishes in his first five tournaments. He tied for 18th at the Shriners Hospitals for Children Open and finished 23rd place at the OHL Classic at Mayakoba. Herman amassed $120,779 in earnings in those two tournaments alone. He had a stretch where he missed the cut in four out of five tournaments. In the tournament where he did make the cut, Herman finished seventh at the Honda Classic. He won $183,763. Herman then made the cut in seven consecutive tournaments, highlighted by the tie for fourth at the Zurich Classic of New Orleans. That tournament performance alone earned him $303,600.

Herman qualified for the FedEx Cup Playoffs for the first time in his career, 89th in the standings. Herman's tie for 13th in the Barclays secured his advancement to the second playoff tournament. Herman's season ended in the 74th position once he missed the cut in the Deutsche Bank Championship. He earned a playoff bonus of $80,000.

In addition to the playoff bonus, Herman earned more than $1.2 million in the 2014–2015 season his first season over $1 million. Herman began the following PGA Tour season with his highest exempt status. Herman cites one other accomplishment as he began the 2015–2016 season. It was his fifth year on the PGA Tour, which qualified him for pension benefits. Herman remarks that he "started the year on a high."

Herman's performance reflected his newly-earned status on the PGA Tour. He made the cut in four of five autumn tournaments with three top-20 finishes, highlighted by a tie for tenth at the CIMB Classic. Herman accumulated $333,262 in prize money in the autumn tournaments. In the weeks leading up to the Shell Houston Open in 2016, he missed the cut at the Honda Classic and the Valspar Championship, before finishing 63rd at the Arnold Palmer Invitational.

At the Shell Houston Open in 2016, a first-round three under par 69 left Herman five strokes behind Charley Hoffman. He repeated his 69 in the second round, gaining one stroke on Hoffman. The third round resulted in a seven-stroke swing between Herman and Hoffman. Herman's 67 vaulted him to the top of the leaderboard after 54 holes for the first time in a PGA tournament. He was tied with Jamie Lovemark at 11 under par, one stroke ahead of Russell Henley, Dustin Johnson, and Henrik Stenson. Hoffman posted a 74 in round three and trailed by three strokes.

Herman, who is confident in his ball-striking ability, points out that he worked extensively to improve his short game. He credits perfectly executing an up-and-down on 18 in round three, when he chipped from 29 yards to less than two feet to save par, as "a big moment." He explains that "it was meaningful to execute in that situation" and that it provided an important "confidence boost" going into the final round.

Herman faced a new experience, the pressure of being in the last group in the final round of a tournament. Before he even played the first hole, Herman had to deal with hearing the reactions of the crowd as golfers moved up the leaderboard. Jordan Spieth, in particular, made his native Texas crowd roar after he birdied five of his first seven holes. Very aware that he needed to shoot a good score to win his first tournament, Herman was anxious to start the round. He explains, "you are just trying to get to the tee. You cannot do anything from the putting green."

Spieth would not continue his torrid play, and he shot two over on the back nine for a two under par 70. Lovemark removed himself from any chance at winning early on when he bogeyed holes 2 and 3 and posted a double-bogey on the 6th. He shot a final-round 76. Hoffman also shot 76 to eliminate himself. On the back nine, a birdie on 10, 12, 14, and 15 was not enough for Dustin Johnson to overcome his double-bogey on 11. After three birdies on the front nine, Russell Henley bogeyed 10, 12, and 17, with only one birdie on the back nine for his final round of 71.

The duel for the 2016 Shell Houston Open tournament championship that emerged was between Herman and Henrik Stenson. A Stenson birdie on 10 was answered by a Herman birdie on 11 to tie for the lead. Both players birdied the par-5 13th hole, with Stenson making a 14-foot putt from just off the green. A bogey by Stenson on the par-3 14th dropped him one stroke behind Herman. Stenson quickly responded with a birdie on 15 to create another tie atop the leaderboard.

The par-3, 191-yard 16th was the hole that forever changed the career of Jim Herman. His tee-shot landed on a hill to the left of the green, approximately 40 feet from the hole. Herman's chip shot landed on the fringe of the green before rolling along the perfect path to drop into the hole for a birdie to take a one-stroke lead. Herman parred on 17.

On the par-4, 488-yard 18th hole, Herman hit his tee-shot 316 yards in the middle of the fairway. His second shot put him only 25 feet from the cup, where he successfully completed his two-putt par. The 38-year-old Herman had his first PGA tournament victory in his 106th start, one stroke better than Stenson and two strokes better than Johnson. Herman explains that while his shots on 16 and 18 get all of the attention, "over a 72-hole tournament, there are many shots along the way that are pivotal." Herman also secured the final spot in that year's Masters, the first time that he qualified. Herman missed the cut at the Masters.

Herman did make the cut in five of his 12 remaining regular season tournaments. His top finishes were 27th at the World Golf Championships—Bridgestone Invitational, 29th at the Dean & DeLuca Invitational, and 43rd at The Open Championship, the first time that he played in that major. Herman ended the regular season 41st in the FedEx Cup standings, with the win at the Shell Houston Open accounting for 500 of his 923 total FedEx Cup points.

Herman posted finishes of 22nd, 33rd, and 24th in the first three playoff tournaments, but fell short of qualifying for the Tour Championship. He was still able to claim $181,522 in FedEx Cup Playoff tournament prize money out of his season total of $2.09 million. Herman finished 42nd in the standings to earn a playoff bonus of $133,000. Herman attained the other tournament entrance benefits of his victory, such as participation in the no-cut, guaranteed prize money Tournament of Champions in 2017. His 12th-place finish in that event earned him another $147,000.

Only 29 golfers who competed at the Shell Houston Open in 2017 already qualified for that year's Masters. Three golfers in the top ten of the points standings participated in the Shell Houston Open: Rickie Fowler, Jon Rahm, and Jordan Spieth as did seven of the top 20 and 15 of the top 30. Other past major winners Henrik Stenson, Keegan Bradley, Justin Rose, and past Masters champions Phil Mickelson, Adam Scott, and Angel Cabrera were part of the 2017 field in Houston. For Mickelson, it was his 13th straight appearance in the Houston tournament.

Sung Kang emerged as the most likely candidate to join the field at Augusta. He topped his seven under par 65 in the first round by matching the course record of 63 in round two. Using a new putter, Kang made six putts longer than 20 feet in the second round. His two-day total of 128 eclipsed the previous course record and was six strokes better than Hudson Swafford and Russell Henley and seven strokes ahead of Rickie Fowler.

Kang started the third round with a birdie on the 1st and 4th holes. After completing a 22-hole stretch when he made nine birdies and an eagle, Kang bogeyed holes 5 and 7. Kang ended the third round one under par, 17 under for the tournament. Fowler had eight birdies on the first 14 holes in round three, but a bogey on 17 and a double-bogey on 18 left him three strokes behind Kang. Swafford took himself out of contention with a 75 in the third round that included four bogeys on the front nine. Henley birdied the 17th and 18th holes in round three to pull him within four strokes of Kang heading into Sunday.

In the final round, Fowler double-bogeyed the 2nd hole and bogeyed the 4th to put him six shots off the lead. Fowler's five birdies over the rest of the round were not enough to overcome the six-hole stretch of six over par from the end of round three through the beginning of round four. Fowler tied for third, along with Luke List, to earn $406,000 and 163 FedEx Cup points.

Henley capitalized on his strong finish in round three by making four birdies in the first seven holes to tie Kang for the lead. Kang played the first seven holes at even par. The winner was determined by Henley and Kang over the final 11 holes. Both golfers birdied the par-5 8th hole to go to 18 under. At the par-3 9th hole, Henley's tee-shot landed in the bunker. After his sand-shot raced past the hole, he needed three putts before reaching the bottom of the cup. The double-bogey dropped him to 16 under par. Kang also had trouble on the ninth hole as he made a bogey, but he did regain a one-stroke lead.

On the back nine, Kang's play was solid, but Henley's was spectacular. Henley proved the 9th hole was a blip as he quickly responded with a birdie on 10 to tie for the lead at 17 under. They remained tied until the 590-yard, par-5 13th hole. There a 14-foot putt for birdie by Kang came up one revolution of the golf ball short of the hole. Henley needed to convert from only two foot, ten inches for a birdie to move into the lead.

At 14, a 225-yard par-3, Kang made par with a seven-foot putt. Henley's five-iron tee-shot left him 36 feet from the hole. His lengthy birdie putt rolled around the entirety of the cup before dropping to extend his lead to two strokes. Henley furthered his lead with another birdie on the par-5, 600-yard 15th. A final birdie on the 17th hole, his tenth of the day, moved him to 21 under par and completed a 19-hole stretch with 12 birdies. Henley shot a final-round 65 as Kang shot an even par 72. After finishing in the top seven of the leaderboard at the Shell Houston Open in 2014, 2015, and 2016, Henley was the 2017 tournament winner.

For Henley, it was his third PGA tournament win and his first since the Honda Classic in 2014. His $1.26 million payout for winning the Shell Houston Open was the highest for his career. Henley, a native of Macon, Georgia, and a graduate of the University of Georgia, returned to play in the Masters in 2013, 2014, and 2015, with his best result 21st in 2015. He failed to qualify for the Masters in 2016. Henley finished in a tie for 11th with four other golfers at the 2017 Masters and earned $233,200. By finishing in the top 12 of the 2017 Masters, he qualified for the 2018 tournament.

For the season, Henley made the cut in 22 of 27 starts. He had 11 top-25 finishes and five top-ten performances. Henley finished the regular season 19th in the FedEx Cup standings. He made it to the Tour Championship, where he tied for third place. He ended the season 13th in the standings to collect a bonus of $280,000. He won more than $3.41 million in prize money in 2016–2017.

Kang made the cut in 18 of his 29 regular season starts. He had eight performances in the top-25, with three top tens. Finishing second at the Shell Houston Open was his best result of the season. Kang completed the regular season 45th in the standings but missed the cut at the Northern Trust and tied for 35th and 53rd in his other playoff appearances. Kang's season ended after the BMW Championship at number 59 in the standings. He collected a playoff bonus of $110,000, in addition to his earnings of more than $1.94 million.

There are certainly other examples of the pre-major/post-major tournament field dynamic. Two golfers recently repeated as champions in tournaments played in between elite events: Daniel Berger won the FedEx St. Jude Classic in 2016 and 2017, and Jhonattan Vegas won the RBC Canadian Open in 2016 and 2017.

When Berger won the FedEx St. Jude Classic in June 2016, it was scheduled between the Memorial and the U.S. Open. It was his first career PGA tournament victory in his 50th career start. A first-round 67 left Berger two strokes off the lead. In round two, Berger stamped his mark on the tournament as his six under par 64 vaulted him to a three-stroke lead. He would hold that advantage after the third and final rounds. The win earned Berger more than $1.1 million.

In 2015–2016, his second season on the PGA Tour, Berger made the cut in 23 of 26 tournaments. He had 12 finishes in the top 25, with six in the top ten. Berger earned just under $3.3 million for the season and finished 22nd in the points standings. After participating in all four FedEx Cup Playoff tournaments, highlighted by tying for tenth at the BMW Championship, Berger ended the playoffs 26th to earn a bonus of $195,000.

The FedEx St. Jude Classic in 2017 was once again between the Memorial and the U.S. Open. The tournament field had six of the top 30 golfers in the current FedEx Cup standings and eight of the top 30 in the Official World Golf rankings. Berger grinded a bit in the first two rounds as his four-birdie, four-bogey first day produced an even par 70, and his five-birdie, three-bogey second day put him at two under par for the tournament, tied for 34th place, seven strokes behind the leaders.

Berger quickly got back into contention when he birdied holes 2 through 4 in round three. He ended the day with a 66 and was now only three shots off the pace. He chipped in from just off the green to save par on the 1st hole in round four. He went on to post another round of 66. When Berger birdied the 15th hole, he took sole possession of the lead as those ahead of him after 54 holes stumbled. Rafa Cabrera Bello shot 71, and Stewart Cink and Ben Crane both shot 73. Berger finished the tournament at ten under par to repeat as tournament champion, defeating Charl Schwartzel and Whee Kim by one stroke.

The RBC Canadian Open in 2016 was sandwiched between The Open Championship and the PGA. Only nine of top 30 golfers in the current FedEx Cup standings and 13 of the top 50 of the Official World Golf rankings played in the RBC Canadian Open. The number one and number two golfers on both lists, Jason Day and Dustin Johnson, were part of the field.

Jhonattan Vegas started the 2015–2016 season in the past champions group. He participated in all four of the opposite tournaments, with a tie for fourth at the Sanderson Farms Championship and the Barbasol Championship, a tie for 26th at the Puerto Rico Open, and a tie for 53rd at the Barracuda Championship. Vegas earned $320,208 and 161 FedEx Cup points in those four tournaments. It was at the RBC Canadian Open where Vegas secured his second career victory with a one-stroke victory over Jon Rahm, Dustin Johnson, and Martin Laird. His other tour win occurred at the 2011 Bob Hope Classic.

Vegas ended the first round of the 2016 RBC Canadian Open at one over par. He responded quickly in round two when he birdied the 3rd, 6th, and 7th holes before a bogey on the 9th. He added four birdies on the back nine, but he made three bogeys, including on 17 and 18. Vegas shot three under par, and a third-round score of two under par 70 had him entering the final round five strokes off the lead.

In the final round, Vegas moved into contention with a blistering front nine score of 31. He birdied holes 2 through 6, with a bogey on the 8th the only blemish on his scorecard. In position now to win the tournament, Vegas continued his rally with four more birdies on the back nine. He birdied 16 to tie for the lead, and his birdie on 17 moved him into sole possession of first place. A birdie on 18 finished the day for Vegas with an eight under par 64. He earned more than $1.06 million for the win and 500 FedEx Cup points. The next week, Vegas finished 22nd in the PGA Championship, claiming $75,636 and 44 FedEx Cup points.

Vegas did not play again on the PGA Tour until the beginning of the FedEx Cup Playoffs, opting instead to represent Venezuela in the Olympics. Quoted by Mike McAllister at pgatour.com, Vegas stated

> Just to be part of the Olympics itself is something that, as a golfer, you never dreamed of. It puts golf in a different perspective. Instead of playing for yourself, you've got the whole country behind you. It's been a fun experience thinking about being there with all the other Olympic athletes. It's more than just being a golfer playing another event. It's being part of the Olympics, the biggest sporting event in the world. Should be a fun week.

As the first player from Venezuela on the PGA Tour, the opportunity to compete in the Olympics and spread the game of golf internationally added significance for Vegas.

> The game is going to be exposed to more people around the world. It's going to be great for the game. In Venezuela itself, it's going to be super-important. People are going to know that I'm part of the Olympics. They'll start researching more about golf. Peo-

ple who otherwise might not thought they could get to the Olympics will now know they can through golf. Golf is not a big sport in Venezuela, so having an Olympian from that country will be pretty nice.

Vegas tied for 50th at the Rio games tournament.

Vegas amassed more than $2.47 million in prize money in 27 tournaments in 2015–2016. He entered the FedEx Cup Playoffs 31st in the standings. He performed consistently well in the playoffs with finishes of 22nd, 33rd, and 24th in the first three tournaments. He survived a double-bogey on the 18th hole in the final round of the BMW Championship to finish 29th and reach the Tour Championship for the first time in his career. Vegas was quoted by Adam Schupak on golfweek.com saying that qualifying for the Tour Championship is "about the same pressure as trying to win a golf tournament." After a 24th place finish at the Tour Championship, Vegas earned $329,422 for the four FedEx Cup Playoff tournaments. His position in the final points standings earned him a $180,000 playoff bonus.

In 2017, the RBC Canadian Open was again positioned between two elite tournaments, The Open Championship and the World Golf Championships—Bridgestone Invitational. The field consisted of seven of the top 30 golfers in the current FedEx Cup standings, including number two, Dustin Johnson. The tournament field had seven of the top 50 golfers in the Official World Golf ranking.

Charley Hoffman entered the final round with a three-stroke lead over Vegas. Hoffman chipped in on the 1st hole for a birdie and added a birdie on the 2nd and 6th holes. He did bogey the 7th for a two under par front nine. Vegas, however, showed that the final round magic he displayed in 2016 was not a one-time occurrence. Vegas made up for the gap in the lead with a five under par performance on the front nine. Both birdied the 11th hole, but Hoffman gave a stroke back on the 12th. Vegas had the lead after he birdied the 13th and 16th holes, to overcome his bogey at 15. Vegas ended the round with a 65.

Hoffman now had to rally. He birdied the 16th hole. Trailing by one stroke, Hoffman had a chance to win the tournament with an eagle putt on 18, but his attempt from 25 feet slid just to the right of the cup. Hoffman's tap-in birdie set up a playoff with both golfers at 21 under par.

Back at the par-5 18th hole, both drove into the fairway bunker. Vegas was able to get his second shot into the rough just off of the green. Hoffman chose to lay up, hitting to 111 yards from the flagstick. Hoffman's third shot landed in the bunker near the green. Vegas, meanwhile, placed his third shot less than two feet for a tap-in birdie. Hoffman needed to hole out from the bunker. His sand-shot headed toward the cup, but raced past it on the left. Vegas won the RBC Canadian Open for the second consecutive season.

After the RBC Canadian Open, Vegas tied for 17th at the World Golf Championships—Bridgestone Invitational, but he missed the cut at the PGA Championship. He entered the playoffs in the 29th position and quickly solidified his position in the FedEx Cup standings with a tie for third at the Northern Trust. He earned $507,500 for that tournament. His tie for 65th and tie for 63rd at the next two playoff tournaments did not derail his advancement to the Tour Championship for the second consecutive year. Although he finished 30th in the Tour Championship, for the four FedEx Cup events he earned $684,251 of his season total of $2.94 million. For finishing 23rd in the standings, Vegas collected a bonus payment of $210,000.

19

The Open Championship Qualifying Series

The Quicken Loans National tournament occurred at the point of the 2016–2017 season when the calendar turned from June to July. Including the Quicken Loans National, ten tournaments remained in the regular season, to be played over an eight-week span. There were two majors, one World Golf Championships event, and two opposite tournaments left in the season. Then both the FedEx Cup Playoffs and the Web.com Tour Finals would occur. Critical opportunities existed for all golfers. No matter what type of season a golfer was having or where he was positioned in the FedEx Cup standings, the outcome of the current season and the prospects for future seasons were still very much to be determined. As Jim Herman, winner of the 2016 Shell Houston Open, states, and many golfers can attest, "one week can move you from a mediocre season to an outstanding season."

One of the opportunities presented at the Quicken Loans National was that it served as the first of three tournaments in The Open Championship qualifying series, followed by the Greenbrier Classic and the John Deere Classic. With the goal of inviting golfers who are playing well at that point in the season, The Open Championship qualifying series has 44 spots that are filled through the outcomes of 15 tournaments played in ten countries. Four go to the top finishers of the Quicken Loans National who have yet to qualify for The Open Championship, providing that they finish the Quicken Loans National in the top 12, including ties. The same criteria are used for the Greenbrier Classic. Played the week before The Open Championship, only one qualifying spot is available to the highest finisher of the John Deere Classic who has yet to qualify, providing that he finishes in the top five.

The Quicken Loans National tournament in 2017 was played at TPC

Potomac at Avenel Farm in Maryland. The golf course was an annual stop on the PGA Tour from 1987 through 2006, hosting what was known as the Kemper Open for most of those seasons. After a major renovation in 2009, the golf course hosted tournaments on both the Champions Tour and the Web.com Tour before the return of the PGA Tour. Justin Thomas, who was third in the FedEx Cup standings and in prize money earned, described the conditions of the golf course at his pre-tournament press conference.

> You could 100 percent host a U.S. Open here starting tomorrow. It's not very often we play greens this firm on Tour other than majors. I'm having a hard time seeing double-digits under par win. It's real difficult. Firm greens change everything. It's just the little things like chipping the ball, instead of staying close around two, three-feet, rolling out to five, six. Stats show you're going to miss those (putts) at some point.

Rickie Fowler also commented, "it does have the feel of a little bit more than just a normal Tour event as far as what the difficulty level is out there."

Kyle Stanley and Charles Howell III found themselves in a tie for seventh place at three under par after the third round. They were four strokes behind leader David Lingmerth, who after spectacular back-to-back 65s at the par-70 course, shot 73 in the third round. Howell had not won a tournament since he defeated Phil Mickelson in a playoff at Riviera in 2007, a span of 293 tournaments entering the Quicken Loans National. Howell also won the Michelob Championship in 2002. In addition to his two tournament wins, Howell entered the 2016–2017 season with 14 career second-place finishes.

One of the most consistent golfers on the Tour, Howell is one of 13 golfers who qualified for the Fed Ex Cup Playoffs in every season of its existence. In 16 consecutive seasons from 2002 through 2017, Howell earned no less than $1.2 million in a season, and in six seasons he eclipsed $2 million. At the conclusion of the 2016–2017 season, Howell earned more than $33.4 million for his career, 22nd on the PGA Tour career list.

Entering the Quicken Loans National, Howell was making his first start in nine weeks after recovering from a rib injury. He made the cut in 13 of 14 tournaments prior to the injury with seven top-20 finishes. The 38-year-old Howell ranked 33rd in the points standings when he arrived in Maryland.

Kyle Stanley entered the 2016–2017 season with a career marked by far less consistency. He qualified for the FedEx Cup Playoffs in 2011, 2012, and 2013, making it as far as the third playoff tournament in 2011 and 2012. It was in 2012 that Stanley had his only victory, a one-stroke victory over Ben Crane at the Waste Management Phoenix Open when Stanley's six-birdie, no-bogey, final-round 65 bettered Crane's 66.

Stanley had 28 starts on the PGA Tour in 2013–2014, his final season in the tournament winners group. He made 16 cuts, with three top-25 finishes and one top-ten finish. He earned $473,581, but he ended the regular season at number 158 in the FedEx Cup points standings. He was not successful in improving his exempt status group for the following season through the Web.com Tour Finals.

Stanley started the 2014–2015 PGA Tour season in the past champions group. He split time between PGA Tour and Web.com Tour events that season. He played in 12 PGA Tour events and made the cut in eight, but without a top-ten finish. Stanley ranked 181 in FedEx Cup points at the conclusion of the regular season. Stanley also competed in six regular season tournaments on the Web.com Tour, making the cut in three. His $36,717 was not enough to put him among the top 25 on the Web.com Tour money list. Unlike the previous season, however, Stanley used the Web.com Tour Finals to improve his exempt status for the following season. Stanley finished with one top-20 and two top-ten performances in the four Web.com Finals tournaments. His $81,875 was good for 15th on the money list.

Stanley made 17 cuts, with five top-25 finishes, in 27 PGA tournaments in the 2015–2016 season. He earned his way into the FedEx Cup Playoffs when he jumped from 127th to 116th in the points standings with his tie for 14th in the regular season-ending Wyndham Championship.

Playing out the top 125 in the FedEx Cup points standings group for the 2016–2017 season, the Quicken Loans National was Stanley's 20th start of the season. He made the cut in 16 of 19 tournaments, with four top-ten finishes. His season was highlighted by a tie for fourth at The Players Championship that earned him $462,000 and 135 FedEx Cup points. Stanley was 38th in the FedEx Cup points standings when he entered the Quicken Loans National tournament.

The crowded leaderboard in the final round on the back nine at the Quicken Loans National included many golfers who could use being in the top four as the pathway to the 146th Open Championship at Royal Birkdale in Southport, England. Stanley opened the fourth round with a bogey, but he birdied 5, 6, 8, and 10. Stanley completed erasing the four-shot deficit that existed at the start of the round when he made the birdie at the 10th hole. Stanley was at six under par for the tournament and tied for the lead with David Lingmerth and Sung Kang.

Lingmerth, the 54-hole leader, started the fourth round with a bogey on the 1st and another at the 5th, before making a birdie at the 8th hole to get to six under par. Lingmerth could not regain the form that he displayed earlier in the tournament. He pulled his tee-shot left into the hazard on the 10th hole, but the ball was playable and he scrambled his way to a par. On 11, he again pulled his tee-shot left, but this time the ball landed in the water. He hit his third shot from back at the tee. His drive did find the fairway, but the best that Lingmerth could manage was a double-bogey to drop him to four under.

Martin Laird was one of several golfers chasing the leaders. Laird was at five under par as he arrived at the 284-yard, par-4 14th hole. Laird's tee-shot found the high rough at the bottom of a mound that protruded into a bunker. It was not possible for Laird to stand facing the hole and get a club to the ball. He had to stand awkwardly in the bunker with his back to the hole to hit his second shot. He pitched the ball sideways back into the fairway. Now facing the hole he more than made up for his errant tee-shot as his pitch from 39 yards miraculously found the bottom of the cup for a birdie. Whereas a few minutes ago it seemed that saving par would be a welcome outcome, Laird's improbable birdie caught the leaders at six under par. That would remain his score until the 18th hole, when a bogey removed him from contention.

The 14th hole was not as forgiving for Rickie Fowler. His tee-shot went into the water to the right of the green. His third-shot chip from the drop zone landed short of the green and rolled back to the same position. Fowler's fourth shot finally arrived on the putting surface. He could not convert his seven-foot bogey putt and made double-bogey at the easiest hole on the course. For Fowler, the six at the 14th hole was part of a final-round, five under par 65 that also included a bogey on the 4th and 11th holes, offset by his career high of nine birdies in one round. Fowler concluded the tournament at five under par, in a tie with Laird for third place.

The results at the 14th hole continued to shape the volatile leaderboard. Charles Howell III arrived at the 14th at five under par. His tee-shot reached the green, and he converted his eagle putt of 27 feet to go to seven under par. Kyle Stanley put his tee-shot on the green and had a tap-in birdie to join Howell at seven under. Sung Kang also found success at the 14th hole as his birdie moved him to seven under.

On the 15th hole, Kang dropped back as his bogey did not match the par of Howell and Stanley. They maintained their steady play with par on the 16th hole, but Kang was about to have continued troubles.

Howell placed his tee-shot on the green at the par-3, 199-yard 17th hole. Using a six-iron, Stanley flew his ball over the green into the thick rough. An unexpected rain storm then made its way through the area. With no rain predicted, some golfers were completely caught off-guard without rain gear or an umbrella. In the heavy rain, Stanley was able to pop his chip up out of the thick rough and onto the green. The rain, however, seemed to affect Kang, who did not have an umbrella in his golf bag. With the rain becoming more torrential, Kang even turned his hat backward to prevent the bill from dripping in his face as he was about to putt. Kang missed his six-foot birdie putt on 16.

Tournament officials decided to suspend play with all golfers held in their positions on the course until the rain subsided. After a nine-minute delay from when Stanley chipped onto the green, play resumed. Stanley was faced with a ten-foot, six-inch putt on a green that after the downpour was different from the previous 16 putting surfaces that he navigated on the day. Unfazed by the changed weather conditions, Stanley dropped his putt to dramatically save par. Howell equaled Stanley on 17 after securing a two-putt par. Kang, perhaps still reeling from the short putt he missed in the rain on 16, hit his tee-shot into the water on the 17th hole. He made a double-bogey five on 17 to drop to four under par and eliminate the opportunity for his first PGA Tour victory.

The championship would now be decided between Howell and Stanley, who remained tied as they went to the par-4, 473-yard 18th hole. Stanley hit his tee-shot into the fairway bunker. With 191 yards to the hole, his six-iron put him on the green in regulation. Howell also reached the green in regulation with his eight-iron from 177 yards stopping inside Stanley's ball. Stanley, putting from 36 feet, executed another lengthy lag that led to a tap-in par. Howell now had a putt from 21 feet to win the tournament. The putt went across the front face of the cup from right to left, but did not find its way into the hole. Jim Nantz quizzically exclaimed on the broadcast, "how did it not drop?" Howell tapped in, and he and Stanley remained at seven under par. They would have to settle the Quicken Loans National tournament championship in a playoff.

Howell and Stanley did so with one accomplishment secure, entrance into The Open Championship. For Howell, it would be his ninth appearance at The Open Championship and his first since 2014. Stanley would be making his fourth start at the European major and his first since 2013.

As for the other two tickets into The Open Championship, with a final-round 67, Martin Laird received entrance for his tie for third. Laird's heroics at the 14th hole were now significantly amplified as he played his way to Royal Birkdale for his sixth appearance in The Open Championship and his first since 2013. With Fowler having already qualified for The Open Championship, one final spot was available.

If eligible golfers tie in the tournaments used in qualifying series, the Official World Golf rankings determine which golfer receives the entrance. Eight players tied at four under par at the conclusion of the Quicken Loans National tournament. Sung Kang responded to troubles at 16 and 17 with a par on the 18th hole to complete a final-round 70 to finish four under par. Kang earned the final entrance into The Open Championship thanks to an Official World Golf ranking of 87.

Kang was almost eclipsed by Spencer Levin, the 369th player in the Official World Golf rankings. Levin started the final round at five under, in third place. He bogeyed the 18th hole when his par putt from eight feet, six inches rolled around the cup but did not drop. Levin completed a final-round 71 to drop to four under par. He would have qualified for his third start at The Open Championship had he converted the putt on 18.

Kang now only had to worry about David Lingmerth, who needed a birdie on the 18th to move ahead of Kang. Lingmerth's second shot made the green, but the ball was more than 39 feet from the cup. When his birdie putt came up short, Kang got the final entrance into The Open Championship through the pathway of the Quicken Loans National. He would be playing in The Open Championship for the first time.

In the playoff, back at 18, Stanley teed off first. He hit his drive to the right of the fairway near a couple of utility boxes. Howell's tee-shot placed him just off the fairway on the right, 191 yards from the hole. Howell hit his second shot prior to Stanley, into the thick grass just off the green. Stanley debated whether to take relief, but with a good lie, and perhaps seeing that Howell was not on the green, he decided to play the ball from where it was. At 175 yards away, Stanley shaped a six-iron from right to left with the ball going just off the green, up against the edge of the rough.

With both golfers hitting their third shots, Howell played first. His chip-shot left him a difficult 11 feet from the hole. Stanley had to get another ruling as his ball was near the CBS broadcast microphones. After removing the microphones, Stanley placed his chip-shot inside of Howell's ball. When Howell's par putt drifted wide right, the door was open for Stanley to win the tournament. Stanley buried the five-foot, straight uphill putt to earn his first PGA victory in a span of 135 starts.

Stanley earned more than $1.27 million, the highest earning for his career. He moved into 14th place in the FedEx Cup points standings. For Howell, it was the second time of the season that he finished in the runner-up position, having done so at the Farmers Insurance Open. It was Howell's 16th second-place finish of his career. Howell did jump to 18th in the FedEx Cup points standings.

The third round of the Greenbrier Classic ended with PGA Tour rookie Sebastian Munoz atop the leaderboard at 14 under par. Munoz fired an opening-round 61 that featured ten birdies and only one bogey. He then carded rounds of 67 and 68 at the par-70 Greenbrier course. Munoz held a two-stroke lead over Robert Streb and a three-stroke lead over Xander Schauffele and Jamie Lovemark.

Munoz earned his way onto the PGA Tour by finishing 22nd on the Web.com Tour regular season money list in 2016. Munoz played in 20 regular season tournaments on the Web.com Tour that season. He made the cut in only seven events, but one of those was a win. The Bogota, Colombia, native gained entrance into the Club Colombia Championship played in his hometown on a sponsor exemption. He birdied the 18th hole in the final round to win that tournament by one stroke. Munoz earned $126,000 of his Web.com Tour regular season prize money total of $156,671 for that victory. Munoz missed the cut in all three tournaments of the Web.com Tour Finals and entered the 2016–2017 PGA Tour season 46th in the Web.com Tour priority ranking group.

Munoz played in 11 tournaments on the PGA Tour prior to the Greenbrier Classic 2016–2017. He made the cut in six tournaments, but he finished 35th or better only twice. His best performance was a tie for 27th at the Valero Texas Open. Munoz was tied for the lead after two rounds of the FedEx St. Jude Classic that was played four weeks earlier than the Greenbrier. He posted rounds of 64 and 67, but he could not sustain that level of play. At the par-70 course, Munoz shot a 75 in the third round and a 76 in the final round to finish two over par and tied for 60th. He earned $13,952 for that performance. Munoz also participated in three tournaments on the Web.com Tour in 2017. He missed the cut in two events, but he finished second in the El Bosque Mexico Championship. Munoz earned $70,200 for that performance.

Munoz started the final round of the Greenbrier Classic with three pars. His bogey on the 4th hole was balanced by a birdie at the 5th. His lead over Robert Streb remained at two strokes. On the 6th hole, Munoz began to run into trouble. His tee-shot landed in the rough, and his second shot only found the fringe of the green. He completed the hole with a bogey. On that same hole, sitting in the fairway with 131 yards for his second shot, Streb hit a sand-wedge onto the green. He made his birdie putt to tie Munoz for the lead at 13 under.

In his PGA Tour rookie season in 2013, Streb just missed out on the FedEx Cup Playoffs when he finished 126th, only ten points out of the final playoff position. Streb did qualify for the playoffs in 2014, 2015, and 2016. At the McGladrey Classic in the autumn of 2014, Streb used a final-round 63 and consecutive birdies on the 14th through 17th holes to force a playoff with Brendon de Jonge and Will MacKenzie. While MacKenzie was eliminated on the first hole, Streb emerged victorious against de Jonge on the second extra hole when for the second time that day he birdied the par-3 17th hole. Streb went on to have 16 top-25 finishes and nine top-ten performances in the 30 tournaments that he played in the 2014–2015 season. He qualified for the Tour Championship and earned more than $3.94 million, along with a bonus of $235,000 for finishing 18th in the FedEx Cup points standings.

Streb had his own unique history at the Greenbrier Classic. In 2015, on the 9th hole in the final round he tossed his putter toward his golf bag. The shaft of the putter bent, making the club no longer usable. Streb played the last nine holes using a sand-wedge to putt. He was miraculously able to convert five birdie putts, including a 26-foot, eight-inch effort at the 13th hole, to make a four-man playoff. Streb could place a new putter in his golf bag for the play-off, but his attempt at victory came up short when he was eliminated on the first extra hole. Danny Lee emerged as the 2015 Greenbrier Classic champion.

Streb and Munoz both parred the 7th hole, but they were achieved far differently. Streb missed the green on his approach shot, but he executed an up-and-down to save par. Munoz continued to have problems with his putter when a three-foot birdie opportunity lipped out. Munoz missed another putt of less than five feet on the 8th hole to fall out of the lead. On the 9th hole, after hitting his tee-shot in the left rough and his approach short of the green, another missed par putt concluded the front nine for Munoz at three over par. He was 11 under for the tournament and two strokes behind Streb.

Meanwhile, Xander Schauffele, playing in the group ahead of Munoz and Streb, joined the top of the leaderboard. Schauffele made his second birdie of the day at the par-3, 213-yard 8th hole to tie for the lead at 13 under par. On the 11th hole, Schauffele found the bunker on the right with his tee-shot. With the ball up against the edge of the trap, Schauffele was forced to lay up for his second shot. Although his third shot was on the green, his par putt lipped out, and the bogey dropped him to 12 under. At the par-5, 574-yard 12th, Schauffele found himself in trouble off the tee for the second consecutive hole. Schauffele, who eagled the 12th hole in the third round, was able to scramble his way to a par in the final round.

Munoz regained his composure as he birdied the 11th and 12th to get to 13 under par. He was one stroke ahead of Schauffele and one stroke behind Streb, who birdied the 12th hole to get to 14 under par. The 13th was the hole where Streb ran into trouble. Streb's tee-shot went far left into the deep, high weeds, forcing him to take a penalty stroke. His third shot rolled through the green. He had to chip onto the green, but he remained more than 20 feet from the hole. When that putt did not roll in, the double-bogey dropped Streb to 12 under par. A par by Munoz on 13 put him back into the lead. Streb did quickly rebound with a birdie on the 14th, making a putt from just inside 35 feet, to once again match Munoz at 13 under. Both players parred the 15th hole.

Schauffele found his way back into the co-lead position at 13 under par when he birdied the par-4 16th hole. Munoz's volatile day continued on the 16th. His tee-shot ended up against the first cut of the rough. He could not recover on his second shot as it missed the green. Munoz was able to chip to eight feet, but he missed his par putt to drop him out of the lead for the final time. Streb's attempt at birdie on 16 was only one or two revolutions short of going in the hole. Streb and Schauffele were tied with two holes to play.

At the par-5, 614-yard 17th hole, Schauffele hit his second-shot two-iron from 295 yards to the left, finding the thick rough near the spectators. He successfully managed that difficult lie and chipped onto the green, where he converted a two-putt par. For his second shot on the 17th hole, Streb played a three-wood from 290 yards. A few inches away from what might have been the perfect shot, Streb's ball hit the edge of the bunker and kicked right to land in the trap. Streb did get his third shot onto the green, but he could not convert his birdie putt from 13 feet, six inches. He too made par on 17.

The 18th at the Greenbrier is a par-3, 161-yard hole. It was the only tournament on the PGA Tour in 2016–2017 that concluded with a par-3. Schauffele stuck his pitching wedge three feet from the hole. When Schauffele converted his birdie, he took sole possession of the lead for the first time at 14 under par. Streb needed to match the birdie by Schauffele to force a playoff. He used a nine iron, and while his tee-shot hit the green, it jumped into the rough. Streb was not able to chip in and finished 13 under. The 23-year-old Schauffele, who three weeks earlier tied for fifth at the U.S. Open, now had his first PGA Tour victory. He jumped from 94 to 27 in the FedEx Cup points standings. He also qualified for the trip to compete in The Open Championship.

Streb did have the consolation prize of gaining entrance into The Open Championship for the third consecutive year. He also moved up in the FedEx Cup points standings from 137th to 68. Overall, for the 2016–2017 season Streb made the cut in 20 of his 30 appearances. He had six top-25 and three top-ten finishes. He entered the playoffs 79th in the standings. He tied for tenth at the Northern Trust and for 73rd at the Dell Technologies Championship. He was able to advance to the BMW Championship, where a tie for 53rd completed his season. Streb won a bonus of $110,000 for finishing 63rd in the standings. He won more than $1.58 million in tournament prize money.

Schauffele and Streb were joined in qualifying for The Open Championship by Munoz, who completed a final-round 72 to finish at 12 under par, and Jamie Lovemark, whose final-round 69 also put him at 12 under.

For Munoz, it would be his first major tournament appearance. Munoz also moved himself up 58 spots in the FedEx Cup Playoff standings, advancing from 198 to 140. Munoz finished 153rd in the FedEx Cup standings and played in the Web.com Tour Finals. He qualified for the Finals through two paths, the top 200 in the FedEx Cup standings and the top 75 on the Web.com Tour regular season money list. He earned $20,800 for his tie for eighth at the WinCo Foods Portland Open. Added to his previous amount of $70,200, Munoz was 54th on the Web.com Tour money list. He earned $13,713 in the Finals over the first three tournaments, but missed the cut in the Web.com Tour Championship. Munoz attained fully exempt status on the Web.com Tour for the 2018 season by being in the top 75 of the regular season money list.

For Lovemark, it was his second consecutive season of qualifying for The Open Championship and making the FedEx Cup Playoffs. Lovemark entered the playoffs 47th in the standings. After missing the cut at the Northern Trust, he tied for 40th and for 33rd at the next two events. Lovemark received a $110,000 bonus for finishing 57th and earned more than $1.88 million in prize money.

The John Deere Classic was played the week before The Open Championship, on the same weekend as the Scottish Open, a tournament more similar in playing style to The Open Championship. The field at the John Deere Classic in Illinois included only two of the top ten golfers in the points standings. Only five of the top 20 and seven of the top 30 golfers comprised the John Deere field.

Bryson DeChambeau was trying to overcome missing eight straight tournament cuts from the RBC Heritage in April through the U.S. Open in June. He was 141st in the FedEx Cup standings after the U.S. Open. DeChambeau shot rounds of 66, 65, and 70 at the par-71 course to be one of a trio of golfers at 12 under par entering the final round of the John Deere Classic, in fifth place, four strokes behind tournament leader Patrick Rodgers at 16 under par. Daniel Berger and Scott Stallings were 14 under, while Nicholas Lindheim was 13 under entering the final round. A marker was set early in the round when 50-year-old Steve Stricker shot a seven under par 64, to put him in the clubhouse at 15 under. Wesley Bryan eclipsed Stricker's score and went to the clubhouse at 16 under par. Bryan completed a final round of 64 that featured a five-hole consecutive birdie stretch from the 13th through the 17th holes and a back nine score of 30.

Rodgers played the front nine at one over par. He birdied the 10th hole and the par-3 12th to go to 17 under par to re-take the lead. DeChambeau had yet to make his charge. DeChambeau played the front nine at even par, with a bogey on the 4th hole and a birdie on the 8th. He birdied the 10th and 11th holes to go to 14 under and move into a tie for seventh. After a par on the 12th hole, DeChambeau birdied the 13th and 14th holes to move to 16 under par and join Bryan and Stallings, who just birdied the 13th hole. They were now one stroke behind Rodgers. Stallings bogeyed the 15th hole, and he finished at 15 under, tied for fifth with four other golfers.

At the par-4, 13th hole, Rodgers converted a 28-foot, four-inch birdie putt to extend his score to 18 under. Rodgers, however, gave that stroke back when he bogeyed the 357-yard 14th hole. Rodgers' tee-shot found the fairway bunker.

Unable to see the green or the flagstick on his second shot, he flew his approach over the green and down a hill into the rough. Rodgers' chip went past the cup, and he missed a 13-foot par putt.

Now again only one stroke back in his chase of Rodgers, DeChambeau hit his tee-shot at the par-5, 560-yard 17th hole to the right of the fairway at the bottom of a hill just inches from the cart path. From 259 yards away, DeChambeau ran up the hill after striking the ball to see where it landed. He liked what he saw as the ball ended up on the green, but still more than 40 feet from the hole. DeChambeau put his eagle attempt to four feet, two inches before making the birdie putt to go to 17 under. Rodgers responded to his bogey on 14 with a birdie on the 15th and a par on the 16th. Rodgers was at 18 under par and had a one-stroke lead with two holes left.

DeChambeau played the par-4, 482-yard 18th hole with scores of par-par-bogey in the first three rounds. He placed his tee-shot in the fairway in the final round. His second shot, from 194 yards away, landed near the hole and rolled 14 feet away. DeChambeau's birdie putt rolled across the face of the hole from left to right, appearing as if it would not go in, before dropping on the right side of the cup. DeChambeau completed a final round of 65, 30 on the back nine, to put himself at 18 under and into a tie with Rodgers for the lead. The exuberant DeChambeau slapped hands with fans as he went to sign his scorecard.

DeChambeau had to wait for Rodgers to finish his round. At the 17th hole, Rodgers hit his tee-shot far left into the trees. From behind a tree, Rodgers was forced to pitch out for his second shot. The ball rolled through the fairway and into the primary rough on the right side. For his third shot, Rodgers had 180 yards to the front of the green and 205 yards to the hole. His seven-iron got him on the right front of the green, but the putting surface is shaped in such a way that a bunker protrudes into the green. With the pin tucked in the back right corner, although Rodgers was on the green, putting directly to the hole was not possible. Instead, his fourth shot from the green had to be executed with a wedge. After pitching over the bunker, Rodgers saw his par putt hit the hole, but bounce out. He bogeyed the 17th hole.

Rodgers was down one stroke going to the 18th hole. Again, his tee-shot got him in trouble, into the gallery on the right. Rodgers, who led after the third round and for much of the final round, now had to go up-and-down to force a playoff. With a tree intruding on a clear path to the hole, Rodgers had to shape the ball around the tree that was 167 yards from the hole. His seven-iron hit the green but ran through it to the bottom of a hill. He needed to chip in for any chance of victory. The ball appeared that it might roll in as it moved toward the cup, but it stayed left of the hole. Rodgers shot 70 in the final round and finished 17 under par, in sole possession of second place. Rodgers did advance from 107th to 52nd in the FedEx Cup points standings. He earned more than $1.34 million for the season and a bonus of $80,000 after participating in two playoff tournaments.

DeChambeau, in his 40th start on the PGA Tour, had his first victory. He also earned the final entrance into The Open Championship through the qualifying series format. DeChambeau headed to the Quad City International Airport to join the other golfers on the charter flight to England.

DeChambeau jumped from 114th to 34th in the FedEx Cup points standings with the win. He concluded the regular season 43rd in the standings. After missing the cut in the Northern Trust, DeChambeau tied for 30th at the Dell Technologies Championship and tied for 33rd at the BMW Championship. For the season, he made the cut in 14 of his 31 tournament starts. He had four top-25 finishes and two in the top ten. His total prize money for 2016–2017 was more than $1.81 million, and he was awarded a playoff bonus of $126,000 for 49th place in the FedEx Cup standings.

20

July 23, 2017

The Open Championship at Royal Birkdale in 2017 will long be remembered for the exploits of Jordan Spieth. Spieth started the final round with a three-stroke lead over Matt Kuchar. He squandered his lead with bogeys on three of the first four holes. Spieth and Kuchar shared the lead at eight under par as they arrived at the par-4, 503-yard 13th hole. From this point in the tournament, Spieth displayed all of his skills as a champion golfer: course management acumen, ball-striking, short game, and putting.

As Spieth struck his drive on 13, he immediately put his hands to his head in disbelief at a shot that landed an estimated 75 yards to the right of the fairway. The ball was found in an unplayable position, and he absorbed a penalty stroke. Spieth had three options from where he could play his next shot. He could drop the ball within two club lengths of the unplayable ball, hitting his next shot from similar, difficult terrain. He could return to the tee and hit his third shot from there. Or he could take the ball back on a straight line from the flagstick and where his unplayable ball landed, back as far as he desired.

In seeking a ruling, Spieth went all the way back to the practice range. With golf equipment trucks obscuring the direct line, Spieth was able to drop his ball two club lengths, no closer to the hole, from that position. Finally, with a completely blind shot to the green, Spieth's caddie, Michael Greller, could stand in a position to help align Spieth with the flagstick. This human alignment aid is permissible in shot preparation, but a two-stroke penalty if Greller remained in that position when Spieth hit the ball. Spieth alerted Greller to move as he was about to play his shot.

Approximately 22 minutes after hitting his tee-shot, Spieth hit his third shot. Spieth again reacted with dismay, but this time, although the ball did not reach the green, it was on line with the flagstick. Spieth then executed a perfect up-and-down to record one of the more memorable bogeys in major championship golf. Doug Ferguson of the *Associated Press* wrote, "Spieth showed his golfing brain is as valuable as any club in his bag."

Now down one stroke to Kuchar, Spieth hit a tee-shot at the par-3 14th hole that bounced within inches of the cup. He made a birdie to once again tie for the lead. Sitting 257 yards away from the pin for his second shot at the par-5 15th hole, Spieth found the green. Spieth made an eagle at the 15th in round two. In the final round, he did so again by draining a 48-foot putt. Kuchar birdied 15, but he suddenly trailed by one stroke.

Spieth missed the fairway on the 16th hole, but from 153 yards away his approach shot put him in the center of the green, 30 feet from the cup. Spieth made another improbable birdie putt. He added a birdie at the par-5, 565-yard 17th hole when he hit his second shot to 56 yards from the hole before executing another up-and-down.

Spieth won The Open Championship, his third major championship, by three strokes. Of Spieth's five under par performance over the four-hole stretch after the 13th, Johnny Miller stated on NBC that it was "the greatest finish I have seen in championship golf." Jack Nicklaus posted on social media, "to follow that bogey on 13 with great golf shots and great putts, and play the final five holes in five under par, I was just happy for him and very impressed to watch all that guts, determination and skill."

Of the nine golfers who entered The Open Championship through the qualifying series, six did not make the cut. Xander Schauffele had the best performance with a tie for 20th at one under par. He earned $104,500 and 49 FedEx Cup points. Jamie Lovemark finished even par to tie for 22nd. He took home $88,000 in prize money and accumulated 42 FedEx Cup points. Sung Kang tied for 44th upon shooting three over par. Kang earned $31,070 and 11 FedEx Cup points.

One other golfer's career significantly changed on the final day of The Open Championship, but it did not happen in England. Instead it occurred a continent away in Auburn, Alabama, at the PGA Tour's Barbasol Championship. Scott Stallings was the leader at 19 under par entering the final round. Stallings shot a third-round 60 at the par-71 course when he hit all 18 greens in regulation. He had a one-stroke lead over Grayson Murray, who posted rounds of 67–64–64. Murray made 17 birdies with only three bogeys in the second and third rounds.

Stallings had a two-stroke lead over Tag Ridings and Chad Collins. The 42-year-old Ridings was seeking his first win on the PGA Tour in his 236th start. Ridings' best finish was a tie for second at the Michelin Championship in Las Vegas in 2004. In 2016–2017, prior to the Barbasol Championship, Ridings played in 15 PGA tournaments and made the cut in ten. He had one top-

25 finish, a tie for 11th in the Zurich Classic of New Orleans team event where he partnered with Xander Schauffele. Ridings entered the Barbasol Championship in 175th place in the FedEx Cup points standings. He earned $257,036 at that point in the season.

Chad Collins had not won a tournament in 175 Tour starts. Prior to the Barbasol, Collins had 22 PGA Tour starts, but he made the cut on only four occasions. His season highlight was a tie for fourth at the Honda Classic for which he earned $232,000. Collins posted a 60 in the second round of the Barbasol Championship when he birdied six consecutive holes, 11 through 16. At some point in the final round, Stallings, Murray, Ridings, and Collins found themselves atop the leaderboard.

Murray opened the final round with a bogey on the 1st hole. He birdied the 2nd and 7th holes before missing a short par putt to bogey the par-3 8th hole. Murray's tee-shot at the par-4, 432-yard 9th hole drifted right, striking a tree branch but ricocheting onto the left side of the fairway. His second shot from 83 yards found the green, and his birdie putt from six feet found the bottom of the cup. Murray, one under par on the front nine, joined Stallings in the lead at 19 under par. Stallings shot even par on the front nine with a bogey on the 1st hole and a birdie on the 5th.

Both Ridings and Stallings birdied the 394-yard, par-4 10th hole. Ridings improved his score to 19 under and Stallings to 20 under, as he regained the sole lead. On 11, Stallings squandered an opportunity to extend his lead to two strokes when his three-and-a-half-foot birdie putt rolled around the cup and out.

The 13th hole, a 536-yard par-5, playing as the second easiest hole on the course, dramatically altered the leaderboard. As Murray struck his second shot, he dropped his head, unhappily thinking that his ball was going into the greenside bunker. The shot from 185 yards, however, just cleared the trap and bounced before perfectly rolling along the contours of the green to less than five feet from the cup. Murray buried the eagle putt to take the lead at 21 under par.

Ridings birdied the 13th hole to move to 20 under par. Stallings was not able to execute his short-game on that hole. His drive went to the left of the fairway, and he chose to lay up for his second shot. His third shot did put him on the green, but more than 48 feet from the hole. Stallings' putt still left him 12 feet away, and when he could not make the par putt, he dropped to 19 under par. The play at the 13th hole produced a three-stroke swing between him and Murray.

The shakeup of the leaderboard continued on the 435-yard, par-4 14th hole. Both Murray and Ridings drove into the fairway bunker. Murray's second shot was hit well right of the hole into a barren area of weeds beyond the green, the rough, and the announcer tower. With a stick touching the ball, Murray's pitch, his third shot, came up short of the green. Murray settled for a tap-in bogey.

Ridings, meanwhile, hit his bunker shot from 117 yards onto the green and made his birdie putt to complete the two-stroke swing with Murray. Ridings took a one-shot lead at 21 under par. Stallings parred the 14th hole to remain at 19 under par, two strokes behind Ridings.

The par-4, 442-yard 15th hole resulted in a par for each golfer. While Ridings' par offered no drama, Murray once again found the fairway bunker with his tee-shot. Unlike the previous hole, Murray perfectly executed his second shot, placing it on the green, where he two-putted for par. Stallings' second shot on 15 almost went into the water. He had to hit his third shot from an incredibly awkward stance with his right leg in the water up to his knee and his left leg bent on the hill next to the water. Stallings, amazingly, was able to punch the ball onto the green, stopping only three feet away from the hole. He sank the par putt.

Ridings' one-stroke lead with three holes to play showed no signs of being in jeopardy when his tee-shot at the par-5, 581-yard 16th hole found the fairway. From 240 yards out on what appeared to be a rudimentary second shot, Ridings immediately dropped his club after he struck the ball. Ridings inexplicably hit the ball short of the green, to the right and into the hazard area. It was the only place on the hole that presented trouble. Short and left would have Ridings well positioned to reach the green in regulation.

After being assessed a penalty stroke, now hitting his fourth shot, Ridings put the ball on the green more than 41 feet from the hole that made salvaging par unrealistic. His par putt left him with an eight-foot, three-inch putt for bogey. When that putt also missed, Ridings walked away from a hole that started with a tee-shot in the fairway with a double-bogey seven. He was now 19 under and out of the lead.

Other golfers took advantage of the Ridings miscue. Playing one group ahead of the final trio, Chad Collins rallied with a birdie on the 13th hole and three consecutive birdies on 15 through 17 to get to 20 under par. Stallings birdied the 16th to also get to 20 under par. Their gaining a share of the lead at 20 under par was only momentary. On 16, Murray placed his drive in the fairway. His second shot from 210 yards from the flag, using a five-iron, rolled through the green to the back fringe. He wedged the ball into position to tap in for a birdie and take the lead at 21 under with two holes left.

Murray, Ridings, and Stallings all parred at the par-3, 156-yard 17th hole. Collins, playing the par-4, 476-yard 18th, missed the fairway with his tee-shot.

He recovered by hitting an eight-iron from 176 yards onto the green. Back at the tee on 18, Stallings hit his drive way right into the trees, essentially removing himself from contention. Stallings had to avoid the trees by punching out into the rough and bogeyed the hole. Stallings' final-round 71 was 11 strokes greater than his score the previous day. Ridings parred the 18th hole to end the tournament at 19 under par.

Murray's drive on 18 ended up on the edge of the first and second cuts of rough. While waiting to hit his approach shot to the green, Murray asked Golf Channel on-course reporter Gary Christian if Collins' putt on 18 was for birdie. When Collins came up short on his tying birdie attempt, Murray only needed to par the hole for the victory. From 176 yards away, Murray put his second shot onto the green with two putts for the win. His first putt stopped four feet, seven inches short, certainly not a simple tap-in. Murray, though, buried the putt, and the 23-year-old Tour rookie had his first PGA title in his 24th start. Murray set the 72-hole tournament record for low score with a total of 263.

Murray played in 23 tournaments and made the cut in 13 prior to the Barbasol Championship. He started the season by making only three cuts in his first 11 tournaments but made the cut in his next ten starts. He ranked 124th in the FedEx Cup standings before the tournament in Alabama. With the win, Murray jumped to 58th.

Murray missed the cut at the RBC Canadian Open the following week. He was not part of the field at the World Golf Championships—Bridgestone Invitation, and he also skipped the Barracuda Championship held that same weekend. He tied for 22nd at the PGA Championship, his first appearance in that major tournament. Murray earned $87,167 and 41 FedEx Cup points for that outcome. After missing the cut at the Wyndham Championship, Murray ended the regular season 69th in the standings.

Murray made the cut in all three playoff tournaments he played. He tied for 62nd at the Northern Trust, tied for 25th at the Dell Technologies Championship, and tied for 51st at the BMW Championship. He earned $108,151 for these three playoff performances and a bonus of $110,000 for finishing 66th in the FedEx Cup standings. Murray earned more than $1.46 million for the season, far above his previous season's winnings of $407,963 on the Web.com Tour.

One week after a tie for fifth at the John Deere Classic, Scott Stallings had his second consecutive top-five finish with a tie for third at the Barbasol Championship. Stallings advanced from number 132 to 108 in the FedEx Cup points standings after the John Deere Classic. He now advanced to number 96 with his performance at the Barbasol Championship. After making the playoffs every season from 2011 through 2014, but missing the playoffs in 2015 and 2016,

Stallings ended the 2017 regular season 102nd in the standings. He tied for 43rd at the Northern Trust to earn $28,058, but he did not advance any further. Stallings was awarded a playoff bonus of $70,000 for finishing 101st. Stallings played in 27 tournaments in 2016–2017, with 14 made cuts. He had six performances in the top 25 and three in the top ten. He earned $955,337 for the season.

The tie for third at the Barbasol Championship was the best performance of the season for Tag Ridings. He advanced his position in the FedEx points standings 21 spots, up to number 154. Ridings won $182,000. Ridings competed in 20 PGA tournaments and made the cut in 13, finishing 155th in the standings. He was 32 points behind the 150th position of Rick Lamb that would have provided him with a bonus and status on the PGA Tour for the following season. Ridings earned $489,927.

Ridings did compete in the Web.com Tour Finals, where the previous season he finished 23rd on the prize money list to earn his PGA Tour card. In 2017, however, Ridings would not have the same success, winning only $15,235. Without having won a tournament or having made 150 PGA Tour cuts in his career to claim a veteran member status, Ridings was looking at entering the 2017–2018 season with conditional status on the Web.com Tour. He competed in the Q School final stage tournament to try to upgrade that status. He tied for 57th place. If Ridings finished one stroke better in the Q School final stage tournament, he would have joined the other 15 golfers who tied for 42nd. If he had finished in the top 45 of the Q School final stage, Ridings would have been fully exempt on the Web.com Tour for the first eight tournaments of the season.

Chad Collins did advance from 170th in the FedEx Cup points standings to number 127 for finishing alone in second place at the Barbasol Championship. He would not gain the few needed positions to advance into the FedEx Cup Playoffs. After the Barbasol, Collins tied for 48th at the RBC Canadian Open. He then missed the cut at the Barracuda Championship and the Wyndham Championship. Collins completed a regular season in which he played in 26 PGA tournaments but made the cut in only six. Collins earned $693,743 on the PGA Tour and received a $32,000 bonus for finishing 143rd in the standings.

Collins was able to improve his exempt status group for the following season through his performance at the Web.com Tour Finals. He opened the Finals with a tie for 41st. After missing the cut at the second tournament, Collins tied for sixth at the DAP Championship to earn $31,300. His tie for 20th at the Web.com Tour Championship added another $9,348 for his Finals total of $44,348. Collins finished 22nd on the Finals prize money list. After the alternate selection process, Collins entered the 2017–2018 season 45th in the top finishers of the Web.com Tour group.

21

The Wyndham Championship

As demonstrated, while some golfers are rallying to qualify for the FedEx Cup Playoffs, others are coming up short. The fate of the PGA Tour's system is such that being on the wrong side of its dividing lines will happen to some golfers each season. Considering how close the conclusion of the season-long points race typically is, the difference in qualifying for the playoffs could literally be one stroke, making one more tournament cut, having the opportunity to compete in one more tournament, or even deciding to participate in one more tournament. One late-season win or strong performance can vault a golfer to an improved playoff position, or simply be the difference in qualifying for the playoffs.

In the PGA Tour system, a golfer is never out of playoff contention. In comparison, when teams in other sports are having a poor season, many of their remaining games will have no bearing on that season's outcome. For a golfer, the opportunity to qualify for the playoffs is not determined until the final regular season tournament concludes. Much the way that the WinCo Foods Portland Open has additional drama and pressure as the final tournament of the Web.com Tour regular season, so too does the Wyndham Championship on the PGA Tour. While a PGA Tour card or entrance into the Web.com Tour Finals is at stake in Portland, with FedEx Cup Playoff positions still to be resolved, the Wyndham Championship provides unmatched intrigue and finality on multiple dividing lines.

The 2014–2015 season for Will MacKenzie ended in July when he had knee surgery. In his first five tournaments, MacKenzie won $747,511 and accumulated 382 FedEx Cup points. He collected $492,800 in the tie for second at the McGladrey Classic when he, along with Brendon de Jonge, lost in a playoff to Robert Streb. He earned $141,171 after a tie for ninth at the OHL Classic at Mayakoba, and $97,125 for a sixth-place tie at the Puerto Rico Open. Overall,

MacKenzie played in 16 tournaments with these three top-ten finishes. With the successful season he was having, despite not playing in one month, MacKenzie still found himself 116th in the FedEx Cup points standings prior to the Wyndham Championship.

At the Wyndham in 2015, Ryo Ishikawa shot a fourth-round 66 that included three birdies in the final six holes. Ishikawa's rally put him in a tie for 31st and earned him 37 FedEx Cup points. With that finish, Ishikawa ended the season tied with MacKenzie and Jeff Overton at 458 points. Overton missed the cut at the Wyndham. The golfers' position in the Official World Golf ranking was used to break the tie. With that criterion applied, it was Ishikawa awarded the 124th position, Overton finishing at number 125, and MacKenzie ending up 126th.

Although he couldn't compete in the FedEx Cup Playoff tournaments with his injury, the initial significance of MacKenzie getting the 126th position instead of position 124 or 125 was that he received a smaller bonus, $32,000 instead of $70,000. What helped lessen the negative consequences was that MacKenzie did end 2014–2015 115th on the PGA Tour money list with $863,563. MacKenzie had an exempt status for the 2015–2016 season in the top 125 finishers in prize money priority ranking group. This achievement meant that MacKenzie did not have to apply for a medical extension.

The 2015 Wyndham Championship also provided one of the more improbable outcomes when then 51-year-old Davis Love III won the tournament. Love entered the 2014–2015 season with an exempt status as a life member. Love first won a PGA tournament in 1987 and won the PGA Championship in 1997. His most recent title was in 2008. Love had 20 PGA tournament championships and career winnings of just under $42.8 million in prize money as he began the 2014–2015 season.

Love arrived at the Wyndham Championship 186th in the FedEx Cup points standings. He participated in 15 PGA tournaments and made the cut in five, with a tie for eighth at the CIMB Classic as his best finish. Love even competed in three events on the Champions Tour that season. He made the cut in all three tournaments, including a tie for fifth place, to earn a Champions Tour total of $87,125.

Love entered the final round of the Wyndham Championship trailing Jason Gore by four strokes. Love started his round with a bogey but followed with a five-hole stretch that he played at six under par. Love made four birdies and eagled the par-5, 529-yard 5th hole. After a 345-yard tee-shot in the fairway, Love stopped his shot from 188 yards inside of five feet before converting the eagle putt. Despite a bogey on the 7th hole, Love completed the front nine with a 31. He added his second eagle of the day on the 15th when he hit his second shot from 211 yards to just over 12 feet from the pin. He shot a final-round 64. Love defeated Gore, who carded a 69, by one stroke.

It was Love's third win at the Sedgefield County Club in Greensboro, North Carolina, having won in 1992, when the tournament was called the Kmart Greater Greensboro Open, and in 2006, when it was the Chrysler Classic of Greensboro. Love became the third-oldest player to win a PGA tournament at 51 years and four months. He trailed only Sam Snead, who also won the Greensboro tournament in 1965 at 52 years and ten months old, and Art Wall, who at 51 years and seven months won the 1975 Greater Milwaukee Open.

With the win and the 500 FedEx Cup points, Love vaulted from 186th to 76th in the FedEx Cup standings. He qualified for the playoffs for the first time since 2012. He missed the cut at the Barclays, but he won $22,344 with a tie for 44th at the Deutsche Bank Championship. He earned more than $1.26 million on the season plus a playoff bonus of $75,000 and a two-season exempt status in the tournament winners group.

Si Woo Kim won the 2016 Wyndham Championship in his 30th start of the season. Kim certainly could have skipped the Wyndham Championship, sitting 41st in the standings. Instead, the 500 FedEx Cup points for the win moved him into 15th in the final points standings. By playing and winning the Wyndham Championship, Kim gained entrance into all four FedEx Cup playoff tournaments. After missing the cut at the Barclays, Kim finished 15th at the Deutsche Bank Championship, 20th at the BMW Championship, and tied for tenth at the Tour Championship. Kim earned $449,395 for his performance in the FedEx Cup Playoff tournaments. His prize money total was $3.08 million, and his final finish of 17th brought a playoff bonus of $240,000.

In 2016, two golfers used their Wyndham Championship performance to qualify for the FedEx Cup Playoffs. Shawn Stefani and Kyle Stanley finished the Wyndham Championship in a tie for 14th place, earning 55 FedEx Cup points. They replaced Matt Jones and Whee Kim, who both missed the cut. Stefani was assisted by a hole-in-one at the 16th during the third round and moved from 133 to 123. He finished with 459 points, only 14 ahead of Matt Jones in 126th place.

Stanley moved from 127th to number 116 with 497 points. For Stanley, his rally to qualify for the FedEx Cup Playoffs included earning 47 points at the John Deere Classic the week before the Wyndham Championship.

Although they both made the cut at the Barclays, neither Stefani nor Stanley advanced past the first tournament of the FedEx Cup Playoffs. Stefani, tied for 64th, earned $17,765, and Stanley, tied for 74th, earned $16,150 at the Barclays. Qualifying for the playoffs did earn each a $70,000 bonus.

The Wyndham Championship in 2017 once again delivered spectacular drama with results that would reverberate through the upcoming post-season and the following season. First, Henrik Stenson won the tournament by shooting a record 22 under par, 258, to break the record of 259, set by Carl Pettersson in 2008 and Si Woo Kim in 2016. Stenson needed every one of those strokes as Ollie Schniederjans finished only one stroke off the lead at 259.

Stenson posted rounds of 62–66–66–64. He made eight birdies in his opening round of eight under par 62. Stenson still needed a 31 on the back nine in the final round with a birdie on 13, 15, 16, and 17. Schniederjans shot a final-round 64 with a birdie on 16 and 17 to apply pressure on Stenson. At the 18th, Stenson came out of the rough to save par and win the tournament. Stenson moved from number 75 to 23 in the FedEx Cup points standings. Schniederjans jumped from 74th to 39th.

Four golfers moved into the top 125 in the points standings and into the playoffs at the Wyndham. This result, of course, meant that four golfers who held positions in the top 125 prior to the Wyndham were eliminated from the playoffs. Rory Sabbatini had the greatest jump when he moved from number 148 to 122. Sabbatini was a six-time winner on the PGA Tour with more than $29 million in career earnings as he entered the 2016–2017 season. In 2007, Sabbatini won more than $4.5 million in a season that included a victory at Colonial in a playoff over Jim Furyk and Bernhard Langer, as well as top-ten finishes in all four FedEx Cup Playoff tournaments.

Sabbatini played in only 20 tournaments in the 2015–2016 season due to neck surgery in May 2016. He made eight cuts, with a tie for 25th at the Shriners Hospitals for Children Open as his best finish. He ended the regular season 191st in the FedEx Cup standings. With the prospect of being relegated to the past champions group, for the first time in his career Sabbatini put a tee in the ground at a Web.com Tour event when he participated in the Finals. At the DAP Championship, the first Finals tournament, Sabbatini made a hole-in-one in the third round on his way to a tie for sixth. That result provided Sabbatini $32,375. Despite missing the cut in the other two Finals tournaments, Sabbatini was able to finish 21st on the Finals prize money list. He began the 2016–2017 season in position number 43 in the top finishers of the Web.com Tour ranking group.

In the 2016–2017 season, Sabbatini had a stretch from the Valero Texas Open, which concluded on April 23, through the Travelers Championship, which concluded on June 25, when in seven tournaments, he missed the cut in six and withdrew from the other. Sabbatini had 95 FedEx Cup points and was in 175th place after the Travelers Championship. He responded with a four-tournament stretch in which he finished every event in the top 25. He tied for

14th at the Greenbrier Classic, tied for 19th at the John Deere Classic, tied for 23rd at the RBC Canadian Open, and 17th at the Barracuda Championship. This flurry got Sabbatini to 148th place in the standings.

At the Wyndham Championship, Sabbatini played his only tournament of the season with all four rounds under 70. He posted scores of 65–68–66–64. In the fourth round, after switching his putting grip earlier in the week, Sabattini needed only 24 putts after hitting 11 greens in regulation. He finished the Wyndham in a tie for fourth place, his only top ten of the season.

Overall, for the regular season, Sabattini played in 22 tournaments with 12 made cuts. The Wyndham capped his late-season rally that produced six made cuts and five top-25 finishes. He completed the regular season 122nd in the standings. Sabbatini, who played regularly on the PGA Tour since 1999 and completed his 472nd tournament at the Wyndham, explained to CBS reporter Amanda Balionis, "considering as long as I've been out here it brings back a lot of memories from being a rookie. It was a rough year. You can't really make a schedule coming out of the Web playoffs. It was tough. Over the last couple of months I really had to grind."

Harold Varner III finished the 2015–2016 season 75th in the final points standings. He made it to the second playoff tournament and earned an $80,000 bonus. In 2016–2017, Varner participated in 28 tournaments and made the cut in 16 prior to the Wyndham Championship. He had five top-25 finishes, highlighted by a tie for 19th at the Memorial. Varner entered the Wyndham number 138 in the standings.

Varner had his best finish of the season when he tied for tenth at the Wyndham. Varner opened with an eight-birdie, one-bogey round of 63. He followed with rounds of 68 and 66 at the par-70 course. Varner shot a 32 on the front nine in the final round with a birdie at the 5th, 6th, and 9th holes. He shot 11 under on the front nine holes over all four rounds of the tournament.

Varner was projected to be at number 107 in the FedEx Cup points standings with nine holes remaining in the regular season, but bogeyed the 10th and 11th holes. He did birdie the 15th hole, but he followed that up with a bogey on 16. His back nine score was a 37. Varner's fourth-round score of 69 left him at 14 under. It was good enough for him to end the regular season at number 123 in the FedEx Cup standings. Varner's first two seasons on the PGA Tour concluded with the FedEx Cup Playoffs.

J. J. Henry entered the 2016–2017 season with career earnings of more than $15.4 million. He is a three-time winner on the PGA Tour. His first win occurred at the Buick Open in 2006, and his most recent at the 2015 Barracuda Championship. In his final season in the tournament winners ranking group, Henry arrived at the Wyndham Championship 134th in the points standings.

Henry shot a 66 in the opening round and an even par 70 in round two. He was one stroke inside the cut line total of 137. A third-round, four under par 66 still had Henry projected outside of a playoff qualifying position as he stood at number 129. The 42-year-old Henry shot a two under par 33 on the front nine in the final round. He posted a bogey at the 12th hole, his only one of the day. Henry stabilized his round with a par on the 13th through 15th holes. He needed to rally with three holes left to play. Henry birdied the 16th when he converted a putt of 13 feet. Henry still only projected into the number 127 position as he parred the 17th hole.

Henry's tee-shot at the par-4, 504-yard 18th hole found the rough. The stance for his second shot placed his left heel in the fairway and his right foot in the rough. He delivered his approach shot from 185 yards to five feet from the cup. It was Henry's 16th green in regulation in the final round. His birdie putt rolled along the side of the hole before it dropped. Henry shot a 34 on the back nine as part of his final-round 67. After a season in which Henry played in 28 tournaments, making the cut in 16, he was now in the projected 125th position. In an interview with CBS reporter Amanda Balionis, Henry stated, "I'm very proud of the way I finished today. I've won three times and played on a Ryder Cup team, and it was probably some of the most pressure I've felt, playing today."

Henry would have to wait for Johnson Wagner to complete his round. In the second round, Wagner became the eighth golfer on the PGA Tour since 1983, and the first since 2005, to make an albatross and an eagle in the same tournament. The albatross came on the par-5, 531-yard 5th hole when he holed out from 214 yards. He eagled the par-5 15th hole when he drained a putt from 29 feet. Wagner found himself tied for ninth after rounds of 67 and 64. His third-round 65 included holing out from 95 yards on the 1st hole. Wagner ended the third round in sole possession of fifth place, only two strokes behind eventual tournament champion Henrik Stenson. Wagner also now projected into the 115th position in the FedEx Cup points standings after beginning the Wyndham Championship 141st.

Wagner's fourth round, however, produced no birdies. At the 15th hole, where he went birdie-eagle-birdie in the previous rounds, his second shot from 215 yards found the water. Wagner made a double-bogey on the hole. He had one last slim chance to earn his way into the playoffs, but he needed to hole out on his second shot from the fairway at 18. When Wagner's shot landed in the bunker, J. J. Henry landed in the FedEx Cup Playoffs. Wagner ended the day with a 74 to tie for 24th place. He completed the regular season 140th in the FedEx Cup standings.

No golfer had more dramatic shot-making at the Wyndham Championship in 2017 to produce a jump into the FedEx Cup Playoffs then Martin Flores. After graduating from the Web.com Tour in 2011, Flores made the FedEx Cup Playoffs in three consecutive seasons, from 2012 through 2014. He had 30 tournament starts with 18 made cuts in the 2014–2015 season. He had three top-25 finishes, highlighted by a tie for 16th at the Puerto Rico Open. He entered the Wyndham Championship in 2015 152nd in the FedEx Cup standings. He shot three over on the front nine and four over in the final round of the Wyndham. He finished 156th in the standings and earned $499,274 in prize money. Flores competed in the Web.com Tour Finals. He missed the cut in the first tournament and earned only $23,188 in the other three events. He had to return to the Web.com Tour for 2016.

Flores showed his resolve and quickly rebounded with a spectacular 2016 regular season. He won his first professional tournament, the Lincoln Land Charity Championship. Flores made 15 cuts in 21 starts, with nine top 25s and seven in the top ten. He finished 2016 fifth on the prize money list after earning $281,403. Flores was going back to the PGA Tour, where he had some success in two starts in 2015–2016. He tied for 12th at the Sanderson Farms Championship and tied for 63rd at the AT&T Byron Nelson. He earned $101,576.

Back on the PGA Tour for the 2016–2017 season, Flores played seven consecutive weeks starting with the Travelers Championship at the end of June. He missed the cut there and found himself number 147 in the FedEx Cup standings. Flores simply explains, "I knew I was in a hole and had to keep playing." To deal with the physically grueling schedule, Flores would "take Monday and Tuesday off before going out to practice on Wednesday afternoon." His practice plan was also about trying to stay "mentally fresh."

It turned out that the Travelers Championship was Flores last missed cut of the season. Flores had three top-20 performances in his stretch of seven straight made cuts. He tied for 18th at the Barbasol Championship, tied for 19th at the RBC Canadian Open, and tied for 11th at the Barracuda Championship. After not qualifying for the PGA Championship and having that week off, he was 139th in the points standings heading into the Wyndham. Of his stretch of quality performances, Flores says that although he "didn't have a week where the putter got hot and everything clicked," he felt that he was "building momentum" and that he went into the Wyndham Championship "ready to play." Flores also remembered being in a similar position in the 2015 Wyndham. He was well aware of the stakes, saying, "your job is on the line."

An opening-round 64 was paired with a second-round 70. A third-round 68 left Flores projected outside of the top 125 and faced with missing the playoffs for the third consecutive season. For the first two rounds, Flores played with Johnson Wagner and witnessed first-hand his heroics. He played with

Cameron Smith in the final round. When Smith holed out from 90 yards on the 1st hole, Flores jokingly said to his caddie Don Gadberry, "when is it going to be my time?" It soon became evident that Flores' time to put all aspects of his game together arrived.

On the par-4 1st hole, Flores' approach shot from 117 yards put him eight feet, nine inches from the cup, and he converted the birdie putt. He drained a birdie putt from 22 feet, nine inches on the 2nd hole. At the 174-yard, par-3 3rd Flores put his tee-shot to within six feet of the cup before making his third straight birdie. Flores calls it a "dream start," and at that point his strategy was to "keep being aggressive, but also patient." Flores says that throughout the day he was looking at the scoreboards posted around the golf course, because "I wanted to know where I was." Flores added a birdie on the 5th and 8th holes to complete a front nine 30 and put playoff qualification within reach.

After a bogey on the 11th hole, Flores parred the 12th through 14th holes. With four holes left and still projected to be out of the playoffs, Flores thought he needed two more birdies, with three for sure being enough to get him into the playoffs. He was thinking that each birdie could be worth a move of two spots up in the projections. At the par-5 15th, Flores hit what he calls his "best drive in a long time." It traveled 327 yards and landed in the fairway. However, he hit what he calls "an awful six iron" that stopped short and right of the green. Flores chipped to 17 feet, but he could not convert the birdie putt and settled for a tap-in par.

The 16th hole at the Wyndham Championship is a par-3, 171 yards. Cameron Smith played first and hit his tee-shot a little long. Flores says that after seeing Smith's shot, he "knew exactly how hard to hit it." Flores explains that he was trying to land the ball in the front, middle of the green, where he hoped to get the ball "inside 15-feet of the hole." Flores points out that he "had the shot pictured in my mind." He took dead-aim using an eight iron. His ball hit the green below the hole and took a big hop before rolling perfectly toward the cup and in for an impeccably-timed hole-in-one. Flores points out that he is "normally level-headed and not a big celebrator on the course," but on this occasion, he jumped and tossed his club in the air with both arms raised before exchanging jubilant high-fives with Gadberry and Smith.

After the ace, Flores jumped into position number 123 in the FedEx Cup standings. He just missed a birdie putt on 17 and had another tap-in par. Flores had to wait at the tee-box on 18 and recalls that he hoped there wouldn't be a delay so that he "wouldn't have to think about it." Flores played the 18th hole at par-bogey-bogey in the first three rounds. He hit a monster drive of 367 yards at the par-4 18th hole. Unlike the 15th hole, when Flores did not execute as he desired, on 18 he put his approach shot from 140 yards eight feet from the flagstick. He describes the putt as "ideal, straight up the hill." Flores poured in the putt, pumped his fist, and was well on his way to the playoffs. Upon signing his scorecard, Flores was informed that his making the playoffs was not a certainty with so many golfers still playing, but his chances were probably 90 percent. Flores explains, "I did all that I could" and says that he was "at peace with the outcome."

It turned out that his final-round 63, good for a tie for seventh, was more than enough. Flores' next tournament appearance was the first event of the FedEx Cup Playoffs. With the 85 FedEx Cup points gained in the Wyndham Championship, Flores ended the regular season at number 118 in the points standings, 18 points higher than J. J Henry in 125th place. It should be noted that Matt Every, who finished only two strokes higher than Flores, obtained only 60 points in that tournament.

Overall, Flores had 17 made cuts in 26 regular season tournaments in 2016–2017. He had seven finishes in the top 25 and one other top ten, a tie for tenth in the Puerto Rico Open. In the playoffs, Flores tied for 34th at the Northern Trust but it was not enough to advance to the second playoff tournament. He did get a $70,000 bonus to go along with his prize money winnings of $830,057. Flores entered the 2017–2018 season with an exempt status in the top 125 of the FedEx Cup standings group.

Some golfers had to persevere through the Wyndham Championship to maintain their qualifying position for the FedEx Cup Playoffs. Geoff Ogilvy sat squarely on the bubble in position number 125 heading into the Wyndham. The highlight of Ogilvy's 2016–2017 season was a tie for fourth at the Shriners Hospitals for Children Open in November. During a stretch of five consecutive made cuts, Ogilvy had his second-best performance of the season, a tie for 13th at the Quicken Loans National.

Ogilvy posted a first-round 70 at the Wyndham Championship. In the second round, making the cut was very much in question. Starting at the 10th tee, Ogilvy shot an even par 35 on his first nine holes. He added a bogey at the 2nd hole. The cut line wound up at 137, and Ogilvy needed to complete the final seven holes in 23 strokes to equal that number. He proceeded to complete that stretch of holes in 22 strokes. He birdied holes 3 through 6 and added another birdie at the 8th. The score on his second nine in round two was a 31, and his total of 136 was one stroke inside the cut line.

A third-round 66 projected Ogilvy to 123rd in the standings. He seemed to erase any doubt when on the front nine in the final round he scored a 29 over the same stretch of holes where two days earlier he rallied just to make the cut. Ogilvy birdied 1, 5, 6, and 9, plus an eagle on the par-4 8th hole when he holed his shot from 93 yards. Despite a back nine three-over par 38, Ogilvy ended the Wyndham in a tie for 16th. He finished the regular season number 116 in the FedEx Cup standings.

Ogilvy returned to the playoffs after not qualifying in the previous two seasons. He finished the Northern Trust in a tie for 40th and did not advance. He took home a $70,000 bonus to go along with prize money winnings for the season of $867,249. Ogilvy entered the season using his career earnings exemption. By making 12 cuts in 24 tournaments and qualifying for the playoffs, that calculation by Ogilvy had been validated. Moving forward, in the 2017–2018 season Ogilvy had his exempt status in the top 125 in the FedEx Cup standings group.

Ogilvy spoke to CBS reporter Amanda Balionis after his final round about the pressure of needing to play well at the Wyndham to secure his spot in the playoffs and his exempt status for next season.

> It took me by surprise a little bit. The last couple of months I've been teetering around the edge thinking if I don't make many more points I'm going to be in this situation and I really wasn't that stressed about it. I guess I didn't realize how much I wanted it until I turned up this week and how I felt on the first tee on Thursday. It was true Q School feelings that I haven't had for 15, 20 years. It was very difficult. It's a very difficult thing to do and, I guess, what the situation proved to me is how much I still want to be doing this.

Vaughn Taylor may have felt a little less pressure than some of the other golfers near the playoff bubble, as his exempt status for the following season was secure in the tournament winners ranking group for his victory at the 2016 AT&T Pebble Beach Pro-Am. Taylor began his 2016–2017 season by making the cut in seven consecutive tournaments, including a tie for 15th at the Safeway Open. His other top finish was a tie for 12th place at the Wells Fargo Championship. He was 106th in the FedEx Cup standings after that tournament, held the first week in May.

Taylor played in 24 tournaments, with 16 made cuts, before the Wyndham Championship. He had seven top-25 finishes, but no top-ten performances. He was 118th in the FedEx Cup standings. At the Wyndham, a first-round 63 and a second-round 66 helped him stave off playoff elimination. He shot rounds of 74 and 71 to end the tournament tied for 50th. Taylor held on for the 124th position in the standings and made the FedEx Cup Playoffs for the second consecutive season after not qualifying from 2012 through 2015.

The PGA Tour system of dividing lines produced the annual close calls of golfers who do not surpass the critical threshold of the playoffs. Daniel Summerhays qualified for the FedEx Cup Playoffs every season from 2012 through 2016. He made it all the way to the third playoff tournament all four seasons. Summerhays was coming off of a 2015–2016 season in which he finished 65th in the FedEx Cup points standings to earn a playoff bonus of $110,000. Summerhays now found himself 124th entering the Wyndham in 2017.

Summerhays played in 29 tournaments in the 2016–2017 season and made the cut in 20. His season was highlighted by a tie for tenth at the Memorial, as well as four other top-25 finishes. He also made the cut in all three major tournaments that he played. Aside from the Greenbrier Classic, held the weekend of July 9, Summerhays played every week, 14 tournaments, from The Players Championship, which concluded on May 14, through the Wyndham Championship, which concluded on August 20. After rounds of 67 and 73 at the Wyndham, Summerhays' total of 140 missed the cut by three strokes. Summerhays dropped to 131st in the FedEx Cup standings.

Two golfers on the FedEx Cup Playoff bubble were barely able to survive into the third round at the Wyndham Championship. Both Seamus Power and Zac Blair were among the 20 golfers tied at three under, right at the cut line of 137. Neither could take advantage of his round three opportunity.

Power made it onto the PGA Tour after finishing the 2016 Web.com Tour ninth on the prize money list. The Wyndham was his 25th tournament of the 2016–2017 season. It was his 18th made cut and seventh consecutive. Power's best finish was a tie for tenth at the RBC Canadian Open. He had three other top-25 finishes. Power entered the Wyndham Championship 123rd in the FedEx Cup standings. He began the third round with a two under par 33 on the front nine. However, his PGA Tour season would end on the back nine in round three. A six over par 74 left him with a MDF result at the Wyndham. Power fell to number 130 in the standings with 350 points and missed out on the 125th position of J. J. Henry by 15 points. He earned $646,181 and a $32,000 bonus.

Zac Blair finished the 2015–2016 PGA Tour season 110th in the FedEx Cup standings, earning a playoff bonus of $70,000. In 2016–2017, the Wyndham Championship was his 32nd tournament of the season. He made the cut in 20 tournaments when he advanced to the third round of the Wyndham. Blair had one top-ten finish, a tie for eighth at the Shell Houston Open, as well as one other top-25 finish, a tie for 12th at the Wells Fargo Championship. Blair played in a tournament every week except for the PGA Championship, eight starts from the Travelers through the Wyndham. He arrived at the Wyndham at number 120 in the FedEx Cup standings.

Blair posted a front nine score of three over par 38 in the third round. He could muster only an even par 35 on the back nine. Blair appeared to have some momentum when he birdied the 14th and 15th holes. However, birdie putts on both 16 and 17 lipped out. His 73 did not advance him to play in round four as his three-day total of 210 was two strokes off of the MDF cut line of 208. He was still projected in the 124th position heading into the final day, but his playoff prospects now depended on the performance of other golfers. Blair did not get the help he needed. He ended up dropping to 126 in the standings. Blair's total of 364 was one point less than the total of J. J. Henry.

David Hearn finished the 2015–2016 season 56th in the final FedEx Cup points standings. He claimed a playoff bonus of $110,000. Hearn qualified for the FedEx Cup Playoffs every season from 2011 through 2016. In four of those seasons, he advanced to the third playoff tournament. Hearn's 2016–2017 season started slowly. He made the cut in only two of his first nine tournaments, a tie for 66th at the CIMB Classic and a tie for 58th at the CareerBuilder Challenge.

Hearn responded by making the cut in his next five tournaments, starting with the Honda Classic in February and extending through the RBC Heritage in April. Hearn's best playing of the season was a four-tournament stretch that began in June with a tie for tenth at the FedEx St. Jude Classic. He followed with a tie for eighth at the Travelers, 73rd at the Quicken Loans National, and a tie for 14th at the Greenbrier Classic. He was 112th in the FedEx Cup standings. After the Greenbrier, Hearn played in five tournaments and made the cut in three.

Hearn arrived at the Wyndham Championship ranked 121st in the FedEx Cup points standings. After rounds of 67 and 68, Hearn was two strokes inside the cut line. In the third round, he shot one over on the front nine, with a double-bogey on the 6th hole, and two over on the back nine, with two birdies offset by four bogeys. Although he shot a 73, Hearn did make the 54-hole cut and projected in the 125th position in the points standings heading into the fourth round.

Hearn started well with a two under par 33 on the front nine. That, however, was paired with a one over par back nine. Hearn completed the Wyndham Championship at three under par in a tie for 64th. That result dropped Hearn to number 128 in the FedEx Cup points standings. His total of 359 points was six less than J. J. Henry.

As for the playoff bonus and having some status on the PGA Tour in the following season dividing line of 150/151 in the FedEx Cup points standings, Rick Lamb entered the 2016–2017 season in the top finishers of the Web.com Tour group. He earned $154,368 and was 24th in prize money in the previous regular season. Lamb began the PGA Tour season by missing the cut in his first six tournaments and in nine of his first 11. His only made cuts were a tie for 62nd at the AT&T Pebble Beach Pro-Am and a tie for 60th at the Puerto Rico Open. Lamb entered June with only seven FedEx Cup points. He rallied by making the cut in four of his last five tournaments. This stretch was highlighted by a tie for third at the John Deere Classic. He earned 163 FedEx Cup points for that performance.

Lamb entered the Wyndham Championship at number 150 in the FedEx Cup points standings. He opened the tournament with rounds of 64 and 68, tied for 14th. In the third round, after a two under par front nine, Lamb had to overcome a nine on the par-4 11th hole. He followed that with a bogey on the 12th but responded with a 15-hole stretch in which he shot six under. Lamb double-bogeyed the 17th hole before finishing his fourth round at the Wyndham by draining a 19-foot, eight-inch birdie putt on 18. Lamb shot a 67 in the final round and completed the tournament at nine under par, tied for 28th. Lamb was awarded 25 FedEx Cup points.

Overall for the season, Lamb played in 19 tournaments and made the cut in seven, finishing 150th in the FedEx Cup standings with 269 points. Lamb missed the cut in three of the four Web.com Tour Finals events and earned only $5,475 with a tie for 33rd in the other. Lamb entered the 2017–2018 season as the final golfer in the FedEx Cup finishers 126 through 150 priority group.

Lamb needed every one of those 25 FedEx Cup points that he secured in the Wyndham Championship. The golfers who scored one stroke higher for the tournament were awarded only 17 points. In 2016–2017, Troy Merritt was in his final season with tournament winners exempt status that he obtained for winning the 2015 Quicken Loans National. Merritt started his season with two top-15 finishes followed by a stretch of missing the cut in seven of his next eight tournaments. Merritt competed every week from the FedEx St. Jude Classic in June through the Wyndham. In those ten tournaments, Merritt made four cuts, with his best performance a tie for eighth at the Travelers Championship.

Merritt arrived at the Wyndham Championship number 153 in the FedEx Cup points standings. He shot rounds of 67–70–65–69 and was able to match Rick Lamb in finishing nine under par, tied for 28th, and earning 25 FedEx Cup points. In playing in 28 tournaments, with 11 made cuts, Merritt accumulated 265 points to finish 151st in the standings, four points behind Lamb.

Matt Jones, who in 2015–2016 finished 126th on both the PGA Tour money list and FedEx Cup points standings, came up short on another dividing line in the 2016–2017 season. Jones entered the Wyndham Championship 149th in the standings. He, however, missed the cut by three strokes after rounds of 72 and 68. It was Jones' fourth missed cut in his last five tournaments. He made 12 cuts in 20 starts with three top-20 finishes. Jones fell to 152 in the FedEx Cup points standings after the Wyndham. His 248 points were 21 fewer than Lamb. Rather than earning a playoff bonus and at least being in the 126 through 150 finishers in the FedEx Cup standings heading into the 2017–2018 season, Merritt and Jones would have to improve their position in the Web.com Tour Finals.

Soren Kjeldsen was the golfer who replaced Jones in the top 150. Kjeldsen entered the Wyndham Championship 154th in the standings. At the Wyndham, Kjeldsen had a 28-hole stretch from the 13th hole in round one through the 4th hole in round three in which he had 12 birdies and no bogeys. He shot a 30 on the back nine in round three. Kjeldsen finished the Wyndham at 11 under, tied for 16th, to earn 46 FedEx Cup points. He finished the regular season with 283 points, good for 146th in the points standings.

One last dividing line is finalized at the Wyndham Championship, occurring at position number 200 in the FedEx Cup points standings. For the players at positions 126 through 200, a post-season opportunity awaits at the Web.com Tour Finals if they choose to compete. The four golfers who entered the Wyndham in positions 198 through 201 all played in the regular season finale. For 48-year-old Dickie Pride, winner of the 1994 FedEx St. Jude Classic, his six under par performance at the Wyndham earned him seven points to increase his season total to 85. He moved from 200 to 199 in the FedEx Cup points standings. Pride switched positions with Padraig Harrington, who dropped back to 200. Harrington shot even par over three rounds at the Wyndham to end the tournament with an MDF. Harrington started the tournament with a pair of 68s before a third-round 76 ended his regular season. Harrington finished with 82 FedEx Cup points.

Miguel Angel Carballo and Will Wilcox both concluded their seasons with 81 points. Carballo had an exempt status for the 2016–2017 season in the top finishers of the Web.com Tour group, ranking ninth within that group. He was fourth on the Web.com Tour Finals prize money list on the strength of coming in second place at the Albertsons Boise Open. In the 2016–2017 regular season, Carballo played in 22 PGA tournaments and made the cut in nine. He had one top-25 finish, a tie for 14th at the Sanderson Farms Championship. He also played in four Web.com Tour events, making the cut in two. Carballo entered the Wyndham Championship in 201st place. He remained in that spot after shooting two under for the tournament to collect three points. Carballo earned $186,623 on the season.

Will Wilcox entered the 2016–2017 season on a minor medical extension. He had three tournaments to earn 55 FedEx Cup points or $41,049. When that was not achieved, he played the rest of the season out of the 126 through 150 FedEx Cup finishers group. Wilcox entered the Wyndham Championship having made four cuts in 13 tournaments. He did not have a finish in the top 20. He was 198th in the FedEx Cup points standings. Wilcox did not make the cut at the Wyndham after rounds of 71 and 73. He dropped to 202 in the FedEx Cup points standings. Davis Love III was the player who jumped into the top 200, moving from 209 to 185. Love finished the Wyndham 14 under par, tied for tenth, to earn 70 FedEx Cup points.

22

The FedEx Cup Playoffs

What makes the race to qualify for the FedEx Cup Playoffs so compelling and meaningful is that once those tournament fields are established, all the golfers are capable of getting on a hot streak and advancing to further playoff events. Geoff Ogilvy, quoted by Sean Martin on pgatour.com, stated, "you can be right on the razor's edge, one round away from going home, and then have a chance to go to Atlanta [the Tour Championship]. That's the cool thing about the FedEx Cup."

The FedEx Cup Playoffs offer another opportunity for a golfer to define his season. He can dramatically improve his earnings for that season with the greater prize money for these playoff tournaments. Conversely, not playing well can result in getting jumped in the standings and losing out on playing in the later playoff tournaments. Each FedEx Cup Playoff tournament, therefore, has four unique outcomes: the tournament winner, positioning in the standings toward becoming the season-long FedEx Cup Champion, positioning in the standings to receive a higher playoff bonus, and advancing to the next playoff tournament.

Simply advancing to the third and fourth tournaments of the FedEx Cup Playoffs is significant because these are no-cut, guaranteed prize money tournaments. Despite having the highest score in the BMW Championship in 2017, Wesley Bryan earned $17,675. The 2017 Tour Championship had a total purse of $8.75 million that was dispersed to only 30 golfers. The winner received $1.575 million. Jhonattan Vegas, who finished with the highest score in the Tour Championship, however, still left Atlanta collecting $140,000.

The playoffs offer more chances to get a win and obtain the tournament championship benefits, such as a spot in the Masters, a spot in the no-cut, guaranteed prize money Tournament of Champions, and the multiple-season tournament winners exempt status. For example, Patrick Reed had no concerns about his exempt status as he entered the playoffs in 2016. He won the World Golf Championships—Cadillac Championship in March 2014, and the Tournament of Champions in January 2015. He also ended the 2015–2016 regular season at number seven in the points standings. Still, Reed had not won a tournament that season. Winning the Barclays brought a return to the Tournament of Champions, where Reed tied for sixth to collect $210,000.

Rory McIlroy once again showed his excellence during the 2016 FedEx Cup Playoffs. Coming into the playoffs, McIlroy, a four-time major winner and 11-time PGA tournament winner, had not won a PGA Tour event in the 2015–2016 season. His top finish was third place at the World Golf Championships—Cadillac Championship at Trump National Doral. McIlroy did win the Dubai Duty Free Irish Open, hosted by the Rory Foundation in May 2016, at the K Club in Kildare, Ireland. McIlroy entered the playoffs in 36th place in the standings.

McIlroy tied for 31st at the Barclays, still seemingly well off the pace to win the season-long FedEx Cup Championship. McIlroy's run was not improved after shooting even par in the first round of the Deutsche Bank Championship, six strokes off the lead. A second-round 67 moved McIlroy to four under par, but his distance behind the tournament leader actually grew as Kevin Chappell's 64 put him in first place at 11 under. Chappell was one stroke ahead of Paul Casey and Jimmy Walker. McIlroy's prospects began to change on the 18th hole in the third round. At the par-5, from 210 yards, McIlroy's perfectly hit second shot rolled just off the edge of the cup to set up an eagle. With a 66 in the third round, McIlroy moved to nine under. Despite this performance, McIlroy picked up only one stroke on the lead as Casey's 66 moved him to 15 under par. Brian Harman posted a 68 to move into second place at 12 under par, followed by Chappell, Walker, and Smylie Kaufman at 11 under.

McIlroy displayed his elite skills in the final round of the 2016 Deutsche Bank Championship. He birdied six of the first 12 holes to propel him to a final round of 65. Coupled with difficult rounds by Walker, who shot 70, Casey and Chappell, who both shot 73, Kaufman shooting 76, and Harman posting 77, McIlroy won the Boston region FedEx Cup Playoff tournament for the second time in his career, having also won in 2012. The win moved McIlroy into fourth place in the FedEx Cup standings.

McIlroy's position dropped two spots to number six after the third playoff tournament, when he tied for 42nd at the BMW Championship. The only way now for McIlroy to win the season-long FedEx Cup Championship was to win the Tour Championship.

There is a standings reset after the third tournament of the FedEx Cup Playoffs. The 30 remaining golfers are ranked based on their FedEx Cup points for the regular season and the first three tournaments of the playoffs. Each ranking position is allotted a certain number of points. First place is allotted 2,000 points, and 30th is allotted 115 points. Those points are then added to the points accrued for his performance in the Tour Championship to determine a final FedEx Cup points total.

Mcllroy trailed Dustin Johnson and Kevin Chappell by two strokes going into the final round of the Tour Championship. A birdie by Chappell on 13 moved him into the lead at 12 under par, one stroke ahead of Ryan Moore and three ahead of Mcllroy. Johnson was fading from contention. After shooting one over par on the front nine, Johnson ran into additional trouble on the 12th hole when he made a double-bogey. After rounds of 66–67–69 put him at eight under going into the final round, Johnson's final-round, three over par 73 left him five under. Johnson, however, was still in position to win the season-long FedEx Cup Championship, so long as Rory Mcllroy did not emerge as the winner of the Tour Championship.

Mcllroy arrived at the par-4 16th hole at nine under par. His second shot from 137 yards hopped twice, jumped to the right, and directly into the hole for an eagle. Mcllroy moved to within one stroke of the lead. He was still behind at the par-5 18th as he stood over his third shot from the bunker left of the green. Mcllroy got up-and-down for a birdie. After Ryan Moore missed a birdie putt on 18 that would have won the tournament, and Johnson the season-long FedEx Cup Championship, a three-way playoff between Moore, Chappell, and Mcllroy was needed to decide the tournament and the season-long champion.

Chappell was eliminated with a par on the first playoff hole. Moore made a birdie putt from just over nine feet. Mcllroy hit two perfect shots to reach the green, setting up an eagle putt from five feet. Mcllroy's putt rolled around the cup, but it did not drop, leaving him also with a birdie. Mcllroy and Moore matched each other on the next two playoff holes. The fourth playoff hole was back at the 16th. Moore saved par by making a 17-foot putt. Mcllroy countered with a birdie from 15 feet to secure both the Tour Championship and his first season-long FedEx Cup Championship.

The 2,000 points accumulated with the victory gave Mcllroy 3,120 points, besting Dustin Johnson's 2,380. A second-place finish at the Tour Championship, worth 1,000 FedEx Cup points, would have kept Mcllroy short of Johnson. Adding 1,000 points to either Ryan Moore's or Kevin Chappell's total would have left them short of Johnson's total. Moore finished in seventh place and Chappell eighth in the FedEx Cup standings. Moore earned a playoff bonus of $700,000 and Chappell a bonus of $600,000.

Mcllroy earned more than $3.1 million in FedEx Cup Playoff tournament prize money, plus the $10 million bonus for winning the season-long championship. Dustin Johnson took home the $3 million bonus for second place. McIlroy became the third golfer who entered the Tour Championship from outside of the top five to win the FedEx Cup. The win at the Tour Championship was McIlroy's fourth in a FedEx Cup Playoff tournament, passing Tiger Woods for the most FedEx Cup Playoff victories.

Every season, the FedEx Cup Playoffs produce the weekly drama of which golfers will advance to the next tournament. Again, with the prize money as high as it is for the playoff tournaments, merely playing one extra weekend can significantly increase a golfer's earnings. The golfers who finished the regular season 101st through 125th in the standings are faced with the most pressure in the first playoff tournament, in terms of continuing their season. With only 100 golfers advancing to the second tournament, they need the combination of playing well and others faltering in order to advance. In 2016, there was a slight help to those looking to move up as Shane Lowry, ranked 87th, opted not to play in the first tournament of the playoffs. He instead chose to play in a tournament in Denmark. This created an instant opening for one player.

In the 2016 playoffs, five golfers ranked from 101 through 125 performed well enough in the first playoff tournament to advance in the FedEx Cup Playoffs: Derek Fathauer, John Huh, Sung Kang, Sean O'Hair, and Tyrone Van Aswegen. This meant that four golfers, in addition to Lowry, dropped out of qualifying for the next playoff tournament. Jonas Blixt, Lucas Glover, Peter Malnati, and Robert Streb all made the cut at the Barclays, but were not able to advance. Each received a bonus of $70,000.

The same dynamics play out on the dividing lines of being in the top 70 and the top 30 to advance to the succeeding tournaments. Kang, Fathauer, Huh, and Van Aswegen saw their seasons end the following week after the second playoff tournament. All four earned a bonus of $75,000 for their finish in the FedEx Cup standings.

Sean O'Hair, who ended the regular season 108th in the points standings, capitalized on his entrance into the FedEx Cup playoffs. In the Barclays, O'Hair tied for second, along with Emiliano Grillo, only one stroke behind tournament winner Patrick Reed. The Barclays performance moved him all the way up to number 15. After a tie for 53rd in the Deutsche Bank Championship and 52nd in the BMW Championship, O'Hair finished 17th in the Tour Championship. He earned $954,211 in prize money for his playoff performances and claimed an additional $190,000 bonus for finishing 27th in the standings.

The field at the third playoff tournament in 2016 got one small break when Henrik Stenson did not compete due to an injury. This moved Stenson out of the top 30, guaranteeing an opening for one player to advance to the

Tour Championship. Stenson ended up 36th in the FedEx Cup standings and received a bonus of $140,000.

Four golfers who were outside of the top 30 played their way into the Tour Championship through their performance at the BMW Championship. Roberto Castro moved from 53 to 21 after finishing third. Castro earned $578,000 for that tournament performance. He earned another $166,600 at the Tour Championship when he shot even par and tied for 17th place. Castro collected a playoff bonus of $215,000 for finishing 22nd in the FedEx Cup points standings.

J. B. Holmes advanced from 42 to 28 after he tied for fourth. His first three rounds of 69–65–68 helped overcome a final round of 74. Holmes faltered at the Tour Championship, shooting six over, but he still earned $141,100. Holmes finished 30th in the standings and earned a bonus of $175,000.

Daniel Berger entered the playoffs 22nd, but a tie for 70th and a tie for 41st in the first two tournaments dropped him to number 31. Berger moved up only a few, but incredibly important spots when he jumped to 26 after a tie for tenth at the BMW. It was the second consecutive year that he moved from outside of the top 30 into the field of the Tour Championship. Berger was quoted by Adam Schupak on golfweek.com, stating, "I felt more pressure today than there was when I won Memphis [2016]." Berger tied for 15th at the Tour Championship to earn $183,600. He ended the season 26th in the FedEx Cup standings, which garnered a bonus of $195,000.

Charl Schwartzel claimed the final spot in the Tour Championship when he advanced from the 43rd to the 30th position. He ended the regular season in 30th but he fell back after playoff performances of a tie for 53rd and a 70th. Schwartzel tied for fourth in the BMW Championship on the strength of an eight under par 64 in the final round that featured five birdies on the back nine. He moved past Rickie Fowler by .57 points, the closest margin in determining advancement to the Tour Championship in the ten-year history of the FedEx Cup.

Fowler entered the BMW Championship in the 22nd position. He could not overcome a first-round 75 that had him at four over par after the first eight holes. He ended up 59th, one over par, after a bogey on the 17th hole in the final round. Fowler's 31st-place finish in the standings awarded him a bonus of $165,000.

Schwartzel tied for tenth in the Tour Championship. His best round was the third, when back-to-back eagles on the front nine helped him to a four under par 66. Schwartzel won $218,620 at the Tour Championship and pocketed another $200,000 as his playoff bonus for finishing 25th in the standings.

In addition to Stenson and Fowler, Sergio Garcia and Brooks Koepka lost out on a qualifying position for the Tour Championship. Garcia dropped from

25th to number 32 after final rounds of 76 and 73. He bogeyed the 15th and 17th holes in the final round to finish in a tie for 47th at the BMW Championship. Garcia earned $22,474 in the tournament that concluded his 2015–2016 season. He did receive a playoff bonus of $155,000.

Brooks Koepka played in only 18 regular season PGA tournaments in 2015–2016, yet he finished 19th in the FedEx Cup standings. Koepka entered that season in his first of two in the tournament winners priority ranking group for his victory at the 2015 Waste Management Phoenix Open. Koepka made the cut in 15 tournaments, with eight top-ten and five top-five finishes. His highlight was making the playoff at the AT&T Byron Nelson, where he was defeated by Sergio Garcia. Koepka held the 30th and final Tour Championship qualifying position heading into the BMW Championship. He dropped to 35th as his late rally in the fourth round, playing the final seven holes at six under par, was not enough to overcome a second-round 72 and a third-round 76. Koepka tied for 32nd and collected a playoff bonus of $142,000, as well as tournament prize money of more than $3.32 million.

The 2017 FedEx Cup Playoffs continued to deliver on one its main objectives, having tournaments that feature the best golfers in the world competing against each other with consequential outcomes. The Northern Trust, the first playoff tournament, renamed from the Barclays, saw Dustin Johnson, fourth in the FedEx Cup standings, shoot a final-round 66, with a back nine 32, to make up a three-stroke deficit to Jordan Spieth, third in the standings, and force a playoff. Johnson won the tournament with a birdie on the first extra hole. With the victory, Johnson matched Rory McIlroy for the most FedEx Cup Playoff tournament wins with four. The second playoff tournament had Justin Thomas finishing first and Spieth second.

In 2017, the Northern Trust had three golfers who finished between 101 and 125 in the regular season standings who were able to play their way into the Dell Technologies Championship, the second playoff tournament, renamed from the Deutsche Bank Championship. David Lingmerth entered the FedEx Cup Playoffs 103rd in the standings. After a one over par 71 in the opening round, Lingmerth scored consecutive rounds of 68. He ran into a difficult stretch in the final round when he played the 5th through 8th holes at five over par. He finished the round with a 73. Lingmerth tied for 29th place by shooting even par. He earned $58,188, enough to move him up to 87th in the standings. Lingmerth missed the cut at the Dell Technologies Championship to conclude his season. He received a bonus of $75,000 for being 94th in the points standings.

Bubba Watson entered the playoffs 113th in the standings. He shot rounds of 67–68–71–70 to tie for tenth at the Northern Trust, his eighth top-ten finish in a FedEx Cup Playoff tournament. He collected $187,500 and jumped into

72nd in the standings. Although he was on the cusp of qualifying for the third playoff tournament, Watson was not able to break into the top 70. Watson tied for 69th at the Dell Technologies, earning $17,413, and finished 75th to claim a bonus of $80,000.

For the second consecutive week, Harold Varner III was on the wrong side of a critical dividing line heading into a tournament. For the second consecutive week, Varner played his way into advancing. Varner became the fifth golfer to reach the second playoff tournament after being out of a playoff position heading into the last regular season Tour event. He jumped from position number 138 to 123 in the standings with a 14 under par tie for tenth in the Wyndham Championship. After a tie for 20th in the Northern Trust, Varner catapulted to 91st place. He won $98,350 for his performance.

Varner opened the Dell Technologies Championship with a six over par 77 to put any chance of advancing in serious jeopardy. He responded with a bogey-free, four under par 67 in round two. He followed with a third-round 73. Varner revived his faint hopes of advancing in the playoffs when he made consecutive birdies on the 2nd through 5th holes and seven birdies over the first ten holes in the final round. When Varner bogeyed the 14th through 16th holes, however, his season ended. Varner finished the Dell Technologies Championship in a tie for 47th place to earn $22,779. He moved up to 90th in the standings and claimed a bonus of $75,000.

Byeong Hun An, Robert Garrigus, and Seung-Yul Noh all missed the cut at the Northern Trust to drop out of the top 100. The competition for the 100th and final position to advance to the Dell Technologies came down to a single point. Michael Kim entered the playoffs in 95th place with 483 points, but he missed the cut in the Northern Trust. Kim retained the 100th position by holding off Scott Stallings. At the end of the regular season, Stallings was 102nd but he shot a final-round, three over par 73 at the Northern Trust. His round included a bogey on the 17th hole that created the one-point difference between him and Kim. Stallings earned 44 points for his tie for 43rd at the Northern Trust that brought his total to 482. Kim missed the cut at the Dell Technologies Championship to complete his season. His $75,000 bonus for position number 100 was $5,000 greater than that of Stallings in position number 101.

Perhaps no advancement to the next tournament in the 2017 FedEx Cup Playoffs was as dramatic as Kevin Tway's movement from the Dell Technologies Championship to the BMW Championship. Tway entered the playoffs in the 72nd position. He crept up to 69th after a tie for 43rd at the Northern Trust. He now needed to remain in the top 70 after the second playoff tournament to advance.

Tway's round one at the Dell Technologies was aided by a hole-in-one at the 231-yard 11th hole. He shot an even par 71. Rounds two and three produced scores of 74 and 72. Tway bogeyed the third hole in round four but made six birdies over the rest of the round, including a shot from the sand trap for a birdie on 17. Tway finished with a 66 and completed the tournament in a tie for 40th place. He remained 69th in the standings. Tway finished the BMW Championship in a tie for 53rd place, which did not advance him to the Tour Championship. Overall, he earned $80,593 for the three playoff tournaments and finished with a $110,000 bonus for 69th.

Emiliano Grillo, Stewart Cink, and Rafa Cabrera Bello were the three golfers outside of the standings-position threshold, but were able to play their way from the Dell Technologies Championship into the BMW Championship. None, however, obtained a coveted spot in the top 30 to qualify for the Tour Championship.

Ultimately, five golfers started the playoffs out of the top 30 but gained entrance into the Tour Championship. Justin Rose moved up from position number 32, Patrick Reed from 38th, and Jason Day from 49th place. Patrick Cantlay was the only golfer who advanced two tournaments beyond his initial place in the standings. Cantlay ended the regular season 78th before playing his way into the Tour Championship.

The most consequential advancement to the next tournament in the play-offs was that of Xander Schauffele. As a rookie on the PGA Tour, Schauffele tied for fifth at the U.S. Open and won the Greenbrier Classic by one stroke when he birdied the final hole. Schauffele started the playoffs in the 33rd position. With a tie for 17th at the Northern Trust, for which he earned $131,250, Schauffele rose to number 27. He dropped back out of the top 30, to number 32, after he tied for 53rd at the Dell Technologies Championship.

Schauffele played the first two rounds of the BMW Championship at even par. He birdied four of the first five holes in round three. His eight-birdie, two-bogey performance led to a six under par 65. Schauffele was two over for his final round through 12 holes but rallied in spectacular fashion. Schauffele shot five under par over the next four holes. He added a birdie at the 18th to complete a six under par stretch on the tournament's final six holes. He vaulted to a tie for 20th, the 26th position in the standings, and a spot in the field of the Tour Championship.

Schauffele started the Tour Championship with rounds of one under par 69 and four under par 66. His second round included five birdies and one bogey on holes 13 through 18. After a third-round 65, Schauffele was ten under and tied with Kevin Kisner for second place, two strokes behind tournament leader Paul Casey.

At some point in the final round of the Tour Championship, Casey,

Schauffele, Kisner, and Justin Thomas each had a share of the lead. Casey came back to the field with a bogey on the 4th, 5th, and 9th holes. He and Kisner derailed their chances when they both drove into the water at the par-3, 208-yard 15th hole. Casey produced only one birdie on the day, the 18th hole. His three over par, final-round 73 placed him fifth at the Tour Championship. Casey earned $350,000 and a bonus of $300,000 for finishing 11th.

Kisner shot an even par 70 in the final round to end the Tour Championship tied for third place with Russell Henley, who shot 65. Both earned $511,875 for the Tour Championship. For the season, Kisner finished 12th, which came with a bonus of $290,000. Henley ended up in position number 13 and was awarded a bonus of $280,000.

Schauffele and Thomas were the final two golfers in contention for the Tour Championship. Schauffele was 11 under as he arrived at the 16th hole. Thomas birdied that hole when he stuck his second shot from 151 yards just under 11 feet from the hole. The birdie putt by Thomas hit the left edge and rolled around part of the cup before dropping to move him to ten under. Schauffele was able to complete the 16th hole with a tap-in par.

On 17, a 423-yard par-4, Thomas put his tee-shot in the fairway. For the second consecutive hole, from the comfortable distance of 151 yards, Thomas well-positioned his golf ball for a birdie putt. From five feet, eight inches away, Thomas again used all of the cup as the golf ball rolled around the edge before finding the bottom for a birdie. Thomas was now tied with Schauffele at 11 under par.

Schauffele had some drama on the 17th as his tee-shot found the left rough. From behind a tree at 95 yards from the green, Schauffele was forced to punch out right of the green, just short of the putting surface. Pitching uphill, he flopped his third shot onto the green, where he was able to save par.

Thomas went birdie-eagle-birdie at the par-5, 567-yard 18th hole over the first three rounds. He would not match that excellence in the final round. Thomas drove into the thick rough left off the fairway. With 244 yards to the hole, his second shot kept him left off the fairway, just short of a bunker. His third shot did find the green, but when he missed the difficult left-to-right putt from 23 feet, Thomas settled for a par at the 72nd hole.

The opportunity to win the tournament was there for Schauffele. All he needed was to match his birdies at the 18th hole in rounds two and three. He smoked his drive 347 yards down the fairway. With 219 yards to the hole, his second shot was on line with the green but ended up just short. He was still able to use his putter for his third shot, which rolled two and a half feet past the hole. Although from that short distance he scorched the ball and it rolled around the lip of the cup, the ball did drop and Schauffele was the winner. Schauffele sank the putt to become the winner of the 2017 Tour Championship.

Schauffele earned $1.575 million for the victory. He claimed more than $1.81 million in prize money for the four FedEx Cup Playoff tournaments. Schauffele also vaulted up to third in the final FedEx Cup standings to win the $2 million bonus. One year earlier, Schauffele was fighting to get his PGA Tour card in the Web.com Tour Finals after being denied his Tour card by finishing 26th on the Web.com Tour regular season money list. Schauffele now had high-priority exempt status for three seasons, through 2019–2020, as the winner of the PGA Tour Championship.

Thomas earned $945,000 for finishing second at the Tour Championship. As Thomas was battling Schauffele to win the tournament, he was also competing with Jordan Spieth to resolve the other title to be determined on the season's final day, the FedEx Cup Champion.

Thomas entered the playoffs in second place, and Spieth was third. Spieth jumped into second after he made it to the playoff in the Northern Trust. Thomas slipped to third. Both Thomas and Spieth started slowly at the Dell Technologies Championship. Thomas shot an even par 71, while Spieth carded a one over par 72, in the first round. Thomas' bogey on the 5th hole in round one would be the last blemish on his scorecard over the next 59 holes. He had his second and final bogey on the 11th hole in round four. Thomas made 14 birdies and an eagle in that stretch. He posted scores of 67–63–66 in rounds two through four to win the Dell Technologies Championship by three strokes over Spieth, who himself rebounded with rounds of 65–66–67. Spieth took the top spot in the standings after the Dell Technologies Championship and held it heading into the Tour Championship. Thomas moved up to second place and remained in that spot with one tournament to play.

Thomas was tied for fourth after the third round of the Tour Championship at seven under par. Spieth was tied for 13th at four under. The projections had them alternating the top position in the season-long points race during the final round of the Tour Championship as their play, as well as the play of other golfers, altered the leaderboard. With Spieth having one hole left and Thomas four, Thomas was tied for third and Spieth tied for sixth. They were projected to be tied for first in the FedEx Cup standings if that remained their final positions on the Tour Championship leaderboard. In that scenario, to determine the FedEx Cup Champion and the $7 million bonus difference between first and second place, the most expensive playoff hole in golf would be held. The compelling drama of extra holes between Thomas and Spieth with that amount of money at stake did not materialize.

When Tony Finau birdied the 18th hole to tie Spieth on the Tour Championship leaderboard, it put Thomas in the FedEx Cup lead. Spieth did have one more opportunity to regain the lead, but at 18 his tee-shot landed in the heavy rough left of the fairway. From 249 yards away all Spieth could do was blast the ball out to 121 yards from the hole. He found the green on his third shot to give him a birdie chance from 14 feet, eight inches away. As his birdie putt sailed wide right of the hole, NBC lead golf announcer Dan Hicks explained, "that could have been a $10 million putt."

Thomas extended his lead over Spieth with a birdie on the 16th and 17th holes. The culmination to Thomas' five-win season was the FedEx Cup Championship. Thomas earned more than $9.92 million in prize money for the season plus the $10 million bonus. Thomas, who began 2016–2017 in the tournament winners group, solidified himself as one of the PGA Tour's elite players. As Thomas held up the trophy to celebrate winning the FedEx Cup, there was still one more piece to the 2017–2018 PGA Tour exempt status group puzzle.

23

The 2017 Web.com
Tour Championship

The weekend of Saturday, September 30, and Sunday, October 1, 2017, was incredibly busy on the sports calendar. The NFL was playing its fourth week of the season, college football was in full competition, and the Major League Baseball regular season was coming to a close. Even the focus of the golf world was on the Presidents Cup being held at Liberty National Golf Club in Jersey City, New Jersey. Meanwhile, at the Atlantic Beach Country Club in Florida, the Web.com Tour was holding its Tour Championship, the last of its four Finals tournaments. The Web.com Tour Championship would conclude with 25 golfers celebrating their advancement onto the PGA Tour for being one of the top 25 golfers on the Finals money list.

Sam Saunders, grandson of Arnold Palmer, first played in a PGA Tour event as a professional in 2010. Saunders appeared in 28 tournaments and made the cut in 13 in the 2014–2015 season. He had four finishes in the top 25. His best was a tie for second at the Puerto Rico Open. That performance earned him $198,000 of his season total of $578,571. Saunders finished 137th in the FedEx Cup standings. He did play his way into the top finishers of the Web.com Tour group for the following season through his performances in the Web.com Tour Finals.

Saunders appeared in 24 PGA tournaments and made the cut in ten in the 2015–2016 season. He had five top-25 and two top-ten finishes, highlighted by a tie for eighth at the Barbasol Championship. The regular season ended with Saunders 148th in the FedEx Cup points standings. He earned a $32,000 bonus by being seven points better than the 151st-place finisher, Will MacKenzie. Unlike the previous season, Saunders did not improve his status group in the Web.com Tour Finals. He entered the 2016–2017 season in the 126 through 150 finishers in the FedEx Cup standings group.

In 2016–2017, Saunders appeared in 24 events and made the cut in 13, with seven top-25 and two top-ten finishes. The highlight of his season was a tie for fifth place at the Puerto Rico Open. He arrived at the Wyndham Championship with an opportunity to break into the FedEx Cup Playoffs well within his grasp, at 127th in the standings. Saunders was tied for 33rd after the third round of the Wyndham. He improved one spot in the projections and was only two points behind the projected 125th-place total. Saunders posted a final-round, one under par 69, but that was not good enough to make up the difference. His Wyndham Championship tournament ended in a tie for 37th.

Saunders, who made the cut in his last five tournaments, drifted back to settle at number 129 in the standings. His 354 points were 11 behind J. J. Henry in the 125th position. It would have been Saunders' first appearance in the FedEx Cup Playoffs. Of his final round at the Wyndham Championship, as quoted by Sean Martin on pgatour.com, Saunders stated, "it was the least enjoyable round of golf I've ever played in my life. You don't know if you're going to throw up or have a heart attack. It's worse than trying to win a tournament, tenfold. I've never had to birdie one hole to change my life for the entire year. And that just kills me." For the PGA Tour season, Saunders earned $678,117 and received a $32,000 bonus for finishing in the top 150.

Saunders returned to the Web.com Tour Finals for the third consecutive season. The opportunity to advance his exempt status group for the following season remained. Saunders completed the first Finals tournament, the Nationwide Children's Hospital Championship, in a tie for 11th for which he earned $24,000. A tie for 40th at the Albertsons Boise Open added $3,900 to his Finals total. He then missed the cut at the DAP Championship. He entered the Web.com Tour Championship 24th on the money list. His $27,900 was only $1,070 better than Zac Blair's total in the 26th position. Saunders did have one advantage in that the Web.com Tour Championship was played at his home golf course.

Starting on the 10th hole in round one, Saunders quickly addressed his position on the PGA Tour card bubble as he shot an astounding 28 on his first nine holes. Saunders finished the first round with a 12 under par 59. He needed only 20 putts to complete his brilliant, 13-birdie performance. Saunders became the seventh player in the history of the Web.com Tour to shoot under 60 in a round.

Saunders was near the top of the leaderboard throughout the Web.com Tour Championship as he posted rounds of 59–66–70–69. He would, however, end the tournament in a tie for second to earn $88,000. Saunders finished sixth on the Web.com Tour Finals money list. After the alternate selection process, Saunders entered the 2017–2018 PGA Tour season 13th within the top finishers of the Web.com Tour group.

Jonathan Byrd was the winner of the Web.com Tour Championship. The five-time PGA winner played the 2016–2017 season out of the past champions group. Byrd had only nine starts on the PGA Tour. He made the cut in seven, highlighted by a tie for fifth at the John Deere Classic. Byrd earned $189,840 of his PGA Tour total $328,337 for that performance. He finished the season 170th in the FedEx Cup standings.

Byrd competed in 14 regular season events on the Web.com Tour. He made the cut in ten, with five top-25 finishes and two in the top ten. Byrd earned $87,178 in the Web.com Tour regular season, 55th on the money list. By splitting time between the PGA Tour and the Web.com Tour, and producing those results, Byrd actually qualified for the Web.com Tour Finals through two paths, the top 200 in the FedEx Cup standings and the top 75 on the Web.com Tour money list.

Byrd tied for 31st at the Nationwide Children's Hospital Championship to earn $5,480. He then missed the cut at both the Albertsons Boise Open and the DAP Championship. He arrived at the Web.com Tour Championship with seemingly only the dimmest hope of improving his status on the PGA Tour, as he was 66th on the Finals money list.

Although Sam Saunders set the pace at the Web.com Tour Championship with his first-round 59, Byrd was within striking distance as he posted a seven under par 64. After Byrd carded rounds of 65 and 64, the third round ended with him at 20 under par with a two-stroke lead over Saunders.

The final round was postponed until Monday when heavy rains made the golf course unplayable. Some golfers who already secured their PGA Tour card decided to leave Florida to travel to Napa, California, for the first event of the PGA Tour season that would be played the following week. One could only speculate about how those golfers who withdrew from the Web.com Tour Championship might have altered the leaderboard and the Finals prize money lists.

On Monday, Byrd birdied the 1st, 5th, and 7th holes to extend his lead to five strokes over Saunders, Rob Oppenheim, and Bronson Burgoon. Saunders pulled to within two strokes, but got no closer. Byrd finished the tournament at 24 under par for a four-stroke victory. Instead of being in the past champions group for the third consecutive season, Byrd vaulted to number three on the Finals prize money list. He entered the 2017–2018 PGA Tour season at number five in the top finishers of the Web.com Tour group, 67 spots ahead of the top golfer in the past champions group in the tournament priority selection process.

Byrd was one of five golfers who started the Web.com Tour Championship outside of the top 25 on the Finals prize money list but left Florida with a PGA

Tour card. Three finished the Web.com Tour Championship on the top five of the leaderboard. Like Sam Saunders, Cameron Tringale already secured a status on the PGA Tour for the following season in the 126 through 150 FedEx Cup points standings group.

Tringale played the 2016–2017 season as part of the top 125 in the FedEx Cup standings group. In 2016–2017, he made the cut in 12 of his 28 PGA Tour starts. His best performance was a tie for sixth at the Barbasol Championship in July. Tringale was within the top 125 of the FedEx Cup standings after the Barbasol Championship, in 119th place, but he missed the cut in two of his final three tournaments, and his tie for 45th at the Barracuda Championship yielded only seven points. Tringale ended the regular season 133rd in the standings. He did earn $792,814 on the PGA Tour.

Tringale opened the Finals with a tie for 50th at the Nationwide Children's Hospital Championship, followed by a tie for 25th at the Albertsons Boise Open. He accumulated $10,944 in prize money. After missing the cut at the DAP Championship, Tringale found himself 49th on the Finals money list heading into the Web.com Tour Championship.

Tringale posted rounds of 65 and 66 with 12 birdies and only one bogey over the first 36 holes. A third-round 65 left Tringale in third place at 17 under par, three strokes behind Jonathan Byrd. A final round of even par 71 was sufficient for Tringale to end the Web.com Tour Championship in a tie for fifth. He earned $36,500. Tringale entered the 2017–2018 PGA Tour season in the 37th position in the top finishers of the Web.com Tour group.

Joining Tringale in the tie for fifth at the Web.com Tour Championship was Matt Jones. After finishing 126th in the FedEx Cup points standings and on the PGA Tour prize money list in 2015–2016, Jones played the 2016–2017 season out of the 126 through 150 points standings group. In that season, Jones made 20 PGA Tour starts and made the cut in 12. He had five top-25 finishes, but none in the top ten. Jones finished number 152 in the FedEx Cup standings. He missed a return to the 126 through 150 finishers group by 21 points while earning $510,622 on the PGA Tour season.

Jones missed the cut in four of his final five tournaments in the PGA Tour season. His trend of missed cuts continued in the Web.com Tour Finals in the first two tournaments. Jones finally broke through with a tie for 20th at the DAP Championship. He earned $11,240. Jones was 47th and looking at being relegated to the past champions group as he began the Web.com Tour Championship having to finish in the top ten. Jones opened the tournament with a six under par 65. Rounds of 67 and 68 left him 13 under par and on the cusp of returning to the PGA Tour. A good performance in the fourth round was still needed.

Jones started the final round with a front nine 32 that included an eagle on the 6th hole. When Jones converted a long birdie putt on the par-3 12th hole, he was tied for sixth and projected into the 20th position on the Finals money list. Jones added a birdie on the par-4, 369-yard 14th hole when from in front of the green, using his putter, he navigated the ball through the fringe and into the cup. His projected spot on the money list advanced to 14. Despite a bogey on 16, Jones had a short tap-in par putt on both the 17th and 18th holes. He finished the final round with a 67. Jones ended up 17th on the Finals money list. He played his 11th season on the PGA Tour in 2017–2018.

Entering the Web.com Tour Championship tied with Jones at 47th on the Finals money list was Shawn Stefani. Stefani made it to the FedEx Cup Playoffs in the previous season when he tied for 14th at the season-ending Wyndham Championship. Stefani played in 26 PGA events in 2016–2017. He made the cut in 11, with two finishes in the top 25 and his season-best tie for tenth at the Shriners Hospitals for Children Open. Stefani endured a stretch from February through April when he missed the cut in six of seven tournaments. He also missed the cut in his final three tournaments of the season. Stefani finished at number 165 in the FedEx Cup standings. He did earn $404,377.

Stefani missed the cut at the first two Finals tournaments before a tie for 20th at the DAP Championship. He earned $11,240. Stefani's status was at stake in the Web.com Tour Championship as he faced only conditional status on the Web.com Tour for the following season. Stefani excelled at the Web.com Tour Championship with a 66 in each of the first two rounds and a bogey-free, third-round 67. He was 14 under par, but six strokes behind Jonathan Byrd. Stefani played another bogey-free round on the final day, shooting a six under par 65. He joined Sam Saunders in tying for second. He earned $88,000 for the Web.com Tour Championship plus his PGA Tour card.

The final golfer who rallied at the Web.com Tour Championship to earn his PGA Tour card was Tom Hoge. Hoge finished 144th in the FedEx Cup standings in the previous season. He competed in 17 PGA Tour events in 2016–2017, playing out of the 126 through 150 finishers in the standings group. He made the cut in ten events, with three top-25 and two top-ten finishes. He finished 166th place in the points standings and earned $373,092.

Hoge made the cut in the first three Finals tournaments, amassing $23,798. He was 31st on the money list heading into the Web.com Tour Championship, $4,057 behind the 25th position total. Hoge began the tournament with an even par 71 in which his four birdies were countered with two bogeys and a double-bogey on the par-5 10th hole. He began to make his move with a bogey-free, eight-birdie 63 in round two. Round three produced a one under par 70.

Starting the final round on the 10th hole, Hoge bogeyed the same hole that he doubled in the first round. Hoge had a stretch of four consecutive birdies from the 16th hole through the 1st. He added another birdie on the 3rd hole. He was projected in the 29th position on the money list with three holes left.

Over the first three rounds, Hoge played the 7th, 8th, and 9th holes at a combined total of four under par. He would need similar success. Hoge's second shot at the par-5, 575-yard 7th hole left him off of the green. He was able to convert the up-and-down for birdie and vaulted up to number 21 on the projected money list. He parred the par-3 8th hole, and on the par-4, 435-yard 9th hole, he found the bottom of the cup in three strokes. Hoge pumped his fist in jubilation as he connected on his second birdie in the final three holes. With a final-round, six under par 65, Hoge was headed back to the PGA Tour.

As with all of the PGA Tour and Web.com Tour dividing lines, it is the race for the final position that brings the most drama, relief, joy, frustration, and disappointment. At the Web.com Tour Championship, several golfers flirted with getting into the top 25 of the Finals money list before falling short. The five golfers who were inside the top 25 heading into the Web.com Tour Championship produced different ways of dropping below that dividing line.

Ben Crane is a five-time tournament champion on the PGA Tour. His first victory came in 2003 at the Bell South Classic, and his last win was at the FedEx St. Jude Classic in 2014. The 41-year-old finished 147th in the FedEx Cup points standings in 2016–2017. In the Finals, he finished sixth at the Nationwide Children's Hospital Championship to earn $34,750. Crane was disqualified at the Albertsons Boise Open for having a driver and a six-iron in his bag that had stickers on the clubs that are used for data gathering when practicing. Crane did not use either club in the tournament, which would have resulted in an immediate disqualification.

The rule is such that even a decal on the clubface is considered an attachment, with the penalty being two strokes per hole, up to four strokes. Crane was penalized eight strokes in Thursday's first round when both clubs were deemed to be non-conforming. Starting his round on the 10th hole, Crane had an eight on his scorecard for both the 10th and 11th holes. It was Crane himself who reported the infraction to a rules official regarding the driver after playing the 10th hole. Had Crane noticed the stickers before completing his first hole, he would have endured only a two-stroke penalty. Crane did remove the driver from his bag immediately but did not pull the six iron from his bag until the 14th hole. After Crane spoke with rules officials prior to the second round, he was disqualified when it was determined that he should have reported the violation with the six-iron sooner.

Crane tied for 45th at the following week's DAP Championship. He added $3,120 for a Finals total of $37,870, 24th on the Finals money list. It was reported on the Golf Channel that instead of playing in the Web.com Tour Championship, Crane was in attendance at festivities at the Presidents Cup. Crane began the 2017–2018 season on a Web.com Tour minor medical extension. He had one tournament to earn 84 points, which when added to his 2016–2017 points total of 281 would equal the 125th position in the standings at the end of the 2016–2017 regular season, the 365 points total of J. J. Henry. Crane would drop to the 126 through 150 finishers group should he not meet that required points total.

Matthew Southgate and Adam Svensson dropped out of the top 25 by missing the cut at the Web.com Tour Championship. Svensson totaled $37,937 in prize money in the Finals. Although he missed the cut at the Web.com Tour Championship by several strokes, it is interesting to point out that the golfer who received the smallest prize money for the tournament earned $2,710. Had Svensson just been able to make the cut and play in the final two rounds of the Web. com Tour Championship, that amount would have been good enough for him to obtain the 25th position on the Finals money list.

Ryo Ishikawa entered the Web.com Tour Finals tournaments after finishing 175th in the FedEx Cup standings. Ishikawa made the cut in the first three Finals tournaments, including a tie for ninth at the Albertsons Boise Open. He was 22nd on the Finals money list with $30,622. Ishikawa finished the Web.com Tour Championship at nine under par, but that was only good for a tie for 40th and an additional $4,300. Ishikawa needed another $5,663 in prize money to get to the PGA Tour.

The 25th position entering the Web.com Tour Championship belonged to Cameron Percy, who accumulated $27,855 in the Finals. At 43 years old, Percy finished at number 144 in the FedEx Cup standings. He earned $623,694 on the PGA Tour and was awarded a $32,000 bonus. Despite rounds of 69–67–66, Percy's faint hopes of remaining in the Finals top 25 rested on his making an eagle on the 18th hole in the final round. The 18th hole at the Atlantic Beach Country Club has water along the left side of the fairway that extends to just a few yards off of the green. Aware of this danger on the left, his second shot hit the hospitality tent right of the green. He needed to chip in to break into the projected top 25 Finals money list. When that did not happen, Percy settled for a tie for 20th. Percy did earn $9,348 to raise his total to $37,203, but that amount was short of the 25th position by $3,422. Percy entered the 2017–2018 PGA Tour in the 126 through 150 finishers in the FedEx Cup points standings group.

One other golfer made a late run at position number 25. Roberto Castro, in the prior season, tied for 17th at the PGA Tour Championship and ended the season 22nd in the FedEx Cup standings. Castro was not able to repeat that success in 2016–2017. He appeared in 25 tournaments and made the cut in ten. Castro had only one top-25 performance, a tie for 20th at the Greenbrier Classic. He had one stretch from the Waste Management Phoenix Open in February through the Wells Fargo Championship in May, in which he missed the cut in nine of ten tournaments. His lone made cut was a tie for 45th at the World Golf Championships—Mexico Championship, for which he won $59,000. Castro ended the regular season earning $367,362, 172nd in the FedEx Cup standings.

Castro entered the Web.com Tour Championship tied for 54th on the Finals money list. He would have gotten into the projected top 25 if he made an eagle three on 18 in the final round. Instead he made a birdie four. Castro ended the Web.com Tour Championship in a tie for eighth, but without a PGA Tour card for the 2017–2018 season. He began 2018 with conditional status on the Web.com Tour.

The 25th and final PGA Tour card would come down to Seamus Power and Matt Harmon. Power had an MDF at the Wyndham Championship to drop from 123rd to 130th in the FedEx Cup standings. Power quickly put himself in a good position in the Web.com Tour Finals as a tie for 13th at the Nationwide Children's Hospital Championship gave him $18,750. He added $3,900 to his Finals total with a tie for 40th at the Albertsons Boise Open. When Power tied for 17th at the DAP Championship, he added $15,000 to his Finals prize money. He entered the Web.com Tour Championship 19th with $37,650, $9,795 better than the number 25 position total.

Power's four under par in the first round of the Web.com Tour Championship seemed to put him in a comfortable position, but in rounds two and three he shot only one under par, putting his opportunity to improve his status for the next season in jeopardy. Starting on the 10th hole in the final round, and still projected at 19th on the money list, Power played the first nine holes at two over par. The remainder of the final round saw Power drift above and below the projected top 25 on the Finals money list dividing line. A birdie at the 2nd, 4th, and 5th holes had him within the top 25.

Power had a birdie putt on the 6th slide past the left edge of the cup. He now found himself in the 26th projected position with three holes left. Power made things worse at the par-5 7th hole. His third shot was from off the green on the left with a bunker in the direct line between the ball and the flagstick. He aggressively played to go over the bunker, but he came up short and landed in the trap. He was able to get out of the bunker on his fourth shot, but he missed his par putt. He did recover to par both the 8th and 9th holes.

Matt Harmon played exclusively in regular season tournaments on the Web.com Tour in 2017. He was part of the U.S. Open field, but he missed the cut. Harmon earned $96,296 on the Web.com Tour, which placed him at number

48 on the regular season money list. He made 17 cuts in 25 events, with nine performances in the top 25 and two in the top ten. Harmon's last chance in 2017 to obtain status on the PGA Tour for the first time in his career was through the path of the Finals.

Harmon missed the cut at the Nationwide Children's Hospital Championship, and his tie for 40th at the Albertsons Boise Open accounted for only $3,900. Harmon posted rounds of 68–68–67 and was the 54-hole leader at the DAP Championship. He then stumbled with a final-round 73 that included a bogey on the 16th, 17th, and 18th holes. Harmon lost out on considerable prize money. He settled for a tie for 11th and $20,500. Harmon entered the Web.com Tour Championship in 29th place on the Finals money list.

Harmon opened the Web.com Tour Championship with a four under par 67 and a bogey-free, seven under par 64. He posted a third-round 70 that left him at 12 under par for the tournament. Harmon played the front nine at two under in the final round. He added another birdie at the 12th hole. His Finals money list projection reached as high as number 15. Even a bogey on 13 still had Harmon with a projected 20th-place finish on the money list. Harmon parred the 14th through 16th holes. On 17, he stood over a three-and-a-half-foot birdie putt that would have advanced him to the 17th projected position. The putt, however, rushed past the hole. Harmon was now in the precarious 25th position.

The play of other golfers caused constant fluctuation in the projections. For example, when Ethan Tracy made a birdie putt on the 17th hole to go to 15 under par, he shifted Power into the projected 25th position and dropped Harmon into 26th.

Harmon still controlled his PGA Tour opportunity. He was projected into the 18th position if he could birdie the par-5, 545-yard 18th hole. A par would put him in the 25th spot and onto the PGA Tour. Harmon had played the 18th hole in par-par-birdie in the first three rounds. Perhaps overly conscious of the water to the left of the green, Harmon hit his second shot to the right, where it struck the hospitality tent. He got a free drop but had a tricky third shot. His chip barely made it onto the green. He now had a lengthy birdie putt over a mound that ran through the putting surface. His putt went eight feet past the hole. Harmon now had one putt to reach the PGA Tour. He could not convert his needed par putt. He slammed his putter and walked off the 18th green with the club broken in two pieces.

Harmon tied for 20th with ten other golfers to win $9,348. His Finals total was $33,748. Seamus Power finished the Web.com Tour Championship tied for 48th. His effort yielded $2,975. Power, who made the cut in all four Web.com Tour Finals tournaments, had a Finals total of $40,625, which was good enough for the 25th and last entrance onto the PGA Tour.

24

In Three Days

After a process which began in October 2016, spanned 28 states, Puerto Rico, the Bahamas, and eight other countries over 47 tournaments on the PGA Tour and 26 tournaments on the Web.com Tour, it took the final 18 holes on Monday, October 2, 2017, at the Web.com Tour Championship in Florida to settle all of the PGA Tour's dividing lines. For some golfers, the result was that their following season would be as a member of the PGA Tour. Their hopes would be for tournament victory and, in late August 2018, to be in New Jersey as part of the field for the first FedEx Cup playoff tournament. For other golfers, the conclusion to 2016–2017 meant another season of trying to prove themselves on the Web.com Tour and graduate onto the PGA Tour.

As illustrated in this book, things could change for the positive very quickly in the life of a professional golfer. As poorly as things may be going, golfers are aware that their stories of achievement, redemption, or perseverance might be as close as the following week's tournament—or perhaps the next tee box. They also know that crossing a critical dividing line will in all likelihood be accomplished by the narrowest of margins. It will take a supreme level of focus, flawless execution, and, perhaps, a little luck.

No matter what a golfer accomplished last season, whether it was his first major championship, his first PGA tournament win, or the last position in the Web.com Tour Finals money list to get onto the PGA Tour, the reality is that every golfer is aware of one important thing: the magnitude of the next opportunity. Every golfer will start this magnificent quest of a golf season seeking his next personal achievement: to be on the positive side of professional golf's many dividing lines, to change his career, to change his life…. The season begins in three days.

Epilogue: 2017–2018

The 2017–2018 season was the last before significant changes were made to the PGA Tour schedule, creating new challenges to navigating the PGA Tour system. As mentioned earlier in the book, the PGA Championship will now be played in May instead of August, The Players Championship will move from May to March, and the FedEx Cup Playoffs will conclude in August. Among the other schedule changes for 2018–2019: the Valero Texas Open replaces the Houston Open as the tournament the week before the Masters, the FedEx St. Jude Classic moves from the week before the U.S. Open in June to July and becomes a World Golf Championships event, replacing the Bridgestone Invitational, and the RBC Canadian Open moves into the spot before the U.S. Open.

The Wyndham Championship remains the final tournament of the regular season. In addition to being the final deciding event for playoff qualification, the tournament will determine the newly formed "Wyndham Rewards Top Ten" that pays a bonus to the top ten in the FedEx Cup standings at the end of the regular season. A total of $10 million will be awarded. The regular season leader will receive a bonus of $2 million, with second place earning $1.5 million and the tenth-place finisher getting $500,000. The Wyndham Championship will take place the first week in August beginning in 2019.

The most notable changes will occur to the FedEx Cup Playoffs structure. Beginning in 2018–2019, there will be three playoff tournaments instead of four. The top 125 golfers will play in the Northern Trust, with the event rotating between the New York and Boston regions, 70 golfers will compete in the BMW Championship, and 30 golfers will form the field in the Tour Championship. The Tour Championship will also have a new format. The "FedEx Cup Starting Strokes" system will put golfers at a certain score in relation to par prior to the start of the Tour Championship. The golfer in first place in the FedEx Cup standings will begin the tournament at ten under par, second place at eight under, third place at seven under, fourth place at six under, and fifth place at five under par. The golfers who are sixth through tenth in the standings will start the Tour Championship at four under par, those in 11th through 15th at three under, 16th through 20th at two under, 21st through 25th at one under, and the golfers 26th through 30th at even par. The winner of the Tour Championship becomes the winner of the FedEx Cup, eliminating the possibility of having two different golfers holding up trophies at the end of the tournament, one as the winner of the Tour Championship and one as the winner of the FedEx Cup, as happened in 2017 and 2018. The FedEx Cup will also have a larger total bonus pool, increasing from $35 million to $70 million. The winner of the FedEx Cup will be awarded a bonus of $15 million.

The golfers' stories in this book from the 2016–2017 season often end by providing their exempt status for the 2017–2018 season. This epilogue provides a brief detailing of some of those prominently mentioned golfers' results from the 2017–2018 season.

Brendan Steele entered the FedEx Cup Playoffs in 2017 16th in the standings. After a missed cut, a tie for 56th, and a tie for 44th, he dropped to 33rd. Steele missed qualifying for the Tour Championship, which blocked one entrance pathway to the Masters. Steele, however, repeated as the winner of the season-opening Safeway Open. He returned to Augusta National for his third time to play in the 2018 Masters, although he missed the cut. For the 2017–2018 regular season, Steele made the cut in 15 of his 19 tournaments, with seven top 25 and three ten finishes. Steele made it to the third tournament of the FedEx Cup Playoffs for the fourth consecutive season, but he has yet to qualify for the Tour Championship. He finished 56th in the 2017–2018 standings to earn a $110,000 bonus, to add to his prize money total of $2,291,128.

The Sanderson Farms Championship, played opposite the World Golf Championships—HSBC Champions tournament, produced a first-time PGA Tour winner for the fourth consecutive season when 41-year-old Ryan Armour won in his 105th start. The golfer who came in second in that tournament was Chesson Hadley who returned after a season on the Web.com Tour. Hadley quickly reestablished himself on the PGA Tour. In the first three tournaments of the 2017–2018 season, Hadley tied for third at the Safeway Open, was second at the Sanderson Farms Championship, and tied for fourth in the Shriners Hospitals for Children Open. Hadley won more than $1.1 million in those three starts. He went on to have four other top ten finishes, and for the 2017–2018 regular season he made 21 cuts in 27 tournaments. Hadley played through the first three tournaments of the FedEx Cup Playoffs. He earned $2,768,863 and a bonus of $131,000 for finishing 44th in the FedEx Cup standings.

There were 45 regular season tournaments scheduled for the 2017–2018 season. However, the 2018 Puerto Rico Open, played opposite the World Golf Championships—Mexico Championship, was canceled after hurricanes ravaged the island. The Corales Puntacana Resort and Club Championship in the Dominican Republic was a new tournament introduced for the 2017–2018 season. This tournament became the fifth opposite event on the PGA Tour schedule, played the same week as the World Golf Championships—Dell Match Play.

The winner in Puntacana was Brice Garnett, the 2017 regular season prize money leader on the Web.com Tour. It was Garnett's first PGA Tour championship. Garnett made it to the third playoff tournament after he finished in a tie for 12th in the Dell Technologies Championship. He earned $1,466,224 and a bonus of $110,000 for finishing 61st in the standings.

Garnett defeated Keith Mitchell by four strokes in Puntacana. Mitchell finished 26th on the Web.com Tour regular season money list in 2017 before qualifying for the PGA Tour through the Web.com Tour Finals. Mitchell began the season by missing the cut in his first three tournaments. He then made the cut in eight of his next nine tournament starts. One week after the tournament in Puntacana, Mitchell had his second consecutive top-ten finish when he tied for sixth place at the Houston Open. Mitchell posted two other top-ten finishes later in the season when he tied for third at the AT&T Byron Nelson and tied for seventh at the John Deere Classic. For the season, including the FedEx Cup Playoffs, Mitchell played in 29 tournaments with 21 made cuts. He earned $1,641,260 and a $110,000 bonus for finishing 67th in the standings.

Joel Dahmen was one of the last golfers to graduate from the Web.com Tour to the PGA Tour in 2015–2016 and 2016–2017. Dahmen started the 2017–2018 season by making the cut in five of his first ten tournaments. He then made the cut in his next eight tournament starts. In July, Dahmen had five consecutive top 25 performances, including a tie for fifth at the Greenbrier Classic that was followed the next week with a second-place finish at the John Deere Classic. He ended the month with a tie for eighth at the RBC Canadian Open. He earned $923,440 over the five-tournament span. Dahmen qualified for the FedEx Cup Playoffs for the first time in his career. Although Dahmen missed the cut in the two tournaments that he appeared, he won $1,476,838 for the season and a bonus of $80,000 for finishing 80th in the standings.

Similar to Joel Dahmen, Troy Merritt was on the PGA Tour in 2016–2017, but he needed to secure his Tour card for the 2017–2018 season through the Web.com Tour Finals. Merritt was outside the top 125 in the FedEx Cup standings when he arrived at the Barbasol Championship in July, played opposite The Open Championship. Merritt scored a 62, ten under par, in the first round and had a three-stroke lead. The lead evaporated by the conclusion of the third round and Merritt was in a four-way tie atop the leaderboard. Merritt shot a five under par, 67, in the final round to win the tournament by one stroke. For the season, Merritt earned $1,326,989 and a bonus of $80,000 for finishing 75th in the standings. Merritt has his PGA Tour priority status as a tournament winner through the 2019–2020 season.

Seamus Power was the 25th and final golfer to qualify for the PGA Tour from the Web.com Tour Finals in 2017. In 2017–2018, he was the final golfer to qualify for the FedEx Cup Playoffs, securing the 125th place finish by six points. Power played in 27 regular season tournaments, with 14 made cuts, six top 25, and two top ten finishes. He finished the first playoff tournament tied for 34th place but did not advance. Power earned $791,018 for the season, a $70,000 playoff bonus, and his Tour card for the 2018–2019 season.

As always, some golfers who had their PGA Tour card in 2017–2018 had to reclaim it by competing in the Web.com Tour Finals in 2018. Robert Streb played on the PGA Tour for six consecutive seasons, making it to the Tour Championship in 2015. He came up one stroke short to Xander Schauffele of winning the Greenbrier Classic in 2017. After qualifying for the FedEx Cup Playoffs for four straight seasons, Streb ended the 2017–2018 regular season in 178th place in the standings. Streb made the cut in only ten of his 29 starts. His return to the PGA Tour would have to be earned by his performance in the Web.com Tour Finals. Streb quickly secured his PGA Tour card when he won the first Finals tournament in a playoff.

In his rookie season on the PGA Tour Roberto Diaz made 11 cuts in 25 tournament starts. His best performance was a tie for 25th place. Diaz earned $235,635 and finished 189th in the FedEx Cup standings. In the Web.com Tour Finals, Diaz posted a tie for 24th, a tie for 25th, and then a fifth-place finish to get him back to the PGA Tour.

Matt Jones ended the 2017–2018 PGA Tour regular season in a familiar position, barely on the negative side of a critical dividing line. Jones finished 151st in the FedEx Cup standings, only two points out of a position that would have provided a $32,000 bonus and some status on the PGA Tour. Jones made 11 cuts in 23 tournament starts, with a tie for 12th in the John Deere Classic as his best result of the season. He won $538,681 in prize money. Jones again earned his PGA Tour card through the Web.com Tour Finals when he tied for tenth and tied for second in the first two Finals tournaments.

The Web.com Tour Finals represented the last opportunity for Rob Oppenheim and Martin Flores to reclaim their PGA Tour card. Oppenheim finished his PGA Tour season in 180th place in the FedEx Cup standings after making 11 cuts in 26 tournaments, with two top 15 performances. He earned

$279,019. Oppenheim was in 39th place on the Web.com Tour Finals money list when he failed to make the cut in the fourth Finals tournament.

Flores finished his PGA Tour season in 164th place in the FedEx Cup standings after making 17 cuts in 29 tournaments, with two top 15 performances. He earned $449,266. Flores did not make the cut in any Finals tournaments.

Ben Kohles ended the Web.com Tour regular season in 45th place on the money list, earning $113,520. He entered the Web.com Tour Championship in 61st place on the Finals money list. He started the last round of that tournament in the projected 56th position. Kohles was projected in the 25th position after making a birdie on four of the first seven holes. He drifted back to 46th place, but a birdie on 17 moved him up to 27th. Any chance of Kohles getting into the top 25 and earning his PGA Tour card was dashed at the par-5, 18th hole when his drive and his third shot went into the water. Kohles finished 49th on the Finals money list, sending him back to the Web.com Tour for 2019.

Wesley Bryan, Cody Gribble, Mackenzie Hughes, Rod Pampling, D.A. Points, and Chris Stroud were among the golfers who won tournaments in 2016–2017 but did not make it to the FedExCup Playoffs in 2017–2018. They enter 2018–2019 in their final season in the tournament winners priority group. They will have to win a tournament, qualify for the FedEx Cup Playoffs (or at least finish in the top 150 in the standings), or qualify for the PGA Tour through the Web.com Tour Finals to avoid being dropped to the past champions group. Sergio Garcia too won a tournament in 2017 but failed to make the playoffs in 2017–2018. Of course, with Garcia's win at the Masters, he is exempt as a major champion through 2021–22.

Greg Chalmers, Jim Herman, and Billy Hurley were golfers in their final season with exempt status as a tournament winner, but they were not able to qualify for the FedEx Cup Playoffs. Chalmers and Herman will start the 2018–2019 season playing with a medical extension. Hurley will play out of the past champions group.

J.J. Henry will find himself using a one-time exemption for making 300 PGA tournament cuts. His placement is after the top finishers of the Web.com Tour group. Henry was in the 125th and final qualifying position for the playoffs in 2016–2017 thanks to his performance in the season-ending Wyndham Championship. In 2017–2018, Henry finished in 158th place after making 13 cuts in 28 starts with one top ten finish.

Geoff Ogilvy, too, used his Wyndham Championship performance in 2017 to help him qualify for the FedEx Cup Playoffs in a season in which he used his one-time top 50 career earnings as his exempt status. In the 2017–2018 season, Ogilvy was able to make only four cuts in 18 tournament starts. He is in the past champions group in 2018–2019.

Ken Duke will once again be in the past champions group after competing in 15 tournaments in 2017–2018 and making the cut in six. Duke, who will turn 50 in January 2019, can also seek opportunities on the PGA Champions Tour.

Brian Stuard also was in his final season with status as a tournament winner in 2017–2018. Stuard played in five autumn tournaments and he made the cut in all, including a tie for fourth and a tie for ninth place. Stuard added his second tie for fourth place in his sixth tournament start of the season, the Sony Open in Hawaii in January. Stuard earned $704,276 of his season total prize money of $1,089,763 in his first six tournaments of the season. He qualified for the FedEx Cup Playoffs for the fourth time in his career, entering in 118th place in the standings. Stuard played his way into the second playoff tournament with a tie for 25th place finish in the Northern Trust. He ended the FedEx Cup Playoffs at 86th in the standings to earn a bonus of $75,000.

Multiple second place finishes were the best tournament performances of the season for Kevin Kisner, Kyle Stanley, and Xander Schauffele. Kisner came in second in the World Golf Championships—Dell Match Play and tied for second in The Open Championship. Kisner earned $2,972,285 and a bonus of $128,000 for his 47th place finish in the standings.

Stanley tied for second in the Memorial and finished in second place at the World Golf Championships—Bridgestone Invitational. He qualified for the Tour Championship for the second consecutive season, where he tied for 15th place. For the season, Stanley earned $3,916,001 in prize money and $190,000 as his bonus for finishing 27th in the FedEx Cup standings.

Schauffele made 19 tournament cuts in 23 starts in the regular season. He tied for second at The Players Championship and The Open Championship. When Schauffele finished tied for third in the BMW Championship, he played his way into the Tour Championship. After winning the Tour Championship the year before, Schauffele finished in a tie for seventh at that tournament in 2018 to earn $279,900 of his season prize money total of $4,047,538. Schauffele earned a bonus of $250,000 for finishing 15th in the standings.

Appearing in the Tour Championship was the result for Patrick Cantlay, continuing his comeback story. Cantlay claimed his first PGA title when he won the Shriners Hospitals for Children Open on the second hole of a playoff. Overall, he made the cut in 21 of his 23 tournament starts. He earned $3,963,962 in prize money and a bonus of $225,000 for finishing 20th in the FedEx Cup standings.

Pat Perez, too, continued his successful comeback to the PGA Tour by winning a tournament for the second consecutive season when he won the CIMB Classic. Perez would go on to earn $2,962,641 and a playoff bonus of $136,000 for finishing 39th in the standings.

The meteoric rise as top golfers on the PGA Tour for Jon Rahm, Brooks Koepka, and Bryson DeChambeau were all furthered by their tournament wins in the 2017–2018 season. Rahm won the CareerBuilder Challenge when he defeated Andrew Landry on the fourth playoff hole. Rahm earned $3,992,678 in prize money and a bonus of $210,000 for finishing 23rd in the FedEx Cup standings.

Koepka became the first repeat champion of the U.S. Open since Curtis Strange in 1988 and 1989. Koepka also won the PGA Championship to become the fifth golfer, and the first since Tiger Woods in 2000, to win both of those majors in the same season. He earned $7,094,047 and a bonus of $550,000 for finishing ninth in the FedEx Cup standings.

DeChambeau was the winner of three tournaments. He won the Memorial in a playoff against Byeong Hun An and Kyle Stanley. DeChambeau then won the first two tournaments of the FedEx Cup Playoffs, earning $1.62 million for each victory. He had nine total top-ten performances. DeChambeau earned $8,094,489 in prize money and a bonus of $2 million for finishing third in the FedEx Cup standings.

Koepka and DeChambeau were joined by Jason Day, Francesco Molinari, Patton Kizzire, Dustin Johnson, Justin Thomas, Bubba Watson, and Justin Rose as multiple tournament winners.

After winning five tournaments, the PGA Championship, and the FedEx Cup Championship in 2016–2017, Justin Thomas continued his level of excellence in the 2017–2018 season. Thomas won the CJ Cup @ Nine Bridges, a new event on the PGA Tour held in South Korea, the Honda Classic; and the World Golf Championships—Bridgestone Invitational. Thomas earned $8,694,821 and a bonus of $700,000 for finishing seventh in the FedEx Cup standings.

Bubba Watson won at Riviera in 2014 and 2016. He did so again in 2018, his first tournament win since claiming the championship at the same golf course two years earlier. It was Watson's tenth PGA Tour win. Five weeks later, Watson won the World Golf Championships—Dell Match Play, defeating Kevin Kisner in the final match. He then won the Travelers Championship for the third time in his career, having also won at TPC River Highlands in 2010 and 2015. Watson won $5,793,748 in prize money and a bonus of $500,000 for finishing tenth in the FedEx Cup standings.

Justin Rose won twice on the PGA Tour in 2017–2018. He overcame an eight-stroke deficit entering the final round to win the World Golf Championships—HSBC Champions tournament, his first since the 2015 Zurich Classic of New Orleans. Rose achieved his ninth Tour victory when he won the Dean & DeLuca Invitational. He made the cut in 17 of his 18 tournament starts and had a total of 11 top ten finishes. Rose would be the FedEx Cup Champion for the 2017–2018 season. He won the $10 million bonus to go along with his prize money total of $8,130,678.

Several other veteran golfers once again claimed a title after a period without a tournament win. Ian Poulter won the Houston Open when he defeated Beau Hossler in a playoff. It was the first PGA Tour win for Poulter since 2012. The win in Houston gave Poulter the final entrance spot into the 2018 Masters where he tied for 44th and earned $35,200.

Keegan Bradley won the BMW Championship, played in the Philadelphia region, when he defeated Justin Rose on the first playoff hole. It was Bradley's first win since 2012 and his first trip back to the Tour Championship since 2013. Bradley finished 26th in the Tour Championship to earn $150,300 for that tournament. For the season, Bradley earned $4,069,464 in prize money and a bonus of $600,000 for finishing ninth in the FedEx Cup standings.

Bradley and Xander Schauffele played their way into the Tour Championship field through the BMW Championship, replacing Jordan Spieth and Emiliano Grillo. Spieth dropped to 31st in the FedEx Cup standings. The Tour Championship was to be Spieth's 25th tournament of the season. Not reaching that tournament put him in violation of the PGA Tour policy where a golfer has to either add a tournament to his schedule that he has not played in four years or play in 25 tournaments. It was reported in several media outlets that a resolution was agreed to with speculation that Spieth will be appearing in more events in 2018–2019.

After playing in 96 tournaments without a win, 47-year-old Phil Mickelson won a PGA tournament for the 43rd time in his career when he defeated Justin Thomas in a playoff in the World Golf Championships—Mexico Championship. It was Mickelson's first win since The Open Championship in 2013. For the season Mickelson earned $4,595,187 in prize money and a bonus of $220,000 for finishing 21st in the FedEx Cup standings.

Paul Casey won for the second time on the PGA Tour, his first title since the Shell Houston Open in 2009, when he claimed a one-stroke victory in the Valspar Championship over Patrick Reed and Tiger Woods.

Reed had the highlight of his career when he won the 2018 Masters, his first major title. Reed held off Jordan Spieth, who started the final round nine strokes off the lead. Spieth rallied to tie Reed at one point in the final round before Reed birdied the 14th hole. Spieth tied the record for the lowest final round at the Masters with a 64, but he finished two strokes behind Reed. Rickie Fowler finished one stroke behind Reed. Fowler birdied the 18th hole to force Reed to make a par on the tournament's final hole to win the Green Jacket. It was Fowler's eighth top-five finish and his third second-place result in a major.

Finally, after having only one tournament start in the 2016–2017 season, Tiger Woods returned to the PGA Tour for the 2017–2018 season. Woods made the cut in 15 of his 17 tournament starts with six top-ten performances when he arrived at the Tour Championship. He was in 20th place in the FedEx Cup standings. Woods scored a two-stroke victory in the Tour Championship to earn his first tournament win since 2013, a span of 1,876 days. It was the 80th tournament victory for Woods, leaving him two behind Sam Snead for the all-time lead in wins. Woods jumped to number two in the final FedEx Cup standings to give him the $3 million bonus. He won $1.62 million for the tournament win, contributing to his season total of $5,443,841 in prize money.

The 2017–2018 season determined the starting positions in the priority ranking groups for the 2018–2019 season. The next chapter on the PGA Tour where it is the system that creates the dividing lines and the storylines, where the drama has significant season and career consequences, and where the outcomes will all be earned can begin to be written.

Suggested Reading

Feinstein, John. *A Good Walk Spoiled: Days and Nights on the PGA Tour.* New York: Little, Brown, 1995.

_____. *Tales from Q School: Inside Golf's Fifth Major.* New York: Back Bay, 2007.

Gould, David. *Q School Confidential: Inside Golf's Cruelest Tournament.* New York: St. Martin's Griffin, 1999.

Lewis, Chris. *The Scorecard Always Lies: A Year Behind the Scenes on the PGA Tour.* New York: Free Press, 2007.

Ryan, Shane. *Slaying the Tiger: A Year Inside the Ropes on the New PGA Tour.* New York: Ballantine Books, 2015.

Strege, John. *Tournament Week: Inside the Ropes and Behind the Scenes on the PGA Tour.* New York: HarperCollins, 2001.

Index